# Identity Games

# Identity Games

Globalization and the Transformation of Media
Cultures in the New Europe

Anikó Imre

The MIT Press
Cambridge, Massachusetts
London, England

MIT Press books may be purchased at special quantity discounts for business or sales promotional use. For information, please email special_sales@mitpress.mit.edu or write to Special Sales Department, The MIT Press, 55 Hayward Street, Cambridge, MA 02142.

This book was set in 10 on 13 pt Sabon by SNP Best-set Typesetter Ltd., Hong Kong and was printed and bound in the United States of America.

Library of Congress Cataloging-in-Publication Data

Imre, Anikó.
  Identity games : globalization and the transformation of media cultures
  in the new Europe / Imre.
    p.  cm.
  Includes bibliographical references and index.
  ISBN 978-0-262-09045-2 (hardcover : alk. paper)
  1. Mass media—Europe, Eastern.  2. Post-communism—Europe, Eastern.
  3. Globalization.  I. Title.
P92.E95I47  2009
302.230947—dc22
                                          2008041191

10 9 8 7 6 5 4 3 2 1

To two seasoned travelers: Margaret and Hugh (Mac)
McGillivray

# Contents

# Acknowledgments

I am grateful to Doug Sery and the editorial staff at the MIT Press for their fast and efficient work on the manuscript, and the Netherlands Academic Organization (NWO) for their generous support during 2004–2007, which enabled me to do invaluable research in Europe. The help and influence of many friends and colleagues is reflected in this book. I will single out Ginette Verstraete, Huub van Baar, and John Neubauer, my collaborators at the Amsterdam School of Cultural Analysis, for their ongoing encouragement and their honest and constructive critique of work-in-progress, Zsuzsa Kozak, Mari Takacs, and Katrin Kremmler for their research help, and Katarzyna Marciniak, Aine O'Healy, Melinda Szaloky, Lisa Parks, David Crane, Marsha Kinder, and David James as well as MIT Press's anonymous reviewers, for their important feedback on parts of the manuscript.

As is usually the case, my argument crystallized in the course of numerous meetings and collaborations. I am particularly indebted to participants in the Central European University graduate seminar "Media Globalization and Post-Communist Identities," held in Budapest in July 2007; the symposium "Via Transversa: Lost Cinema in the former Eastern Block," held in Tallinn, Estonia, in October 2007; and the symposium "Old Curtains, New Walls," organized in Amsterdam in June 2006. Discussions with my graduate students at the University of Amsterdam and the University of Southern California also informed the book. I could not have prepared the illustrations without Amanda Overton's expert skills; and would still be looking for a cover image without Kamil Turowski's talent and generosity.

Some of the arguments in the book developed from earlier publications. Parts of chapter two revise the article "Globalisation, Nationalism, and Post-Socialist Media Education," *Media International Australia* 120 (August 2006): 117–129. Some of chapter three grew out of two publications: "Roma Music and Transnational Homelessness," *Third Text* 92, 22.3 (May 2008): 325–336, and "Global Entertainment and the European 'Roma Problem,'" *Third Text* 20.6 (Winter 2006): 659–670. Chapter four is a revised and expanded version of "Lesbian Nationalism," *Signs* 33 (2, Winter 2007): 255–282. Parts of chapter five draw on "The Politics of Hiccups: National Cinema without National Language," *CineAction* 64 (2004): 8–17.

Last but most important, I want to thank my boys, Tim, Simon, Finnian, and Fergus for their love and patience over the years of research and writing. I hope someday they will think it was worth the time I spent on it.

# Introduction: Global Media Games in the New Europe

## From Big Brother to *Big Brother*

In the foreword to his dark account of American entertainment culture, *Amusing Ourselves to Death* (1985), Neil Postman compares the two fundamental dystopian narratives of postwar Western culture: George Orwell's *1984* (1949) and Aldous Huxley's *Brave New World* (1932). Contrary to the general belief that the two novels prophesy the same future, Postman explains, Orwell's allegory depicts externally imposed oppression, while "in Huxley's vision, no Big Brother is required to deprive people of their autonomy, maturity and history. As he saw it, people will come to love their oppression, to adore the technologies that undo their capacities to think" (1985, vii). Postman's own words sound prophetic in the early twenty-first century, when television, the very medium he blamed for trivializing public culture, has appropriated the dystopic figure of Big Brother on a global scale: The reality show *Big Brother*, one of the most successful global formats, has become an emblem of what Huxley would call "trivial culture, preoccupied with some equivalent of the feelies, the orgy porgy, and the centrifugal bumblepuppy" (Postman 1985, vii).

Douglas Kellner writes about the U.S. version of the originally Dutch series: "The sight of dozens of microphones and cameras everywhere including the CBS logo of an open eye, recalls the Orwellian nightmare, transmuted into fluff entertainment in the society of the spectacle. Quite possibly *Big Brother* helps to acclimatize people to surveillance, such as is exercised by the FBI 'Carnivore' program, which can intercept private e-mail or round-the-clock video surveillance at work, in public spaces, and perhaps even at home" (Kellner 2003, 18). Mark Andrejevic also singles out *Big Brother* as the site of two converging dystopias. In his reading, the interactive audience participation in the show, realized through viewer voting and often hailed as an example of the democratization of spectatorship, is in fact a form of "interpassivity." The promise of sharing power over the production process plays out more like the interaction with a bank machine: it makes the consumers themselves do the work of submitting data about their preferences and thus facilitates data mining (Andrejevic 2001).

Orwell's and Huxley's narratives have a special relevance for postcommunist cultures. An allegory of totalitarian oppression, *1984* can be read as the story of the communist past. *Brave New World* may be said to describe the future toward which postcommunist cultures are rushing at full speed, in which "there would be no reason to ban a book for there would be no one who wanted to read one," where "the truth would be drowned in a sea of irrelevance," and where people would be controlled not by inflicting pain but by inflicting pleasure (Postman 1985, vii–viii). It is tempting to see the past two decades of the history of Eastern Europe and the former Soviet Union as an accelerated transition from the former kind of totalitarianism to the latter.

This assessment converges with most postcommunist intellectuals' views of the ongoing globalization of local media cultures. Postman's book, published in 1985, acts as a recurring prophetic reference point in the post-Soviet region, a kind of "Media *1984*" imported from the past to explain recent changes in public culture: the partial privatization and globalization of formerly state-owned television, the transnationalization of film production, the advent of the Internet and the increasing digitalization of social exchange, the decline in the culture of reading and the book, and the rise of trivial spectacle—to sum up, what Postman calls the shift from the "Age of Typography" to a—for him, infinitely inferior—"Age of Television" (Postman 1985, 8). For Postman, the medium of television is the *metaphor* (as opposed to McLuhan's *message*) for the trivialization of public culture because it institutes the domination of the image over the written and spoken word.

Lev Manovich extends Postman's assessment into the Age of Global Interactive Media. In a short piece titled "Totalitarian Interactivity," he detects an East-West division in people's relations with interactive media technology. "For the West, interactivity is a perfect vehicle for the ideas of democracy and equality. For the East, it is another form of manipulation, in which the artist uses advanced technology to impose his/her totalitarian will on the people. . . . In contrast," he continues, "*as a postcommunist subject, I cannot but see the Internet as a communal apartment of the Stalin era*: no privacy, everybody spies on everybody else, always present in lines for common areas such as the toilet or the kitchen. Or I can think of it as a giant garbage site for the information society, with everybody dumping their used products of intellectual labor and nobody cleaning up. Or as a new, Mass Panopticum [*sic*] (which was already realized in communist societies)—complete transparency, everybody can track everybody else" (Manovich 1996).

As a postcommunist subject myself, I share Manovich's, Kellner's, and Andrejevic's suspicions about uncritical technophilia and the worrisome ideological links among interactivity, surveillance, and media spectacle. As I elaborate in the chapters that follow, the fast colonization of virtually virginal postcommunist media and information technology markets by transnational corporations should make one very cautious about the democratizing potential of the Internet and other interactive digital technologies. For the most part, the corporate transformation of the postcommunist media landscape has been welcomed by nation-states aspiring to share in the economic and ideological profits, and has been wrapped in EU-phoria over an expanding European audiovisual sphere that can stand up to competition with media and communication industries based in the United States and Asia. The shift to a spectacle culture; the spread of commercial television; and the infusion of education, politics, and other public spheres with entertainment and consumerism leave us plenty to worry about, not the least because there is no identifiable agent to resist behind these new technologies of surveillance and control.

As Kellner writes, drawing on Guy Debord's theorization of "the society of the spectacle," we have now left behind the conditions of state-monopoly capitalism described by the Frankfurt School in the 1930s, which had succeeded Marx's analysis of the stages of market, competitive, and laissez-faire capitalism. The world is entering the new era of technocapitalism, which unites capital, technology, and the information and entertainment industries, producing an infotainment society and spectacle culture (Kellner 2003, 11) where "entertainment is shaping every domain of life from the Internet to politics" (12). The abruptness and awkwardness of these new developments in the countries of the New Europe—leapfrogging as these cultures have across phases of technological and social change that had taken decades in other parts of the globe—has important lessons to offer about media globalization. It gives us opportunities to put into relief and defamiliarize aspects of the global infotainment society that have solidified into "truths" as a result of the longer, more continuous pace of change and the subsequent illusion of organic development in late capitalist cultures.

I remember my own desperate scrambling for an epistemological paradigm, a theoretical crutch, or at least pragmatic help, after being immersed in the flow of commercial television and media culture during my first visit to the United States in 1990, at the beginning of the Brave New Era that afforded freshly postcommunist subjects with travel opportunities. The shock over the unbearable lightness of being was overwhelming for someone unequipped with any kind of advertisement literacy—the most important skill that television teaches, according to John Hartley (Hartley 2004). I did not know to separate junk mail from actual mail, had never before received a sales call, and was in emotional turmoil when beer commercials interrupted serious television programs. Trained in a Prussian-style, hierarchical education system and a centralized, ascetic media economy with an educational-informational mission, my shock spread over the cultural field as I observed other phenomena that were alien to my sensitivities. Over the years, the shock has become manageable. But memories of an alternative media economy and aesthetic have endured and transformed into a critical urge to understand, theorize, and evaluate the collective shock that Eastern Europeans have had to process since the end of communism.

However, I also remember my first encounter with *Sesame Street* in 1990, and the subsequent epiphany that learning can be much more effective if it is done playfully, vividly, and creatively, engaging audiences through humor. During the early postcommunist years, I also discovered that books with large, colorful images motivate children to read much more effectively than the typical communist book of fairy tales or poetry, in tight print, illustrated by the rare, strange abstract image. State-controlled communist television might have prided itself on censoring triviality, but it was also boring and alienating for the most part. And the fact that most films made with state support left theaters without audience support was a running joke across the communist region.

As a transnational subject inspired by poststructuralist feminism, whose life and identity has been constructed in the course of perpetual cultural translation, I am somewhat suspicious of the inevitable simplifications that Postman's binary paradigm or Manovich's universalizing, static "postcommunist subject" imply. While we should heed their caution about technoeuphoria and the numbing pleasures of consumption, I want to be equally cautious about nostalgic projections of a simpler, better media world onto communism. The main reason is not even the fact that state-controlled media lent themselves to state propaganda. In some ways, the evidence of this fact had a positive, Brechtian effect on audiences, which is now missing from or is easily co-opted by the seamless flow of postmodern media entertainment. The reason for my caution is the fundamentally undemocratic ideological construction of communist, and postcommunist, national cultures. Such a construction has been formed and operates according to a rigid set of principles that define artistic value and divide the select few capable of creating such value from the rest, who are relegated to the position of grateful national audiences or, worse, unworthy consumers. The principles of selection are motivated by and naturalize Eurocentric nationalisms, which work through violent mechanisms of homophobia, misogyny, racism, ethnocentrism, and xenophobia.

The Cold War paradigm, and Western Marxists' investment in the socialist utopia, greatly contributed to hiding and protecting this undemocratic, ugly underbelly of nationalism effaced by the heroism of anticommunist resistance, with which art from the Soviet empire was identified. In this sense, even the "postcommunist subject" is an oversimplified, nonviable entity held together by the fantasy of national unity, which continues to inform post–Cold War accounts of the postcommunist media landscape. In the past fifteen years—while this book has been slowly ripening—I have come to question the unbearable gravity of being as it is imposed upon and represented in Eastern European national cultures. In this book, I analyze outstanding instances where the postcommunist experiences of sub- and transnational communities with global media expose and demystify the unspoken "truth" that binds together nationalism and high art.

I find it crucial to acknowledge up front my personal transition from late communism to late capitalism—which coincided with the larger, global transition to a post–Cold War world order—as a motivation for writing this book about identity and the media. Even though my memories are as unreliable as anyone else's when it comes to gaining insight into the battle of paradigms, they help explain the ambivalence with which I approach the subject. This book tries to sustain two parallel, often conflicting critical projects: One aims to understand the consumption and spectacle-centered logic of media globalization and "democratainment," to borrow John Hartley's apt term (2004), from a perspective informed by a particular kind of postcommunist critical sensibility. The other project is to show how subtle forms of exclusion and control often underscore the critiques of media globalization issued by postcommunist critics and theorists. The refusal of trash, the rejection of American cultural imperialism, the call for state or European Union monitoring of media content, and the unexamined preference for a literary, high culture are often grounded in exclusionary and reactionary forms of nationalism, Eurocentrism, and cultural imperialism. While of a different kind, this attitude tends to be no less uncritical than the equation of technological innovation with progress or than consumers' equation of the number of available TV channels with meaningful choices.

More generally, this book challenges ethnocentric assumptions about media globalization in the post–Cold War era, whether these assumptions come from mainstream news or from academic accounts. As Ella Shohat and Robert Stam do in their groundbreaking book, *Unthinking Eurocentrism* (1994), I want to "unthink" various centrisms that continue nurturing the Cold War division or create new global divides under the guise of celebrating globalization. As I have gradually come to accept and unthink my own cultural and theoretical suspension between the gloomy old world and the lite new world as the only paradoxical certainty, I have also found the metaphor that is both broad enough and specific enough to connect the two critical projects I described above in the notion of play.

*Play* performs multiple functions in this book. At one extreme, it gives utterable shape to the ambiguity that characterizes postcommunist cultures' encounters with global media, as well as to my own ambivalence toward these phenomena. Play is the very expression of inaccessability, of the "liminal" or "liminoid," and the paradoxical, to borrow descriptions from Brian Sutton-Smith's study, *The Ambiguity of Play* (Sutton-Smith 1997, 1–2). Play also allows me to discuss diverse manifestations of post–Cold War global media culture that have a ludic dimension, such as the production and consumption of video games, television, music, film, and the Internet; tourism and travel; memory and nostalgia; children's play; war, education, politics, art, eating, sex, and poetry. While "almost anything can allow play to occur within its boundaries" (Sutton-Smith 1997, 3), my choice of *play* as the operating metaphor is motivated by the connections between the recent, historically specific "ludification" of late and postcommunist culture and the emergence of convergent, global media.

The current global media environment is increasingly ludic. All political struggle is filtered through media entertainment. News reporting has merged with advertising into infotainment. Education is being redefined by computerized edutainment practices. Digital games blur the distinction between the real and the virtual in the sphere of economics as much as in warfare. The Internet itself has been described as a vast playground

(Seiter 2005; Sefton-Green 1998, 3). The ludification of culture has been matched by an increasing engagement with play across the disciplines. Communication and media studies, game studies, sociology, mathematics, anthropology, literary studies, art history, psychology, and sports studies have all contributed to "play scholarship." My own discussion combines textual analysis infused by a range of cultural theories with recent research in communication and political science on globalization in relation to the European Union's and European nation-states' audiovisual policies and strategies of governmentality.

Play also functions in the book at a more immediate and politicized level. The five chapters each observe the transition from late communism to postcommunism in terms of the conflict and continuity between two kinds of cultural and political expression, identified by two distinct kinds of engagement with play: One characterizes nationalistic cultures that had reserved the freedom associated with play for modernist and post-modernist artists. The other characterizes a global "game culture" of media convergence, a growing concentration of media ownership, and the simultaneous, increasing accessibility of production and distribution technologies to media consumers, empowering new forms of political activism. Throughout the book, I ask how minority identities have been reconfigured in mediated play and how certain minority groups have actively drawn on changing media technologies and aesthetic forms to interrupt or engage in political games governed by the allegedly universal rules of the capitalist market, European democracy, and national culture. The first two chapters investigate the gaps and continuities between the last communist and the first postcommunist generations in the spheres of education, tourism, and children's media culture. The third chapter focuses on musical entertainment and the changing situation of the "European minority," the Roma. The last two chapters analyze mediated reconfigurations of gender and sexuality by considering a range of media practices and texts including feature films, literature, video games, and independent videos.

The chapters foreground situations where anxieties about the encroachment of global entertainment media and its new technologies on national literature, art film, and centralized education clash and combine with euphoria over the democratizing potential of new technologies, European mobility, and transnational exchange. The argument examines the rich aesthetic hybrids that have grown out of the transitional post-communist terrain in their interlinked global, regional, national, and subnational circumstances of production, distribution, and reception.

While "play" and "games" are tools in explaining cultural change rather than the objects of analysis themselves, I account for my selective engagement with these notions with the following brief historical overview of serious theorizing about the notions of play and games. I linger on post-Romantic theories, which have had the most enduring influence on Eurocentric games of identity and media, and on theories that provide an interdisciplinary platform for understanding ludic media and identities in the post–Cold War era.

## Play as a Serious Concept

As a philosophical notion, "play" is so elusive and general that it is almost synonymous with "life." The historical, linguistic, and geopolitical differentiations in theorizing play therefore yield a wealth of insight. In ancient Greek, the same root is shared by the words for *education* (*paideia*), *play/game/pastime/sport* (*paidia*), and *children* (*paides*). These terms often appear in the same context, along with *pedagogy* (*paidagogia*), whose aim is to encourage learning as a form of play (Livescu 2003). Plato advocated motivated play geared toward the growth of individuals who would contribute to creating a just society and promote the idea of "Good," living life as play. Socrates considered *dialectic*, the final stage of education for a philosopher, serious play (Livescu 2003). But play appeared in classical thought as something to be curbed and directed, rather than as a principle of life or a subject of study in its own right. Theories of play did not begin to appear until Rabelais's work and Erasmus's *In Praise of Folly* (1511), at the same time that the fool became a philosophical figure. The Enlightenment reduced play to childishness, not worthy of the attention of serious philosophers (Connor 2005).

The kind of serious thinking about play that profoundly informed European nationalisms as well as theories of modern and postmodern culture is distinctively modern and had not existed until the late 1700s, the period of the late Enlightenment and early Romanticism (Sutton-Smith 1997, 6; Connor 2005). Kant's notion of "aesthetic judgment" in his *Critique of Judgement* (1790), which began the "serious turn" toward play, is grounded in the "free play" of the imagination, which is unconstrained by rules of thought and preexisting concepts. Modern theories that try to define or rely on play as an operative term are all indebted to Kant's play notion. His idea links play to a kind of freedom that is not entirely unregulated, but liberating because it determines its own rules (Connor 2005). As I argue in the first chapter, Friedrich Schiller's formalization of Kant's notion of play is especially important for discussing postcommunist culture's entry into global game culture. His *Letters on the Aesthetic Education of Man* secures a Romantic bond between play and art, conferring privilege on the select few who are most sensitive to and appreciative of the stuff of art, the Beautiful. A post-Romantic line of thought inspired by Kant and Schiller has helped solidify the link between art and play in the humanities. Some of the most influential works in Europe in this regard have been Matthew Arnold's *Culture and Anarchy*, which defines and valorizes the capacity for the "free disinterested play of thought"; and Martin Heidegger's discussion of poetry as a form through which humankind creates new worlds and new varieties of meaning (Livescu 2003). In chapter 5, I elaborate on the fundamental role of poetry in the self-definition of Eastern European nations.

The modern preoccupation with play also indicates a concern with freedom under the rapidly changing conditions of industrialization, the regulation of life, and the emerging distinction between public and private times, work and leisure. Modernity produced the world of play by threatening it and placing it under special protection from the increasingly encroaching world of work. An important consequence of this development is play's association with childhood. This association inspired the developmentalist theories of Klein, Piaget, Vygotsky, Winnicott, and Gross, who used the metaphor of play in their construction of normativized mental growth, and the evolutionary argument of Karl Groos's *The Play of Animals* (1898) and *The Play of Man* (1901), in which he claims that the function of play is preparation and training (Connor 2005; Sefton-Green 1998, 3). Games and play were proper adult activities in the Middle Ages, but changing patterns of leisure as a result of industrialization relegated leisure to youth. The sense of alarm over play's endangered status led to the idealization of childhood as a play age when innocence needs to be protected (Sefton-Green 1998, 1). It is precisely this notion of the safety of childhood, as well as of individual children, that is widely seen as threatened by television and new media technologies in our age (2). Concerns about the "disappearance of childhood" have resulted in particularly intense debates and radical reforms in postcommunist educational systems, discussed in chapter 1, and in a general sense of alarm over the erosion of educational children's television programming and the onslaught of commercial children's television, discussed in chapter 2.

Two of the most influential modern theories entirely dedicated to defining play are Johan Huizinga's *Homo Ludens* (1938) and Roger Caillois's *Man, Play and Games* (1961). Both volumes have proven to be valuable resources for carving out a disciplinary space for the emerging study of video games. *Homo Ludens* extends the empire of play across the animal kingdom, arguing that play is older than culture because it does not presuppose human society. Both books argue that human activities such as law, poetry, war, culture, and music all encompass play in essence and manifestation. Huizinga's and Caillois's works also mark the play notion's increasing centrality to twentieth-century European philosophy. Jean-Paul Sartre continues the humanistic inquiry that ties play to freedom: "When a man is playing, bent on discovering himself as free in his very action, he certainly could not be concerned with possessing a being in the world. His goal, which he aims at through sports or pantomime or games, is to attain himself as a certain being, precisely the being which is in question in his being" (Sartre 1969, 581). Friedrich Nietzsche and Hans-Georg Gadamer begin to trim the post-Romantic idealism that characterizes even Sartre's play notion and assert the primacy of the game over the freedom of the player. In *Truth and Method* (1960), Gadamer sets out to peel off the subjective meaning that had been attached to play since Kant and Schiller. To Gadamer, play is "the mode of being of the work of art itself." It has an essence independent of the consciousness of those who play. This theory opens the field to the deconstructionist view: playfulness takes place within the work of art itself.[1]

In a similar vein, a number of literary theorists in the twentieth century placed playfulness within the very working of language. Whereas for structuralist thinkers Claude Lévi-Strauss and Ferdinand de Saussure culture and language are structured like a game, with prescriptive rules, the text for Roland Barthes is structured like children's play or musical performance (Barthes 1977). It exhibits the infinite playfulness of the signifier. In the act of reading, the text plays, while the reader also plays the text as one plays a game. Mikhail Bakhtin also denounces the formalist and structuralist views of language as monologic. For him, language is characterized by *heteroglossia*, or the internal stratification of language, the interplay among social dialects, class, and professional languages. The novel is especially apt at displaying these centrifugal forces at work in language. In *Rabelais and His World* (1984), Bakhtin writes about the ludic culture of the carnivalesque that flourished in the Middle Ages, which valued the profane, vulgar, grotesque, and obscene, and used consumption as an expression of resistance to the official high culture of the church and the state. I draw on Bakhtin's concept of the carnivalesque throughout this book to theorize a similarly exuberant, consumption-oriented aesthetic in Roma reality television, ethnicized performances of global hip-hop, and the animated "ghetto film" *The District* in chapter 3; reflections on postcommunist masculinity, violence, and consumption in the work of filmmakers such as Emir Kusturica, Jan Svankmajer, and György Pálfi in chapter 4; and in the videos of lesbian visual activists in chapter 5.[2]

### The Post–Cold War Media Playground

The late twentieth century saw the expansion of postmodern media entertainment on a global scale. Steven Connor observes symptoms of an increasing division between the freedom associated with play in Romantic and modernist thought and contemporary, all-encompassing cultural processes, which are increasingly gamelike:

Ours is a world built around and governed by the production of play and the consumption of leisure and pleasure. Perhaps in such a world the free play of the faculties has become the fluctuation of desires that nobody can be quite sure any more belong to them, and the interior purposiveness of game has become the immanent dynamic of self-replication of our systemacity as such. Furthermore, ours is a world in which the operations of game have become more and more separated from the conditions of play. Money, science, war, pedagogy, sex are all being configured as forms of strategy or game-theory, in the sense marked out by Gadamer, governed by the ludic principle, that which gives itself its own rules and purpose (Connor 2005).

Perhaps play is becoming more ambivalent than ever before, Connor concludes. "And this is for a particular reason, if the function of play has in part been to maintain and multiply ambivalence itself; the condition of play is one in which things both are and are not, both do and do not matter" (2005).

The ambiguity of play has been identified as a key characteristic of the postmodern culture of late capitalism. Anthony Appiah famously argued that "postmodernism" is too complex to define; but in all domains in which it has been evoked, "there is an antecendent practice that laid claim to a certain exclusivity of insight, and in each of them 'postmodernism' is a name for the rejection of that claim to exclusivity, a rejection that is almost always more playful, though not necessarily less serious, than the practice it aims to replace" (Appiah 1991, 341). For Fredric

Jameson, postmodernism is not a question of subject matter but of the merging of art with commodity production. In this sense, the cinema is the true postmodernist art form, because it has more or less done away with distinctions between high and low art, mixing culture and economics, local artistic tradition and global advertising (MacCabe 1992, xi).

Such assessments of postmodernism need continual updating in the new millennium, taking into account the emergence of a new world order at the end of the Cold War, which has resulted in the global dispersion of American consumer culture and qualitatively different cultural, economic, and technological practices on a global scale. Theorists as different as Jean Baudrillard, Andreas Huyssen, Fredric Jameson, Svetlana Boym, or Neil Postman converge in distinguishing contemporary culture from earlier, allegedly more "serious" ages. Postmodern game culture, in these accounts, is abandoned by grand, guiding narratives for ludic principles—consumerism, depthlessness, nostalgia, pastiche, and entertaining spectacle, which saturate public and private spheres alike. Some, like Postman, decry the mediatization of culture and the privileging of entertainment over rational public discourse as a process of infantilization, in which the reign of images and the imagination has supplanted a more discursive, print-based, and, by implication, more mature culture (Postman 1985). According to Thomas Mitchell, the "pictorial turn" necessitates a serious inquiry into the relationship between spectacle and surveillance and a distrust in mass culture's seductive pleasures, a position that should be informed by the Frankfurt School's aversion to mass culture and Wittgenstein's iconophobia (Mitchell 1994, 13). Douglas Kellner claims that in contemporary technocapitalist societies media culture centrally determines social identities and sociopolitical values, performing "pedagogies of everyday life." "A media culture has emerged in which images, sounds, and spectacles help produce the fabric of everyday life, dominating leisure time, shaping political views and social behavior, and providing the materials out of which people forge their identities" (Kellner 2003, 1).

Some social scientists see liberating possibilities in the "cultural turn," to use Jameson's term, where the work of the imagination mediated by electronic media is "a constitutive feature of modern subjectivity" (Appadurai 1996, 2–3), and where fantasy has become a social category and social practice (Appadurai 1994, 327). James Clifford, spearheading a serious engagement with play in the social sciences, proposes to transform ethnography's traditionally ethnocentric methods by acknowledging the increasingly central role of play in ethnographic fieldwork (Clifford 2002).[3] Perhaps the most radical challenge to pessimistic theories of postmodern media culture is now coming from video game theory, many of whose practitioners conceptualize what they see as an ongoing historical transformation from a narrative to a ludic ontology, which proceeds from seriousness to playfulness, from legitimation to participation, from passive consumption to the active construction of identities.[4]

To develop a truly global perspective flexible enough to integrate the study of post–Cold War European media transformations, I find that the most productive approaches are those that actively resist both the overly optimistic and the overly pessimistic projections about the blending of consumption, pleasure, and play with citizenship and politics, and those that acknowledge continuities between digital game culture and more traditional forms of play.[5]

As I argue in chapters 2 and 3, television has rapidly become the playground for identity formation and citizenship training in the New Europe. Television scholars have analyzed this as a phenomenon expanding on a global scale. They have observed new forms of citizenship forming around television watching, creating a "fan democracy" (van Zoonen 2004) of television viewers, or "normal citizens" (Ellis 1982), whose activities take place in the sphere of "democratainment" (Hartley 2004). John Hartley compares television to the medieval church and other premodern media in its teaching functions. Since governments have prevented television from becoming directly politicized, it teaches predominantly advertising literacy and addresses the consumer rather than the student. It promotes among its subjects both identity (sameness) and difference (choice). Television, or, more broadly, media citizenship, challenges the boundaries of traditional political theory, which typically sees citizenship as something prior to, separate from, and eroded by media consumption (Hartley 2004). In a similar vein, Liesbet van Zoonen argues that the interactive consumption that voting affords on reality programs such as the British format *Pop Idol* and the Dutch format *Big Brother* can be seen as civic processes taking place in the public sphere, where entertainment and politics are now inseparable (van Zoonen 2004, 40). *Big Brother* and other shows have mobilized audiences to participate, intervene, judge, and vote—even if the stakes of these negotiations remain unavoidably trivial. There are several analogies between fans and citizens; fandom is forming communities that behave like ideal, consensus-building political constituencies, offering a range of platforms and causes. Furthermore, despite political scientists' insistence on the rational decision-making involved in civic activities, in both cases, it is the participants' emotional investment and the development of affective intelligence that drives activity (van Zoonen 2004).

Nick Couldry also proposes that we break with the model of the passive media consumer holed up in an individual virtual bubble, and reconnect otherwise isolated areas of consumption and citizenship (Couldry 2004, 21–23). He sets out to investigate hybrid objects of research, which cross the "real digital divide" between the languages of markets and politics. This division hides the participatory production practices of consumers, which generate and sustain new spaces of public connection. "Crucial here are precisely the possibilities for more dispersed symbolic production/consumption (themselves connected with aspects of the so-called 'new economy' . . . that may tell us something significant about the current crisis in political and social 'belonging' " (24). Departing from large-scale models of network flows versus local resistance such as Manuel Castells's (1996), Couldry is interested in subnational or other local networks that initiate public connections related to consumption, and which should be studied in international comparative research (27). Similar to Hartley, he wants to foreground the continuities between new, global, and older state-centered forms of citizenship and resist the temptation to suspend the primacy of the nation-state framework (28).

This point is particularly relevant in the postcommunist region, where nation-states have remained active negotiators of media ownership and where media citizenship is channeled through powerful affective relations to national languages and cultures. In chapter 1, I showcase negotiations among the nation-state, European media corporations such as Axel-Springer, and grassroots, not-for-profit media literacy initiatives, all of which harness the new generation's nationalistic allegiances for allegedly educational purposes. Studies of postcommunist media, politics, and identities are very much mired in the traditional frameworks these scholars criticize, in which citizenship is prior to and necessarily damaged by media relations (Hartley 2004, 524). Van Zoonen's proposition that emotional involvement is the connecting glue between participation in public politics and television fandom should also help redirect attention from top-down, elite cultural forms and controls to the affective activities of ordinary citizens in TV land in the era of what George E. Marcus calls "affective citizenship" (Marcus 2002).

However, postcommunist television is inundated with imports—primarily American. The local production consists of reality formats and newly transplanted varieties of established genres such as soap operas. Television programming as a whole, therefore, has a derivative, awkward, distancing quality, where the most indigenous and thus popular shows are the national variations of *Pop Idol*, one of my objects of discussion in chapter 3. State-controlled channels only contribute to this alienation since their programming is widely—and correctly—perceived to serve the political agendas of ruling parties. Therefore, the idea and practice of television fandom is something rather foreign in Eastern Europe. The general and hardly debatable perception that the result of post-1989 commercialization has been a steep decline in the quality of programming has not galvanized political participation. Instead, it proves to citizens—rendered cynical by the frequent turnover of historical "truths," confirmed and compounded by postcommunist governments' recent public blunders and crises of legitimacy—that politics and television are equally trashy, trivial, and untrustworthy shows. As I argued above, one also needs to take to heart Mark Andrejevic's analysis of viewer interactivity in the CBS version of *Big Brother* as a form of voluntary viewer submission to surveillance and data mining (Andrejevic 2001). The postcommunist situation underscores the relevance of Daniel Dayan's question: under what conditions could TV audiences actually become publics (Dayan 2001)?

It is equally questionable whether postcommunist media consumers will ever be included in Henry Jenkins's inspired, but perhaps a bit overly optimistic, account of the "cosmopedia" of online fan communities, an emerging knowledge space that will contribute to the breakdown of geographic constraints on communication, the declining loyalty of individuals to organized groups, and the diminished power of nation-states over their citizens (Jenkins 2006, 137). Jenkins draws on Pierre Levy's idea of "collective intelligence" to work out a model for fan-based politics in a culture where "we are trying out through play patterns of interaction that will soon penetrate every aspect of our lives. Levy, in short, gives us a model for a fan-based politics" (Jenkins 2006, 135). He argues that a new, do-it-yourself media production of this participatory culture is emerging, primarily in subcultures, because consumers are now able to employ new technologies to archive, annotate, appropriate, and recirculate media content. Economic trends favor horizontally integrated media conglomerates and encourage the flow of images, ideas, and narratives across multiple media channels, which demands more active modes of spectatorship (135). Jenkins provides a useful and attractive view of globally converging interactive digital media culture as an interplay of two forces: corporate convergence guarantees the flow of media content across different platforms and national borders, while the grassroots convergence of digitally empowered consumers plays a role in shaping the production, distribution, and reception of media content. However, the alleged global reach of such logic, the assumption that it is only a matter of time before these flows clear away geographical and national boundaries, becomes problematic when one moves outside of the Asian-American framework within which Jenkins's examples of this convergence logic reside (157).

But what do we do with cultures where digitalization has been progressing at a slow and geographically uneven pace (see Lengel 2000)? Where fandom is something new and largely imported? Where there is intense viewer suspicion about American popular culture, and Japanese media mixes seem not to have taken hold? Where traditions of play have valorized the autonomous, creative individual, and originality above all else? Where cultural poaching already has a long tradition, in the form of avant-garde art and an allegorical oppositional culture, which still enjoys a great deal of nostalgic reverie? Will people of these cultures be content with incorporating and modifying what is ultimately seen as Hollywood garbage as the limit of their consumer agencies? Even if there is no place outside of converging commodity culture, perhaps such differences of tradition and collective positioning should be taken into account to refine a model that necessarily filters participatory citizenship through participatory fandom.

Such questions are just barely beginning to inform communication and media studies research in relation to postcommunism. My observations suggest that in many cases, new peer-to-peer technologies and participatory digital possibilities have actually rekindled belonging to national communities. The most populous social networking sites in Eastern Europe are primarily national and operate almost exclusively in national languages.[6] While citizens from these European peripheries participate in global file sharing and networking sites such as YouTube and MySpace, the more meaningful communication is conducted in "secret" national languages, as I point out in chapter 3 in relation to the YouTube presence of Eastern European Roma pop musicians. Instead of entering the happy cosmopedia of fan democracies, citizens of the New Europe are experiencing a selective process of media globalization. Rather than help to build a sense of civic responsibility on the ruins of communist apathy toward politics, the ludic emphasis of this transformation may even discourage political participation. There is no automatic equivalent of the active, politically conscious democratic consumer in the political wasteland left by communism, which Europeanization processes aim further to depoliticize and tame into a quiet, full-stomach market for media entertainment and tourism. The evidence collected in this book supports the argument that digital technologies may be accelerating contradictory tendencies toward globalization and localization (Sefton-Green 1998, 8).

## Agonic Power Games and Postcommunist Identities

I have attempted to lay out some important differences and continuities between contemporary theories of global game culture and earlier attempts that theorize play and to theorize culture through play. The main focus in this book is on the ideological implications of mediated play practices, which play theories often overlook. My approach is not primarily descriptive, although the chapters inevitably contribute to mapping new playing fields in the New Europe through the lens of theories developed elsewhere. I want to use the perspectives of latecomer, peripheral, "modernist" post-Soviet cultures on play in order to hold open to criticism the ethnocentrism that often underscores accounts of interactivity, technologization, and the politically mobilizing possibilities of new media culture. I am thus also interested in the power games that often go unacknowledged in the theories of cultural change themselves. Therefore, a poststructuralist necessity to keep the game open permeates each chapter. Contrary to notions, widely accepted in Eastern Europe, that feminist and postcolonial thinking constitute an ideological closing down of the frontiers of theoretical play, I draw on such theories as a way to keep theoretical horizons open—to illuminate the nationalistic, exclusionary, truth-seeking paradigms that continue to operate under the guise of the "free play" on which European high culture prides itself, often set in opposition to "infantile" and "consumerist" American popular culture.

Chapter 1 draws on the work of game studies scholars who resist the liberatory rhetoric of interactivity and resurrect the Frankfurt School to detect ideological implications in computerized play, which put many digital games in the service of a consumerist pedagogy. I explore the conflict and continuity between the increasingly obsolete emphasis on the nationalized, literature-based play of the imagination and the new uncontrollable world of digital games and the Internet in comparison with similar debates taking place in North American education. The chapter focuses attention on the EU and national educational programs, often cofunded by media corporations, which are designed to sustain print literacy by harnessing the edutainment potential of Internet-based games. The analysis also foregrounds the unspoken agenda of such programs: the symbolic inclusion of postcommunist populations in the European Union, whose citizen identities are limited to the nostalgic evocation of a shared cultural heritage and a touristic European identity.

The second chapter is about postsocialist nostalgia, understood as a play with time—a way to capture, preserve, and process slipping memories of socialism. It discusses the changing relations between children's and adult media cultures in terms of a shift from the small creatures that populated the distinct allegorical children's animation of late socialism, such as *Krtek* (the "Little Mole"), to the postsocialist arrival and triumph of the dinosaur, a symptom of what Svetlana Boym calls the "*Jurassic Park* Syndrome." The little mole and the dinosaur represent distinct nostalgic possibilities, different ways of imagining the past as a source of identity formation in the present. While the postsocialist transformation of children's culture has been radical, I point to continuities between late and postcommunist popular entertainment. As I show, an important site of this continuity is the regional popularity of imported and adapted Westerns, a bridge between children and adult cultures and an important terrain for the imaginative rehearsal of proper gendered and racialized national citizenship.

Chapter 3 examines the racial and class politics of musical play as they are manifested in negotiations among the postcommunist state, the European Union, the global music industry, and Roma minority groups. The argument foregrounds a disavowed register of European nationalisms: the moral majority's ludophilia toward "lazy" and "unproductive" Gypsies. Evoking Stuart Hall's theorization of playful Caribbean cultural identities, the chapter discusses Roma Rap, the Czech and Hungarian Idol series, Roma reality television, minority participation in the European song contest *Eurovision*, various politicized manifestations of Afro-American hip-hop by European minorities, and the animated "ghetto film" *Nyócker* (*The District*, 2004). All of these media texts and practices redefine Roma "truth" as a transnational play of identity. At the same time as they politicize musical entertainment and reappropriate the play-fulness of Roma identities from national moral majorities, however, they are also caught up in the consumerist, corporate logic of world music. This logic, in a paradoxical turn, is often appropriated by the shop-window multiculturalism of nation-states and the European Union.

In chapter 4, I explain why Judith Butler's theory of gender performa-tivity has been taken up so enthusiastically by pockets of feminism that are slowly beginning to identify and distinguish themselves in the New Europe. The discussion places in a transnational context the ambivalence that characterizes the visual activism of the Budapest-based Lesbian Film Collective, one of a handful of queer visual activist groups in Eastern Europe—their profound desire to be represented in the terms of national culture, on the one hand, and their efforts to draw on transnational alli-ances and the ludic strategies of global "infotainment" media, on the other. While the former makes their work comparable to allegorical films about lesbianism made in other postcolonial contexts, such as India and Latin America, the latter incorporates poststructuralist notions of gender identity and invites comparisons with the performative activism of groups such as ACT UP. Homi Bhabha's idea of the performativity of the nation as narration helps explain how the playful visual activism of newly emerging lesbian groups brings such a contradictory thing as "national lesbianism" into representation.

The final chapter draws a trajectory of the hidden gendered dimensions of high art as play in Eastern European film of the past twenty-five years. It takes a close look at the changing relationship between Eastern and Southern European nationalisms and the figure of the playful modernist artist, to whom Rey Chow refers as a "man-child" in the analogical Chinese context. The discussion brings together the crisis of nationalism that began to manifest itself in the 1980s, sexually ambiguous visual representations of artists, and a regional preference for a carnivalistic aesthetic reaction to both ethno-nationalism and global entertainment media. Movies as different as *Hukkle*, a "nature documentary" about postcommunist rural Hungary; *Cabaret Balkan*, Emir Kusturica's mythi-cal history of Yugoslavia and the post-Yugoslav wars; and the surrealist animation of Jan Svankmajer all represent the troubles of the transitional nation as the trouble with men. The discussion demystifies the long-effaced gender privileges attached to art as play in Eastern and Southern European cultures along with a nostalgic Western investment in the freedom of the intellectual's playful masculinity. The last two chapters also assert that the poststructuralist necessity of postcolonial thinking is a productive direction to explore in order to render more flexible the rules of current political and economic power games.

The postmodern condition of *jeux sans frontières*, which organizes the economy, science, war, theory, education, sex, and certainly the media, does not mean the absence of rules, the constant threat of anarchy. To configure the gamelike nature of these activities is, rather, to highlight their interconnectedness and ensure what James Tully calls the "agonic freedom" of the players. Tully outlines the conceptual shift toward seeing human activities as agonic games in twentieth-century political philosophy (Tully 1999). Ludwig Wittgenstein, in the 1930s, rejected metatheories of language as a formal system of representation and shifted the focus to the multiplicity of activities he famously called "language games" (Wittgenstein 1974). He argued that we did not need another theory of the game—another game with signs—but, rather, a representation of what the players do and how they do it. In a similar vein, in the 1950s, Hannah Arendt turned her attention away from the traditional terrain of political science, policies, institutions, routines, and theories of governance (Arendt 1958). Instead, she confronted the activity of politics itself as a game of agonic activities for recognition and rule among participants who, like players in other games, take on citizen identities and interact in the public space.

At its core, this book follows the general reorientation in twentieth-century thinking from grand theories that promise to lead to "truth" toward what Foucault calls "truth games"; from the quest for truth adopted by Orwell and his followers to a representation of politics as "the endless struggle between lots of half-truths, cunning omissions, and competing narratives, which may offset each other, but never entirely produce a single consensus" (Jay 2006, 93–94). Politics, in this extended sense, is an agonic activity (from *agere*, "to begin, rule, and lead" and *gerere*, "to carry a task through together") that encompasses the entire, necessarily mediated, public sphere and politicizes its gamelike practices. Despite the triumphant rhetoric that announced capitalism's victory over communism, what died with communism was the *illusion* of historical "truth" as something one can attain by pursuing the right politics.

Citizens today assemble, dialogue, and contest forms of governance outside the formal institutions of representative democracy in a variety of ways, which include television spectatorship as well as cyberspace exploration. Such an expanded and open-ended conception of the public allows for a synthesis between media citizenship and fan democracy, as well as the older and more restricted idea of politics conceived as prior to and separate from media entertainment. In the post–Cold War era of media globalization, effective political power can no longer be assumed to be invested in representative governments alone (Tully 1999, 177). Governance is dispersed—shared, negotiated, and contested by diverse agencies at local, regional, national, and international levels. In this light, the struggles around the multiple practices of governance can be seen and analyzed as the democratic forms of citizen participation that accompany media globalization and neoliberalism (178). The vision this book hopes to offer is one in which political and cultural participation are seen as games whose rules are permanently open to negotiation.

# 1

## A Euro-American Trip from Aesthetic Education to Educational Games

### Play and the Crisis of Education in the United States

In an episode of the popular CBS sitcom *Everybody Loves Raymond*,[1] Raymond notices that his children have too much homework and no time to play. His wife encourages him to talk to the teacher, who defensively refers him to the "curriculum" and its "standards," which put pressure on her to prepare students for centralized tests. When it appears that his concern is shared by other similarly timid parents, however, Raymond finds himself reluctantly testifying to the school board in defense of play, for which children, overburdened by standardized school tests, no longer have time. He expresses worry that, in their anxious efforts to prepare children for success in the future, adults take away their kids' present. His sincere speech seems to elicit sympathy from the board until he makes a grammatical mistake, which is immediately seen to justify the effort to implement strict standards for teaching "the basics" and dissolves the problem in the ambiguity of the laugh track.

The ambiguity in which the public anxiety about educating children in a global media and information age is allowed to submerge in this episode is symptomatic of confusions about the issue in both popular cultural and scholarly reflections. Like Raymond's, many such reflections lament the loss of freedom that unmediated, unregulated play affords children, particularly in economically prosperous countries. Instead, they point out, there is a tendency to drown children in standardized tests and computer-mediated activities. However, the disciplinary apparatuses that such reflections enlist and the ethical positions they occupy have hardly begun to be mapped. This chapter focuses on education as a contested and sensitive terrain to register recent global changes in the ideological role of play in teaching and learning.

I am interested in the widening gap within educational theory and practice between two senses of play: One is conceptualized as the open-ended, active, and creative essence of the natural process of childhood learning. It is rightly considered by parents and educational experts to be endangered by digital, virtual play and educational reforms enforced by global competition. It is therefore often protectively enveloped in nostalgia for a nontechnological, previrtual, "healthy" past. The second sense of play, seen as rapidly undermining the former, is associated with the Internet, computer games, and other technologies of an increasingly integrated global media culture. Those who are anxious about the disappearance of unregulated play from children's lives worry that technologically mediated play creates isolated, cyborg identities. Even worse, it is thought to allow giant media corporations to wield increasing control over children's imaginations, turning schools into edutaining training grounds for raising the next generation of consumers.

This is a legitimate worry. It needs to be taken seriously and tackled as part of a worldwide transition toward a game culture of entertainment. While proposing and encouraging unregulated play in children's lives is a noble goal in this regard, it will remain ineffective unless its proponents examine the issue in its complex global dimension. Adopting a comparative, worldwide lens is equally important in order to peel off the layers of fear and nostalgia that often keep advocacy for "play" tied to essentialist and conservative affiliations, most prominently nationalism. Mystifying "tradition," "human nature," or "the child" obscures a critical approach to education just as much as blind faith in technological progress and economic competition do, endlessly repeated by policy makers and executives who want to stake out a hold in education.

I start here with a large-scale comparison of recent educational developments caught up in the conflict between open-ended play and game practices enhanced by electronic technology. The comparison focuses on the United States and Europe as two of several centers of economic and political power in a postbipolar, transitional world order. The main question I ask is how mediated education has been instrumentalized in the United States and within an expanding European Union in the service of consolidating neoimperial geopolitical power in the post–Cold War era. In important ways, as I show, educational trends are converging, reflecting and mobilizing anxieties about a global competition in which the economic success of states and individuals is bound up with technological advances and marketable, entertaining representations. However, the transition in educational systems and theories from open-ended, imaginative play to gaming and other electronic edutainment practices builds on different local histories and political developments.

In the second half of this chapter, I present case studies that demonstrate how the dynamic between "unmediated play" and electronic games has informed the transformation of postcommunist educational systems. Such a transformation is indebted to the nationalistic cultivation of the written word, but is also affected by both a U.S.-centered media economy eager to incorporate new consumer markets and the policies of an expanding European Union eager to incorporate a new touristic-cultural market. The last section of the chapter points out the ambiguities of the touristic incorporation of the new member states: tourism functions as a specifically European manifestation of the emerging ontological paradigm of global consumer capitalism. This paradigm builds on and purportedly continues the historical educational mission of nineteenth-century leisure migration and premodern forms of travel for training. At the same time, the playful connotations and gamelike virtualization of tourism cover up the continuing imperial West-East hierarchy within the continent: a nostalgic, touristic, consumerist incorporation within the European Union constitutes the only sphere of equality for the new member states.

## Game Culture and the Corporate Model of Education

The United States is the epicenter of the global media entertainment industry, the source of many innovations in information and communication technology. It also provides a model for foreshadowing the effects of such developments on the education of the next generations worldwide. Public education has long been considered to be in a state of crisis in the United States. One of the enduring debates that frame this crisis is between play-based pedagogies and technologically mediated "edutainment" practices, which typically go along with the political push toward accountability. As an educational expert argues, "The economic, technological, political and social foundations that support the teaching of young children today have become so entangled, contentious, and volatile that I believe no one can possibly pretend to know in any straightforward way what is best for children at this moment in time, or how best to teach them" (Wilson 2003, 111).

Questions of equality and the anxiety over unpredictable and nonmeasurable media influences continue to haunt recent educational initiatives embraced by policy makers and business executives on the right and the left alike. Large-scale, top-down reforms have swept public education in the United States in the past twenty years, touting Standards, Account-ability, Testing, and Technology, with the explicit intention to ensure the United States's competitive edge in an information-based global economy. The reforms began under the presidency of Ronald Reagan, continued under those of George H. W. Bush and Bill Clinton, and reached their most recent epitome under George W. Bush's administration (Olfman 2003a, 2). The single most important actor in the current upheavals in education is agreed to be the computer (Wilson 2003, 112). It is a largely unchallenged assumption among educators, politicians, and parents today that computers and the Internet play a positive role in education, and computer literacy must be acquired at an early age, otherwise the child will be unsuccessful in (professional) life (119). This mythification of the computer—often in favorable comparison to television—harks back to the computer-field breakthroughs of the 1960s. These inspired the "information-processing" model of cognition, which likens the mind to the computer (Olfman 2003a, 7). There is an undeniable synergy between mechanistic models of the mind and the current technological revolution, where the goal of education is to prepare kids to serve global, technology-based industries (8). The universal push for wired classrooms and homes is also popular because the rhetoric of easy access to the Internet and the leveling effect of standardized testing are wrapped in the rhetoric of democracy, embodying and reviving the American Dream (7).

But instead of a quality education for all, many children do get left behind, exposing the economic and political reality that had spawned the push for standards and accountability in the first place. Henry Giroux argues that since the early 1960s, big business corporations have increas-ingly appropriated the goal of making schools relevant to students' lives by reducing the curriculum to job training and consumption (Giroux 1994, 48). Behind the manifest aim of the corporate redefinition of excel-lence as a more rigorous math and science curriculum and a mastery of techniques, there has been a tendency to return to an authoritarian classroom model, where "transmission, standardization, and control are the defining principles of the curriculum" (49). For Reagan conserva-tives, schools became producers of human capital. Reaganite school reforms reflected corporate values and individualist goals and were part of a broader conservative attack on multiculturalism, arts, civil rights, and the democratization of the academic canon. Such an attack capitalized on existing fears of a globalized future in order to promote "imaginary unities" such as common culture and national identity (57).

Giroux contests the corporate model of education by drawing on psychoanalytic theories that conceive of identities as relational, dialogical, and processual (59), constituted in social struggle among different communities over issues of representation, social justice, and the distribution of resources (61). Pyschologists and educational experts similarly concerned about the appropriation of public education by corporate executives and policy makers tirelessly call attention to the fact that the child, unlike the machine, processes information through the uniquely human prisms of emotion, sensory and kinesthetic experience, artistry, and imagination. It is a tragic mistake, they argue, to idealize the computer and teach kids to think like it (Olfman 2003b, 7–10). In addition, the information-processing model does not take into proper consideration the developmental stages described most memorably by Jean Piaget and ignores the rich multidisciplinary literature on the critical role of play in cognitive, social, emotional, and ethical development (Simms 2003, 177). As Eva-Maria Simms puts it, play is not only beginning to vanish from American public life but it has become "antithetical to the goals of Western education" (178).

Some scholars go as far as to associate the dramatic recent rise of psychological disorders such as ADHD and autism as well as the general increase of hyperactivity, impulsivity, and distractibility among school-age children with the decrease in children's unmediated play time and the corresponding rise of computer gaming. Thomas Armstrong defines unmediated play time as an open-ended exploration involving the broad use of the imagination, and computer-mediated play as passive, close-ended, unimaginative, and short on language development and social interaction opportunities (Armstrong 2003, 165). Sharna Olfman links two seemingly opposing trends: the "hurried child syndrome," driven by adult anxiety about tests and technological skills, and the tendency to silence kids by offering them screens (Olfman 2003a, 204). Even more disturbing, David Grossman argues, electronic gaming desensitizes children through a process of classical conditioning, associating violence with pleasure much like military training desensitizes soldiers, increasingly through computer simulation (Olfman 2003a, 206). Setting the Romantic ethic and aesthetic against a positivistic, progress-driven ethos, Olfman warns that the "socially patterned defect" and "pathogenic belief system" that is now becoming normative in the United States may threaten our very survival, since the next generation may not privilege reality over virtual reality and human intelligence over machine intelligence (207–208).

When analyzing current educational trends, it is particularly important to historicize and connect two frameworks, both of which tend to operate through dehistoricized "truth" statements: the social and political context in which corporations and policy makers can intimidate educational professionals and parents into investing in uncritical and expensive technological innovation and a conservative, drill-and-kill model of learning; and psychological accounts of the emotional and cognitive impact and potential of computer culture, especially gaming, in relation to bodies and subjectivities, along with aesthetic-representational analyses of specific computer games. Julian Sefton-Green points out how television and, especially, new media technologies have increased the sense of threat to play. He reminds us, however, that play's status as a safety net around the alleged innocence of childhood was generated only in early modernity, when industrialization divided work and leisure time. The association between play and childhood was further cemented in the nineteenth and early twentieth centuries by child-development theorists and psychologists who used the metaphor of play to construct a normativized model of mental growth (Sefton-Green 1998, 3).

This history seems to have reached a new stage when we consider that the largest area of computer use, and one of the economically most powerful, is that of the computer game and related leisure activities. Equally, much supposedly serious use of the computer, particularly for educational purposes, has become more "frivolous" with the development of info- or edu-tainment genres. . . . Playing computer games or even just playing with the computer is thus a central part of its usage: even, for example, the metaphor of "surfing the Net" carries leisure connotations (Sefton-Green 1998, 3).

Julian Stallabrass, whose argumentative ground is Marxist philosophy, offers another complex analysis of games, with particular attention to their ideological effects. He foregrounds the analogy between the workings of computer games and the very structure of global capitalism: "The computer game enforces on players a mechanization of the body in which their movements and their self-image as alter-ego provide both a physical and a simulated picture of the fragmented, allegorized and reified self under the conditions of capital" (Stallabrass 1993, 87). This depiction of subjectivity is remarkably similar to that of the student shaped by the information-processing, machine-emulating cognitive model of education. For Stallabrass, a marked neoliberal ethic defines most computer games, where the only character who improves is the alter ego and whose growth is always a matter of trade, his self-improvement unambiguously measured by numbers. The problematic assumption that all players start with the same resources—in stark contrast with the actual conditions of capitalism—is naturalized in most games just as much as it is naturalized in the skill-enhancing, test-driven "democratic" model of education that underscores recent U.S. educational initiatives such as "No Child Left Behind."

Stallabrass provocatively argues that trading games only make the latent capitalistic, allegorical content of computer games explicit: their founding principle is the tyranny of numbers, where one progresses by emulating the qualities of machine reaction, regulation, and economy in discrete, repetitive acts, following the rigid and episodic action of games through virtual labyrinths (89). The digital dichotomy 0/1 registers the simple moral dichotomies of these games. They find their most explicit form in military games, where destruction is disturbingly pleasurable (90), exposing the extent to which the military-industrial complex is economically intertwined with the computing and gaming industries (92). For Stallabrass, arcade play recalls Walter Benjamin's analysis of bourgeois culture, particularly his characterization of gambling as a combination of automatic action and affective engagement (95). Stallabrass also evokes Theodor Adorno's argument about the simulation of work in hobbies, where leisure activity cannot liberate itself from the internalized work habits of modernity (97). This is similar to what happens in computer games, where the repetition of small, futile, discrete tasks and the loss of the self in labor are real, but the activity remains unproductive.

For Matt Garite, the "interactive" feature of digital games, which is often referenced in order to distinguish them positively from "passive" media such as television, generally manifests itself as a relentless series of demands, a way of disciplining player behavior. He sees interactivity as an aggressive form of Louis Althusser's "interpellation," which induces autosurveillance, the penetration of information technology within the body and psyche of the individual subject, and a passive replication of its programs. Video games function through subjecting the players to a series of binary choices, a relentless testing logic that Baudrillard considers the distinguishing trait of all digital culture (Baudrillard 1983). Garite argues that testing is the primary means by which contemporary disciplinary mechanisms construct standardized, routine modes of behavior suitable to the working conditions of late capitalism. The buttons function like multiple choices on standardized tests (Garite 2003). In this view, video games, far from providing liberation from control through interactivity, function as the primary means of control and surveillance, whose central institutional site is precisely the educational system, also privileged by Althusser as the most effective Ideological State Apparatus. In a similar vein, Stallabrass is concerned that under the guise of alternative realities, computer games may sneak in a powerful tool of mental conformity (Stallabrass 1993, 104). "In their structure and content computer games are a capitalist, deeply conservative form of culture, and their political content is prescribed by the options open to democracy under modern capitalism, from games with liberal pretentions to those with quasi-fascist overtones" (104).

Indeed, reading such accounts, one cannot help asking whether the technologization and standardization of education are tools in an effort to render education part of an informational-military-entertainment machinery, whose invisible, underlying allegorical structure is best exemplified in (certain types of) computer games, and whose primary purpose is to promote and naturalize individualistic, uncritical virtual consumption. A similar view is suggested by Ellen Seiter in her persuasive analysis of product promotion and consumption training embedded in various levels of Nintendo's interactive kids' Web site Neopets (Seiter 2005, 83–100).

A different set of critics argue that such perspectives harbor a nostalgia for naturalized assumptions derived from a Romantic conception of the world and a model of the human mind hardwired to process information in terms of narrative representation. Gonzalo Frasca suggests that computer games, the first simulational media for the masses, signify a paradigm shift in cognitive skills (Frasca 2003, 224). Although he does not deny the fact that games have an economic agenda, which is most explicit in advergames, that is, downloadable Web-based games created exclusively to enable product placement, he also sees in game technology a new potential for empowering the consumer by providing accessible opportunities for production and for promoting decentralized thinking (223).

For Stallabrass, the gamer is played by the game: he or she is an allegorical figure in a predetermined system of social control. For Frasca, "simathors," or computer game designers, educate rather than train their simulations. They craft the rules of the game but ultimately share control over the outcome with the gamers themselves (Frasca 2003, 229). Frasca's discussion usefully refines Stallabrass's somewhat monolithic view of games: He adopts Roger Caillois's distinction between *paidia* (play) and *ludus* (game) to distinguish between relatively open-ended and closed digital games. The two kinds of games, he argues, carry different ideological agendas. Paidia games such as *SimCity*, with their "fuzzier logic" and their "scope beyond winners and losers," have the potential to become tools of critical learning (230).

James Paul Gee, a scholar of reading education, is even more optimistic about the educational potential of video games. In his book *What Video Games Have to Teach Us about Learning and Literacy*, he argues that games can be used effectively to resist the current trend to favor standardized tests and skill-and-drill curricula devoted to "the basics" (Gee 2003, 3). He analyzes his own gaming practice to prove that many games—even violent ones—require the gamer to think in ways most people are not prepared to, stuck as they are in romanticized, narrative educational models and content-driven ideological frameworks. He writes, "The theory of learning in good video games fits better with the modern, high-tech, global world today's children and teenagers live in than do the theories (and practices) of learning that they see in school" (7). He argues that the semiotic domain of video games successfully transports children beyond that of print literacy and helps them develop adaptable cognitive skills in active and even proactive ways (41). This makes gamer students able not only to read and produce ("write") more successfully but also to acquire critical thinking skills and a sense of social justice. Good games "encourage and facilitate active and critical learning and thinking." Furthermore, rather than producing isolated cyborg consumers, he claims, games even create new opportunities for social learning by virtue of gamers' participation in the affinity groups connected to video games (46–47).

Unfortunately, Gee's provocative argument never quite transcends his own adult gaming experience, which he then problematically generalizes as the model for children's learning processes. Moreover, while he is eager to affirm the decentralized, active, and critical skills that "good" games teach, he is admittedly uninterested in issues of what he dismisses as "content," such as violence and gender. This symptomatic dismissal simply evades discussion of the larger ideological effects of gaming through the replacement of ideology with "content." The latter is then somewhat condescendingly designated as a secondary issue of political correctness, an elective aspect of gaming to study. In this way, Gee is able to avoid discussing how games foster consumerist and narcissistic subjectivities—issues that for Stallabrass, Garite, and others become the very representational and ideological fabric of games and the glass ceiling of the gamer's agency. This omission becomes most obvious in the discrepancy between Gee's universal statements about the teaching potential of computer games and his specific examples of such teaching potential, which are invariably limited to teaching science at school (whose built-in disciplinary limits on critical thinking require and are conditioned on the student's faith in authority and truth), and future careers for gamers in the computer sciences, tech industries, and business (48). His motivated dismissal of "content" reaches the most provocative extreme in his enthusiastic review of the military game Deus Ex, a first-person shooter where the avatar, special agent J.C. Denton, is a member of a UN antiterrorist coalition, and whose primary goal is to enhance his choice of eleven skills: "computers, electronics, environmental training, lock picking, medicine, swimming, skills with weapons of different types, including demolition devices, heavy weapons, low-tech weapons, pistols and rifles" (77). Gee's gleeful account of the fun of blasting robots with a single shot hardly convinces one of the development of critical-thinking skills that may enable and encourage the new generation to understand the mechanisms of neoliberalism and to critique the bond between the entertainment and military complex.

Countless similarly optimistic projections of the educational potential of video games in particular and electronic media in general have been published in the United States in the past decade. Steven Johnson's best-selling book *Everything Bad Is Good for You: How Today's Popular Culture Is Actually Making Us Smarter* (2006), while sensationalist and simplistic, can be reconciled with the views of serious interdisciplinary media scholars such as Marsha Kinder, Ellen Seiter, and Henry Jenkins, who see television, the Internet, and video games as potentially valuable and safe resources to help children explore their own postmodernist identities (see Kinder 1999, 1; Seiter 2005; Jenkins 2006). Others more blatantly replicate the limitations of Gee's argument. *Got Game: How the Gamer Generation Is Reshaping Business Forever* is another popular, statistics-ridden book, whose authors embrace success in business as the ultimate and only legitimate kind for the post-baby-boomer generation (Beck and Wade 2004). The book's tone is celebratory from beginning to end, without any sense of complicity with and happiness outside of corporate profit-making and consumerism.

I have outlined two conflicting approaches to the complexities of educating children in the United States today. In reality, most of those involved are caught up in the radical undeterminability of issues surrounding technological and ideological changes in education in a global age. At the heart of both the "pro-play" and "pro-game" positions is the recognition that the experiences and identities of the current generation-in-the-making will be vastly different from those of their parents. Both sides are invested in defining appropriate emotional and aesthetic experiences in the service of maintaining what they perceive as the best form of social control.

Those who favor a "play culture" model bemoan the devaluation of the role of emotion in formal education centralized on testing and accountability. At the same time, they find threatening the emotional immersion that the video game experience provides. For educational psychologists such as Joan Almon, play is a "natural" and "healthy" tool of social control. Allowing children to play is the best way to prevent the subsequent use of mental hospitals and prisons. Almon proposes to organize a "massive public education campaign about play" to protect children's right to play, to "create a protective circle around childhood" (Almon 2003, 40). For many critics, while the technology of Internet use and computer gaming may not be consciously controlled by politicians and business executives, it is driven by market forces and the computer industry's links with the military. It offers the virtual consumption of empty forms in an ideal and idealized neoliberal market, confining people to their homes, where they are hooked up to sensory feedback devices in an enclosing, interactive environment—a far more powerful tool of social control than television (Stallabrass 1993, 105).

By contrast, for those who believe video games and the Internet have predominantly positive effects on the gamer generation's cognitive skills, neoliberal media capitalism is the inescapable state of affairs. This is so whether such voices uncritically glorify and naturalize consumerism or merely insist one can understand and question the information and communication-based economy only by learning to use its own tools and undermining it from the inside. To those of the latter conviction, yearning for the unmediated play of the past is an escapist and ultimately fruitless exercise in nostalgia, which amounts to a refusal to take a critical account of the present.[2]

## From European Artistic Play to Global Game Cultures

Whether explicitly acknowledged or not, the fact that education has become such a contested issue in the United States has much to do with the erosion of the nation-state's control over the knowledges, skills, and ideological commitment of new generations. The increasing power of transnational corporations has seriously compromised the state's authority to decide what should be taught and how. While business corporations often naturalize their motivations with reference to the only imaginable system of global capitalism, the motivations of the nation-state are often cloaked in naturalized patriotic sentiment or the ideology of neoliberal individualism. Neither the state nor businesses—particularly technological and media industries—are invested in enhancing the critical and analytical faculties of young media consumers. Media literacy education—antithetical to both test-based learning and commercial intervention in the school experiences of children—has been kept on the periphery of public school curricula in the United States. Unlike in other English-speaking countries, media education has remained a growing but fragmented grassroots initiative, the collaborative mission of dedicated educators, activists, local and independent media organizations, and artists.

My hope is that a comparative view of U.S. and European—even more specifically, Eastern European—playing and gaming practices in education will make visible some unexamined and often unspoken assumptions: the covert nationalistic component in arguments for the Romanticized exaltation of innocent and natural play, on the one hand, and the conviction that neoliberal capitalism and technological progress are natural and inevitable, on the other. Unlike in the United States, in Eastern Europe the Romantic idea of childlike, creative play has not only been fundamental to the emergence of the institution of modern national education but has also been instrumental in the ideological neutralization of nationalism. As I argue throughout this book, German Romanticism in general, and the idea that art is the highest and purest manifestation of creative play in particular, have nurtured a peculiarly strong brand of cultural nationalism, whose power and legacy have been successfully instrumentalized by postcommunist nation-states and the European Union.

Far from being natural, the unquestionable link between the innocence of childhood and creative play has a specific history. It was established only in the age of the Enlightenment and then fully cultivated during Romanticism: Jean-Jacques Rousseau famously declared that play is the child's work. Novalis idealized the child's play world as a Golden Age. More recent educational initiatives, such as Friedrich Froebel's play-based kindergarten movement or Erik Erikson's engagement with childhood as a "play age," are direct descendants of such Romantic ideas (Simms 2003, 177). A line of post-Romantic philosophical thought identifies "play" as a cultural phenomenon (Huizinga 1955), as a cornerstone of human cognitive, aesthetic, and affective development, which is now being eroded in various spheres of culture. From Sigmund Freud through Jean Piaget to Stanley Greenspan, play has been characterized as the spontaneous, creative movement of the imagination, "the mother of all habit" (Benjamin 2005, 120), whose early cultivation is essential to creative cognitive and ethical existence. This sense of play is thoroughly linked with the Romantic aesthetic (Olfman 2003a, 206), crystallizing into an aesthetic-pedagogical theory in Friedrich Schiller's notion of "aesthetic education" (Schiller 1954).

As I detail in chapter 5, the formation of the Eastern European nation, ostensibly prompted by Habsburg oppression, was significantly informed by German Romanticism, most of all by Johann Gottfried Herder's prediction of the death of small nations (Barany 1998). By necessity, nationalist historians—Palacky, Iorga, Hrushevsky—were not so much scholars as " 'myth-making intellectuals,' who combined a 'romantic' search for meaning with a scientific zeal to establish this on authoritative foundations" (Hutchinson 1994, 123). The national poet is a paradigmatic figure of the national community and its history. His combination of sensuousness and reason, and the analogy between the creative power of the artistic genius and the imaginative play of children is perfectly compatible with Schiller's (1795) eclectic, Platonic manifesto, which uses play as a metaphor of aesthetic autonomy and proposes that art should be the basis of education (Snell 1954, 8). Besides Kant's evident influence, Schiller's treatise incorporates Montesquieu's and Rousseau's notion of the primitive, aesthetically unawakened man. It also embraces Goethe's exaltation of the natural, his view of the artist as a true man, and his effort to unite the sensuous and the spiritual (Snell 1954, 9–11). In Schiller's scheme, the sensuous drive (*Stofftrieb*) and formal drive (*Formtrieb*) are united and transcended in the play drive (*Spieltrieb*). Man is fully human when he plays, and he plays with beauty (Schiller 1954, 138). Only the Beautiful unites society because it relates to what is common to all its members. The Beautiful exists as a need in every finely tuned soul, but as an achievement it characterizes only a select few (Schiller 1954, 140).

Schiller's valorization of imaginative play is at the core of the notion of "transcendent imagination," which many psychologists who favor imaginative play over electronic games tend to assume. "Transcendent imagination," Marsha Kinder argues, is a historically specific notion associated with Romanticism and high modernism, which is in many ways quite incongruous with our postmodern period (Kinder 1991, 60). Even though very few educators have actually adopted Schiller's ideas, the concept of imaginative education, based on the cultivation of a narrow definition of beauty and creative talent, very much inspired Eastern European educational systems and survived along with the Eurocentric yearnings of cultural nationalism under the layers of Marxist-Leninist materialism. It was in fact sustained by the state's cultivation of the intellectual vanguard during the socialist decades. The freedom of play, at the heart of Romantic and modernist art practices, continued to be considered at once a crucial part of universal—understood as European—cultural heritage and, in its highest form, a sign of supreme imaginative talent and sophistication.

In postcommunist cultures, the pervasive presence of global electronic media is a fairly recent phenomenon. The region's accelerated transition toward an information-processing, entertainment-saturated, consumerist culture has undermined the nation-state's hegemony over media and educational institutions and engendered new, more accessible, deterritorialized, mobile, and arguably more democratic forms of communication. In the sphere of education, instructive new negotiations have emerged among the nation-states, eager to represent the ongoing accession to the European Union as a national project and a part of historical destiny; the EU itself, invested in maintaining the appearance of European unity in diversity and downplaying the imperial division between core and peripheral member states; transnational media corporations, eager to turn Eastern and Southern Europe into a vast consumer market; and various grassroots groups, seeking transnational affiliations to develop democratic media spaces. As John Downey puts it, the postcommunist media landscape is perhaps best seen as a patchwork of alliances and competition for legitimacy among these agents (Downey 1998, 49).

As a result of such radical changes, the gap between the perspectives, skills, and values of the generations who grew up under communism and those for whom communism is an inherited memory is exceptionally large. This gap poses particular challenges and causes great anxiety for political and cultural elites invested in guiding and controlling the institutional training of young people, whose subjectivities are being influenced by new experiences. Dina Iordanova borrows Margaret Mead's notion of "prefigurative culture" to identify one of the consequences of the digital gap that separates generations in Eastern Europe. It is a global divide exacerbated by the postcommunist transitions, which have reversed the traditional process of knowledge transition: the older generations' knowledges have been rendered irrelevant for the most part, while young people are quickly accumulating and even transmitting back to their parents' generation the skills and knowledge validated in a globally mediated consumer society (Iordanova 2000, 126–127).

While no one can possibly predict the future of education in Eastern Europe, some tendencies are evident: Nation-states, which had actively maintained a space for shared experiences and the construction of a national consciousness by validating European and national high culture since their emergence, are now to compete with media corporations for students' attention, often by adopting popular media's own strategies of "edutainment." During communism, educational institutions were an integral and self-contained part of the state machinery, thoroughly intertwined with the military, the police, as well as the judicial, legislative, and health care systems (György 1997b). At present, the desire to "return to Europe" while preserving or reinventing (national) cultural specificity constitutes the common ground among the different factions involved in reforming postsocialist educational systems. "Catching up with Europe" is seen not only as a political transformation that brings about democracy but also, and more importantly, as a way of becoming part of a powerful economic network, which will provide protection from threatening transnational processes of globalization. Uncontested and accelerated technological development is agreed to be the winning ticket to joining Europe. The quest for political and economic progress has also called for a curriculum overhaul in each postcommunist country, which has involved efforts to update content areas and to redefine sites of ideological authority. Preparing students for the European and, by extension, global labor market—and the implied competition with the United States—requires less memorization of facts and more flexibility, creativity, and problem-solving abilities (Lowe 1997).

Much like in the United States, many educators and even more state officials unconditionally celebrate modernist progress represented by information and communication technology.[3] At the same time, new technologies, media content, and literacies induce more anxiety in education in Eastern Europe than they do in the United States. Many critics distrust the electronic media as tools of American imperialism and worry that the visually oriented, entertainment-focused, nonlinear kind of learning that these media encourage undermines the values of language-based rationality, literature, and history on which national education has hinged from the start. Well-intentioned educators have adopted the tone of alarm Neil Postman raised in the United States in the 1980s to lament that children are rapidly being transformed from readers into "vidiots" (Domokos 2004; Horvath 2000, 92–93). The unprecedented degree of visual information that has largely replaced the heavily filtered and centrally censored youth media culture of communism is often represented in pedagogical journals as a threat to children's skills and identities, as the "child's disease" of our time. (American) youth media products, in this scheme, take over kids' (supposedly uncontaminated, pure) imaginations and render such children forever immature and childish—in implied opposition to the mature, rational citizen of a European nation.

A Romantic-nationalistic cultural heritage and the quest for ongoing modern development intertwined with technological progress are embraced as the dual means of turning truly European. To the extent that those are two central ideals touted by the European Union in support of its reinvention of "Europe" as a "reimagined community" (Morley and Robins 1995), the process of revamping Eastern European educational systems continues a long tradition of colonial mimicry rather than taking truly new directions.

### The Internet Playground and the Transformation of Eastern European Education

The role of the Internet remains an elusive "wild card" in this process, with which "the traditional concentrated control over communication and technological grounds effectively ends" (McChesney 1998, 39). While the Internet is currently being developed predominantly on commercial grounds, some scholars speculate that its accessibility and ability to turn virtually any consumer into a producer holds out at least the potential to undermine corporate—or national—control over the media and to introduce an element of instability into the global media industry (McChesney 1998; Boyd-Barrett 1998; Jenkins 2004).

The influence of the Internet on the identities and subjectivities of the future is unpredictable. What seems evident, though, is that while the commitment to modernist technological progress and the insistence on high cultural values regarded as part of a European heritage continue to favor the same narrow pool of players—white men of some status—the Internet introduces an altogether different, transnational playing field that is much less bound by territorial divisions. Dina Iordanova speculates that the Internet will both continue to bring new freedoms and opportunities for civic activism and artistic expression as well as enhance class divides and the penetration of corporate takeover. The European Union's role in wiring the new and prospective member states is crucial in this regard. The European Commission's 1997 Green Paper envisions a Europewide "information society" devoted to promoting civic discourse and democratic participation (Horvath 2000, 78). This directive, as John Horvath notes, rests on the problematic assumption that civic discourse did not exist under communism, when media was entirely dominated by propaganda. This was far from true, as I elaborate in the next chapter. It is undeniable, however, that promoting technological "progress" in the East is accompanied by a certain Western missionary fervor and rests on an unconditional faith in consumerist democracy (Horvath 2000, 85).

There are other obstacles in the way of a progressive use of the Internet and new media technologies. One is the enduring and increasing economic differences within the region, which have created "fast" and "slow" lanes of technological development (Horvath 2000, 86). The speed of technologization depends to a great extent on the attention of investors such as George Soros and his Open Society Institute, which has single-handedly rewritten the technological map of the region. Internet service providers often follow outdated business practices, which are hindered by state-run telecommunication firms (92–93). Another obstacle is an enduring "island mentality," a general fear of engaging in Internet-based civic activism out of a historically internalized caution, which sees change as risky and does not allow much of a margin for what is seen as experimentation and play (97). It is no wonder that universities and other educational institutions remain the main hubs of Internet access in the region, and that most users are men under thirty, working in engineering or tech industries (86).

By contrast, writing from a Western geopolitical perspective that does allow a margin for play and risk, Ellen Seiter describes the Internet as an especially apt medium to explore dormant potentials of individual identity because of its unparalleled ability to create an extension of personality in time and space. This is most evident in online fantasy games, which increasingly blur the lines between work-related and entertaining uses of the Internet. While the amount of time that the trial and error of virtual experimentation requires, a kind of "extended play demanding excess leisure time," disadvantages women (Seiter 2003), the postmodern exploration of identities that such play evokes is markedly different from the modernist, poetic play reserved for the artist.

When it comes to postcommunist educational systems in the "fast lane," such as Hungary, Poland, the Czech Republic, Slovenia, or the Baltic states, the Internet has greatly contributed to breaking down artificially erected walls between practical and theoretical knowledge, the humanities and the sciences, teaching and research, institutional and noninstitutional learning, and place-bound and distance learning (Nyíri 1997). The Internet has been rapidly blurring the line between the world of school and the commercial world, placing what students learn ultimately beyond schools' and the state's control. The only evident option in competing for children's attention is wiring schools and incorporating Internet- and new media–based knowledge into the curriculum. But this further undermines the long-held division between high and popular culture while also prioritizing new cognitive competencies, selection, and problem-solving skills. Instead of building on explicit and collectively held values, advocates of wired schools argue, hypertextual learning may promote critical thinking and self-directedness because it forces one to put together information chains from many choices available at every junction. The task of educational reform in the Internet age is to make schooling more open and flexible. "The Internet, for most students, is a virtual playground that offers a variety of communicational forms," writes Zoltán Czeizer (Czeizer 1997). Learning from and in hypermedia represents the kind of freely chosen, playful element in learning that is usually left out of formal instruction. Institutional learning must offer students the choice to design their own path of learning, much like commercial softwares do, Czeizer argues.

Whereas during socialism the state tried to determine what people should be interested in, now this choice and responsibility is largely that of the individual, even though the options are increasingly limited and regulated by the consumer market. The evolving labor market, which has replaced the predetermined set of clearly distinguishable professions identified by the state, demands individual competence-combinations, all of which involve particular technological and cognitive skills. The very naming of such new combination professions presents an ongoing challenge, which the inherited vocabulary of socialist industrial society is insufficient to meet.

It remains to be seen, however, whether individual choices filtered through market values will lead to the democratization of education and whether the gains can compensate for the evident loss of universal (i.e., national) values encoded into centralized education (Bessenyei 1997).

Here one enters the realm of speculation. Does the Internet undermine or challenge conceptual structures built around ideas of center, hierarchy, and linearity, and if so, how? Is this the end of institutional learning as we know it? What is knowledge to begin with if it is not the metanarratives of the Enlightenment or a universal canon? How can schools remain more valuable sources of knowledge than those readily available for users elsewhere, in much more entertaining formats (Czeizer 1997)? Some Eastern European educators are understandably concerned that the massive amount of virtual information conveyed by hypertext does not represent but, rather, creates and replaces reality, potentially leading to a fragmented, unstructured mess of ideas driven by commercial content, instead of new knowledges and identities. Moreover, the horizontal juxtaposition of information, in some ways liberating after the strict institutional and ideological hierarchies maintained by the socialist state, creates an oppressive sense of the present, undermining the ability for historical reflection and obscuring the horizon of learning as a process (Buda 1997). I elaborate on global media's role in blending historical memory and nostalgia in the next chapter.

## Nationalized Media Education

A brief account of the recent emergence of a national media education curriculum in Hungary, followed by even more specific case studies, should help illustrate the intensity of current negotiations about the future of education in a region undergoing a transition to global capitalist media culture, driven by utopian ideals of a pan-European democracy. Such negotiations invariably involve the state, worried about the transnational reach of global media in general and the Internet in particular, but also eager to channel cultural and social changes through its own cosmetically updated postcommunist nationalistic agenda, which revolves around rejoining Europe. This ambition is often supported by transnational media corporations, who frequently share media ownership with nation-states, but whose own economic interests are always primary. The interests of the European Union lie in harnessing the power of national affiliation within new and prospective member states in order to mobilize loyalty to "Europe." The EU is also invested in collaborating with media corporations to create a protective and competitive European audiovisual space, of strategic importance to both reimagining a European community and to success in the global struggle

among "image superpowers" (Morley and Robins 1995, 34–35). The
very power uncertainty of the situation, along with new opportunities
opened up by changing media technology, leave room for creative
consumers—teachers, students, media activists—to introduce alternative
claims issued by transnational or subnational constituencies, with a
critical attitude toward both nation-states and corporations. In many
such negotiations, the Internet represents an element of ambiguity,
whose resolution has a crucial effect on which identities get to be centered and marginalized in specific instances of post–Cold War European
edutainment.

Soon after the regime change in 1989, responding to the need to rede-
sign an outdated, uniform national system of education, Hungarian
educational experts and policy makers launched what has come to be
known as the "NAT" ("Nemzeti Alaptanterv") or National Base Curriculum. The new design breaks down the rigid walls around former
school subject areas and redefines the elementary and secondary curriculum around larger, intersecting, loosely identified areas of study. It has
taken significant steps toward decentralizing control over instruction,
transferring authority from the state to local schools and individual
teachers. Perhaps the most path-breaking component of this curricular
reform, unique even in Europe, has been the introduction of mandatory
media education in secondary schools (from 2004) and in primary
schools (from 2006).

The new subject area, officially called "motion picture and media
studies," is further embedded in the state's long-term educational
vision by serving as an elective high school graduation exam area. In
Hungary, such exams are particularly meaningful as they double up
as entrance exams for university admission. Students' scores therefore
tend to assign them to particular rungs in the hierarchy of higher
educational institutions. Furthermore, motion picture and media studies
have also become legitimated as an "academic" subject in a high-prestige
annual national academic competition among secondary school seniors.
The winners of this competition are exempt from secondary school exit
exams and gain automatic university admission. While the Hungarian
Motion Picture and Media Education Association and various pedagogical institutions have undertaken new teacher training and the retraining
of teachers originally specialized in literature or visual arts in crash
courses, the goal is to make the instruction of media studies contingent
on a specialized diploma from the year 2014 on (Panek 2004,
250–251).

In comparison with the United States, where the efforts of scattered critical media literacy intitiatives have been able to mobilize only negligible resistance to the corporate commercialization of schools and homes, and even with other countries where such a struggle has been backed by the state, the swift, collaborative response of Hungarian policy makers and educators to challenges that the rest of the world has been facing for a long time is stunningly progressive and worthy of emulation. The Hungarian national media education curriculum seems to have found a middle ground between alarmist and defensive outcries over "trash" media's manipulation of young minds and the uncritical, celebratory embracing of technological "progress." While such merits need to be acknowledged, a comparative perspective reveals formative ambivalences and unspoken political interests that underscore the curriculum.

A recent collection of essays on the past, present, and future of mandatory media education in Hungary was introduced by the minister of education. He begins, in the characteristically nominal and bureaucratic language of state politics inherited from communist times,

[Media education has been introduced in public education] because the use of media, the consumption of media products, and the dispersion of informational and communicational tools has brought up questions which the government has the obvious responsibility to answer. For this reason, the government's educational policies, drawing on opportunities provided by and rising to new challenges set by the media, contribute to raising new generations of citizens who are physically and psychologically healthy, able to stand up for their own interests and assume responsibility for the communities they choose. (Magyar 2004, 6).

The rest of the introduction points to the importance of selective and creative media consumption and of developing new critical and analytical skills to become productive contributors to a new, global workforce within an image-saturated information society. These reasonable goals, the minister leaves no doubt, should be achieved under the guidance of the nation-state, whose ultimate goal is to disseminate knowledges that allow individuals to be "active participants within Hungarian culture." Of course, the "responsibility" that the minister assumes on behalf of the government can also be seen as an effort to unify and continue to control desires and goals that are becoming increasingly divergent under the influence of the global media, particularly the Internet. The media educational curriculum is an opportunity for the state to channel new knowledges so that they continue to maintain nationalistic and Eurocentric values. Far from being transparent, such values are also associated with unacknowledged gendered and racialized hierarchies, selectively efface the ongoing history of imperialism, and impose absolutist aesthetic judgments that place modernist art film above popular media, and written culture above a culture of images.

Upon closer inspection, the textbooks developed for public media education and adopted by the majority of public school teachers expose such assumptions about nationalism and the role of the European nation-state. The core textbooks, written by Klára Muhi and László Hartai, two of the driving motors of the media education movement, are heroic efforts, considering the task of summing up the history of visual communication in a way that evokes interdisciplinary, critical responses and engages with the students' own mediated experiences during a period of rapid social change. At its occasional worst, the result is a mix of information that reflects the creators' personal taste in (art) movies, informed by Eurocentric universalisms. Each page is illustrated by four to ten small images representing a variety of—often confusingly incompatible—media forms and genres as so many quick flashes, reproduced invariably from the Internet. Apart from a brief mention of ancient Egypt in the chapter on the emergence of writing, from this book one surmises that civilized communication has not occurred outside of Euro-America. While it would be a mistake to dismiss the pioneering work of the textbook writers, which allows students to study the psychology of contemporary television shows and the aesthetics of advertising along with early cinema, one can also imagine how hard it must be for teachers to turn the immense quantity and often confusingly assembled fragments into meaningful learning experiences—something that media teachers' own feedback appear to underscore (Panek 2004, 254–259).

But these textbooks are still much more progressive than the collection of theoretical and critical readings that accompany them, which contain for the most part the work of Hungarian film critics and university professors who put the collection together, older pieces on cinema by revered Hungarian writers, and a few translations of classical film aesthetics essays by the likes of Erwin Panofsky, Arnold Hauser, and André Bazin. The collection presents a rather distorted introduction to the history and theory of visual communication, in which the study of the "moving image" is reduced to a male canon concerned with the formal properties of modernist, European, and Hungarian art cinema, whose history abruptly stops somewhere about 1970. This part takes up at least two-thirds of the book. The second, much shorter section, devoted to "media studies," contains subjective reflections on new television genres and—even more briefly—on the Internet by some of the same authors, as well as translated bits by Neil Postman, Umberto Eco, Hans Magnus Enzensberger, and Lev Manovich. Unlike in the textbooks by Hartai and Muhi—which are more practical and open-ended, presenting information much less authoritatively—film as an art form continues to be constructed here as superior to all other forms of (popular) media. This normative and selective view of the media, screened through the narrow interests of a handful of "experts," 95 percent of whom are men, perpetuates an ethnocentric perspective that provides Hungarian students no insight into the waves of transformative new perspectives that have swept across film and media studies in the world outside of Eastern Europe since the 1970s: cultural studies; gender studies; studies of postcolonialism and imperialism; and studies of representation, pleasure, reception, and consumption.

## Print Literacy through Online Games: The "Bridge Project"

In a region where national cultures have relied on literature and print journalism to reinforce and perpetuate collective values, one consistent criticism that has been leveled at the new media education curriculum has been its visual focus—the result of a legitimate and thoroughly argued effort to counterbalance the hegemonic authority of print media in an increasingly visual age. The print-versus-image debate cuts to the heart of the struggle over control among different constituents. While approving of the media education curriculum, the state has also tried to validate its interests by supporting parallel programs that foster print literacy among students. These are cosponsored by print publications—often owned by transnational media companies such as Axel-Springer—and modeled after similar European programs, particularly the German ZEUS, or Zeitung und Schule.

The first such initiative, SÉTA (literally, "WALK," but really an acronym from the words *sajtó*, meaning "press," *és*, meaning "and," and *tanulás*, meaning "learning"), was launched in 2003 and had mobilized fifteen hundred students in fifty secondary schools in Western Hungary by 2005. The Ministry of Education and the four county newspapers that cosponsor the program emphasize the fact that forming regular habits of newspaper reading and becoming familiar with the structure of the paper and its advertising and distribution mechanisms will improve not only print literacy—assumed to be distinct from and superior to visual literacy—but also critical-thinking skills. Only mentioned in passing, but of crucial importance, this habit will also increase the circulation of these regional papers (SÉTA 2004, 218). While ideological questions are carefully minimized in official statements, the ministry of education justifies its decision to allow what easily could be seen as advertising into schools by making a distinction between the interests of regional and national papers: the former, the argument goes, must reach a wide variety of readers and therefore cannot allow themselves to be partisan. The latter, by contrast, have traditionally evolved in affiliation with specific political parties (Zöldi 2004, 16). The ideological influence of corporate media does not qualify as "politics" in this framework. This is an especially conspicuous omission given the fact that the newspapers in question are owned by the Westdeutsche Allgemeine Zeitung (WAZ), which has had a thorough influence on their contents and aesthetics since the early 1990s, when most regional papers were bought up by (or sold out to) German media corporations.

The HÍD ("BRIDGE") Project (Hírlapot a Diákoknak, or "Newspapers for Students"), which was launched in 2004 (http://ultramarin.hu/hid), bears out the contradictions implied in SÉTA even further. The project involves the Hungarian News Publishers' Alliance; the most popular Hungarian national daily *Népszabadság*, which is politically linked with the concurrently ruling Socialist Party (MSZP); the media activist organization Visual World Foundation (VWF); and selected Hungarian high schools, predominantly from Budapest. Like SÉTA's, the manifest goal of the joint initiative is to improve Hungarian teens' print literacy, which has rapidly declined since the end of socialism, by providing high school students with free issues of *Népszabadság*. But this program also harnesses the power of electronic, visual media by engaging students in online edutainment games that are tied to the newspaper's daily issues.

While the manifest goal of joining European initiatives to increase print literacy is admirable, contradictions abound. The official Web site declares that the program wants to contribute to the development of more efficient reading-comprehension and information-processing skills, critical thinking, and creativity in order to prepare a flexible workforce for the global information-processing economy in general and for the new generation's entry into a united EU labor market in particular. The creators also speculate that those who read papers and magazines will also read books and frequent museums, art galleries, and theaters. Reading the paper thus supports not only the transition to a European and global capitalist economy but also art appreciation, which will in turn strengthen traditional national cultural values. Of course, the wider circulation of *Népszabadság*, which has shouldered the lion's share of the costs of the project's first year, directly supports both the governing Socialist Party and the German corporation that owns it. One can then also see the program as the state's and the corporation's joint initiative to permeate and instrumentalize schools for their own purposes, creating a typical postcommunist alliance in which, Colin Sparks argues, no neat division exists between the political and the economic (Sparks 2000).

A further irony here is that the medium for developing linear print literacy skills and raising obedient Euro-national consumers is the decentralized space of the Internet. While the state rationalizes the use of the Internet in such programs as a necessary part of its "National Informatics Strategy," an unquestioned technological bridge to desired European modernity, media corporations are equally invested in competing for students' attention by offering entertaining ways of learning that nurture students' consumerist identities. It is hardly a coincidence that the student assignment in which the HÍD project's first year culminated was the production of a student newspaper devoted to food and eating.

The party that wields the least amount of power in this joint project, and which has essentially acted as a hired gun having to fight for as much as public credit—is Visual World Foundation, a media activist alliance whose members—teachers, scholars, and media professionals—designed the online games. They took seriously the edutainment potential of the Internet playground by creating open-ended online challenges that elicit active selection and creative production. Similar to the way ZEUS, the program's model, operates, the games allow students to explore areas of various mediated interests sometimes only loosely linked with the paper, such as fandom around the popular national Idol television series. Fulfilling John Downey's dire prophecy about the fate of intitiatives seeking to create more democratic media spaces, in the second year of the project, after numerous other publications got on board enthused by the profits *Népszabadság* had made, the program's curriculum and organization became overtly centralized around specific political and economic interests. In the fall of 2005, the Bridge Office was created for the more efficient coordination, control, research, and surveillance of the program, forcing VWF almost entirely out of the collaboration and overtly subordinating the manifest goals of fostering critical print and Internet literacy to corporate profits.

### Euro-Identity Games and Educational Tourism beyond the Iron Curtain

"Welcome! Learning about Europe can be fun!" invites EuropaGO, the "website for young European citizens" launched by the European Commission. It is just one of many ways in which the European Union has utilized the Internet and playful new media technologies to promote a pan-European identity and culture among the next generation, and to help teens see recent waves of enlargement as something that will benefit them with the opportunities it creates for jobs, education, and tourism. In this chapter's last section, I investigate the European Union's role in the education and training of newly accessed and prospective EU citizens. I argue that, notwithstanding all its positive aspects, when it comes to Eastern European member states, the emphasis of such a training falls on consumerism and tourism. I show how welcoming young Eastern EU citizens is contained within a paradigm that we can call touristic, following the work of scholars such as Urry, Bauman, Franklin, and Böröcz, which perpetuates long-standing colonial inequalities within the emerging European empire. I want to foreground the continuity between the explorative, gamelike, cartoonish logic through which Internet-based EU initiatives set out to create an integrated European educational space and the consuming logic of tourism that, Adrian Franklin argues, is becoming the new logic of capitalism (Franklin 2004).

The EuropaGO project aims to disseminate knowledge about the EU—in eleven EU languages, none representing the newest member states—in order to incorporate new generations into the EU "family."[4] This is achieved with the help of online interactive games that allow visitors to "explore Europe" and test their knowledge of European cultural symbols and institutions by clicking on different objects in a friendly and colorful cartoon bedroom. The objects take you through the EU anthem, the Euro currency, the nation-states' flags, and slides of the Louvre in Paris or the Dam in Amsterdam. You can take a quiz about "your neighbours" or click on the poster that invites you to go on a "journey through time" in European history: a self-glorifying and excessively watered-down saga. If you are tempted to time travel, a photograph of a group of all-white children and the sign "Let's

Explore Europe," framed by laurel leaves, welcome you to a journey to "the cradle of civilization": "Hello! Welcome to Europe—our home."

Some of the chapters in the journey are titled "Climate and Nature," "Farming," "The Sea," "Forty Famous Places," "Languages in Europe," "A Family of Peoples," and "Bringing the Family Together: A Story of the European Union." The chapter "A Journey through Time" presents an authoritative and neatly ordered narrative starting in the Ice Age and ending with "The Modern World." The latter encompasses the period roughly from 1880 to today, and for the most part consists of a list of significant technological inventions. The final chapter, "Learning the Lessons of History," reads,

Sadly, the story of Europe is not all about great achievements we can be proud of. There are also many things to be ashamed of. Down the centuries, European nations fought terrible wars against each other. These wars were usually about power and property, or religion. European colonists killed millions of native people on other continents—by fighting or mistreating them, or by accidentally spreading European diseases among them. Europeans also took millions of Africans to work as slaves.

These words are illustrated by a row of tombstones featuring "A war cemetery in Flanders (Belgium)," where "[m]ore than eight million soldiers died in the First World War alone." The narrative ends on an uplifting note, however: "Lessons had to be learnt from these dreadful wrongdoings. The European slave trade was abolished in the 1800s. Colonies gained their freedom in the 1900s. And peace did come to Europe at last. To find out how, read the chapter "Bringing the Family Together: The Story of the European Union.""

The tropes of home and family are employed here with persistency and overwhelming cheer. But one wonders who exactly is welcomed here to whose family home. The simplified information and sensory excess in which such a "home" is packaged reminds one of television ads and evokes David Morley and Kevin Robins's claim that the EU's construction of a pan-European industry and market necessitates the integration and support of large European communications corporations, whose futures are embedded in that of global advertising. "A European audiovisual area is intended to support and facilitate freedom of commercial speech in Europe" (Morley and Robins 1995, 34–35). Such web sites illustrate the EU's goals of "maintaining and promoting the cultural identity of Europe," of "improving mutual knowledge among our peoples and increasing their consciousness of the life and destiny they have in

common," according to the Commission of the European Communities
(Morley and Robins 1995, 35). Such more directly youth-focused,
edutaining computer games fostered by the Internet are integral parts
of a range of intitiatives such as the MEDIA program, the European
Cinema and Television Year (1988), and the RACE and Audiovisual
EUREKA program, all of which try to lay the foundations for a
postnational audiovisual territory that is able to compete in global media
markets (3). This is not simply a matter of technological and economic
self-assertion.

The European broadcasting agenda also has a significant cultural dimension. The
question of new media markets is closely associated with improving mutual
knowledge among European peoples and increasing their consciousness of the
life and destiny they have in common. The European Commission has encour-
aged programme-makers to appeal to large European audiences because such
broadcasts can help to develop the sense of belonging to a community composed
of countries which are different, yet partake of a deep solidarity. This assertion
of a common cultural identity is clearly assuming a strategic importance for the
present attempt to restore European self-confidence (3).

However, Morley and Robins ask, "What is the meaning of this 'sense
of belonging to a community composed of countries which are different
yet partake of a deep solidarity?' Is it possible to translate a multinational
unity into any meaningful identity and solidarity?" (35).

What they identify as the current crisis of European identity is
ultimately the result of the ways in which globalization has been reshaping the contemporary world system, evoking new questions and anxieties of belonging. They distinguish three scales of available alliances
within Europe. The first one is the common European home so graphi-
cally featured in the interactive Euro-edutainment games. It is the result
of a nostalgic attempt to forge a cultural unity as the basis for a
market large enough to enable European competition against Japan
and the United States. Old and familiar motifs of European tradition
and heritage are mobilized to this end: the idea of a common descent
rooted in Greece and Rome solidified in the tradition of two thousand
years of Christianity. The Let's Explore Europe game presents the story
precisely in this simplistic chronological fashion. The second available affiliation is national identity, which has recently returned with a
vengeance in Western Europe and has remained powerful in the east—
its most menacing manifestation in the form of violent ethnonationalism (20). The cultural nationalism of new member states has generated a separatist, anti-EU sentiment but has also acted as a powerful

catalyst to foster an already-existing sense of belonging to Europe. The third kind of affiliation is smaller-scale local and regional identities. These three kinds of affiliations are not simple alternatives. Rather, to be European today is to be continental, national, and regional at the same time.

The bridge to Europe is being rebuilt in the postcommunist region from the bricks of nostalgic longing for a common European cultural heritage. The attractive image of a common European home continues to downplay the economic inferiority of peripheral states and the exclusion of those countries that are not part of the Euro family. This scheme disavows the arrogance with which the EU re-creates itself in the image of Europe's imperial glory, standing for the universal values of the Enlightenment, which the new states support even at the expense of collaborating in their own re-colonization (Böröcz 2001).

Several scholars have recently questioned the political and economic strategies behind Europe's nostalgic reinvention of the idea of unity in diversity, particularly when it comes to integrating the newest eastern and southern member states. Ginette Verstraete writes, "As Western Europe faces the task of extending its common market, represented by the fifteen members of the European Union, to the borders of 'Europe proper,' it needs to address the question of the idea, if not fiction, under which this expansion becomes possible. Who is going to be in or excluded and on what grounds?" (Verstraete 2003, 34). With Edgar Morin, Verstraete sees European history as that of transportation, trade, objectification, and travel, which have converged in the postwar boom of tourism that has helped the European "community" recuperate after World War II (Verstraete 2003, 36). "The recognition of *unitas multiplex*," she writes, is "in line with the corporate mission of parceling the product (Europe) in accordance with the needs of particular consumer types in order to extend the market beyond traditional national divides" (38).

Tourism has played a central role in debates about post–Cold War European citizenship, which is underscored by a global competition for touristic consumption. In this competition, Europe's edge has been the extreme diversity it offers within a relatively small, shared space. Therefore, initiatives such as the Council of Europe's European Cultural Routes Project—much like EuropaGO—deliberately approach the past through the lens of a tourist, representing history as a package tour (39). Verstraete writes, "In contemporary debates about the New Europe tourism and cosmopolitanism function as generalized instruments with which to produce and displace crucial differences and evoke a unique place of collective, indeed global, belonging" (46). One can see a similar motive in the accelerated postcommunist development and European inclusion of former Eastern European cities that hold touristic potential, such as Prague, Bratislava, Budapest, Berlin, or Ljubljana, all packaged for nostalgic consumption, as Svetlana Boym's book *The Future of Nostalgia* (2001) testifies. "Cultural difference" in these cases becomes the means of cashing in on images of Europeanness on a global market (Verstraete 2003, 49).

The edutainment games that promote European identity in the playing field of the Internet draw on and amplify the synergy between a European unity in diversity that is consumption-oriented and touristic and the new and prospective member states' historical construction of their own national identities that are primarily cultural, based on a desire for Europeanness rather than on their actual active participation in European economic and political ventures. Whereas earlier this desire was invested in poetry and music, now it is increasingly touristic, willingly overlooking the processes of exclusion, marginalization, and even exploitation that continue to divide the two Europes horizontally and vertically, distinguishing "real" European citizens from various others.

Verstraete aptly describes the European scene as "an education post-tourism engaged in performances of Unity-in-Diversity in which the practices of heading forward and counterfeiting (imitation) are indistinguishable," a "Grand Tour in an age of Cultural Diversity and Multicultural Disney Theme Parks." One is reminded of Stallabrass's Marxist critique of the ideology of video games, which, to him, inherently promote consumerist identities and social conformity. He compares computer gaming not only to shopping but also to tourism, in that progress is a result of spatial exploration, which can be achieved only in terms of travel, topography, and mapping (Stallabrass 1993, 100). The illusion of control and knowledge and the pleasure of interaction that Euro-identity games—real and virtual—offer can be seen as localized examples of Stallabrass's description. Verstraete writes, "Whatever theoretical labels we apply to this mode of cultural tourism, we learn little about the social identities and differences that are produced along with the cultural routes, and that make cultural Europe a highly asymmetrical geography shot through with shifting racial, gendered and ethnic disjunctures" (Verstraete 2003, 39).

Navigating, surfing, and browsing the Internet, much like the binary choices that determine the gamer's spatial exploration in computer games, have a fundamentally touristic structure of learning. Tourism has been described as an activity in which the virtual and the real are increasingly indistinguishable. John Urry argues that in contemporary society people are tourists most of the time, whether through actual or virtual mobility (Jansson 2002, 430). Tourism and media consumption follow a shared logic. As Urry argues, the mass tourism of high modernity has been gradually complemented by more customer-governed and customized, image-intensive forms. For Urry, this means "the end of tourism," when the mediascape becomes primary to actual mobility (Jansson 2002, 432). André Jansson argues that contemporary, mediatized tourism is increasingly hedonistic, similar to carnival or other festivities, but shifting the emphasis to imaginative, virtual pleasures. The more organized tourism becomes, the more it is turned into simulation through Internet sites, catalogs, travel magazines, and television shows, where the latter are not simply simulations of reality but of already simulated environments, which then become the "originals" for the tourist (439).

Adrian Franklin goes even further when he argues that tourism provides an ontological model of "ordering" in late capitalism (Franklin 2004). Zygmunt Bauman uses tourism as a metaphor to describe contemporary, mediated lives in the conditions of what he calls "liquid modernity," when the dualities that characterized the "solid modernity" of the 1960s and 1970s—home/away, everyday/holiday, fake/real, work/leisure—are no longer able to capture contemporary mobilities, flexibilities, and freedoms (Franklin 2003, 206). Bauman's evaluation of the "tourist syndrome" as a metaphor of daily life in liquid modernity is predominantly negative. Tourists, by definition consumers, adopt a "grazing" behavior. They forego the costly investment in cultivating *desire* and live by *needs*, which follow the logic of branding to cut down on research time and create instantaneous confidence in products and places—or places as products. The global tourism industry works like a mall, aiming at accidental buyers in search of diffuse entertainment, rather than a specific product. The contemporary tourist syndrome abandons the educational aims of nineteenth-century tourism (Franklin 2003). It fails to create contact zones between cultures in which mutual learning can be generated. Rather, the tourist meets natives as servants or as spectacle, selling their otherness. "The right proportion of genuine or pretended 'otherness,' a source of pleasurable experience of novelty, challenge and adventure, and reassuring familiarity, a source of the security feeling, that's the name of the tourist game these days" (Franklin 2003, 213). The tourist syndrome, rather than creating lasting communities, results in substitute, temporary relations, Bauman claims, similar to fan communities forming around media celebrities (214).

Adrian Franklin also sees tourism as the ordering game of modernity and global society, but takes a much less pessimistic view. Drawing on the sociology of ordering inspired by Deleuze, Guattari, Latour, Foucault, and Law, he defines tourism as

> always on the move, ordering new places but also by enrolling new objects and by becoming subject to other orderings it is also unstable. It is open-ended and unbounded. It can bond on to other orderings (say sport, urban design and governance and information technology) and produce new tourism orderings (maybe adrenalin tourism, maybe ordering cities after the likeness of resorts or maybe ordering the Internet site after the manner of a tourist site). (Franklin 2004, 279)

Going beyond the structuralist, binary methodologies that characterize authoritative accounts of tourism, Franklin's theory once again recalls Stallabrass's and Garite's description of the explorative movement of the gamer. In both spheres, (inter)activity translates into a process of interpellation that performs tourism and thus creates the tourist. Touristic exploration is an unceasing process as the tourist/gamer becomes interpellated by and curious about new places that have been opened up and become relevant to him. "It is an ontology of unintended consequences, failure, unforeseen agency and promiscuous enrollment. Orderings are pure process" (Franklin 2004, 284).

World tourism, Franklin argues, can be thought of as an ordering of a global space, a fundamentally connected rhizomic entity. He combines Foucault's ideas of governance with Latour's and Deleuze's notions of network or rhizome in their posthumanist insistence on material heterogeneity, relationality, and the agency of the nonhuman to explain the global development of traveling cultures (Franklin 2004, 285). Franklin emphasizes the role of nationalism in interpellating people as tourists and turning tourism into a process of education. Nationalism's spectacles, exhibitions, and knowledges created a curiosity about the world outside national borders and a desire to belong to this wider world. "Rather than *propelled* to escape by intolerable industrial capitalist conditions, tourists were in fact attracted to or *hailed* by the objects they visited" (298). He suggests that tourism, conceived as an ordering, is intimately linked with a range of globalizing effects including translation, consumerism, aestheticization, and cosmopolitanism. The Internet is a central site for the play of these effects. "With its myriad references to and modellings on touristic practice, [the Internet] shows that in a touristic world we both navigate around it as tourists as we are at the same time navigated by it" (299).

The proliferation of nostalgia—longing for home, tradition, identity, belonging—since the end of the Cold War has been fueled and satisfied to a great extent by electronic media, which are able to address geographically dispersed segments of different national communities (Morley and Robins 1995, 5). Since the 1980s, when the basis for the European media order was laid, regulatory principles shifted from public interest to those driven by economic and entrepreneurial imperatives, where audiences are no longer addressed in political terms, as citizens of a national community, but rather as economic entities, as parts of a consumer market. The imperative of media corporations is to break down old boundaries of national communities, which now present themselves as arbitrary and irrational obstacles to the reorganization of business strategies. Audiovisual geographies are becoming detached from the symbolic spaces of national culture and realigned on the basis of the more "universal" principles of international consumer culture (11). Eastern Europe in fact is often singled out as the shining example and target of such expansionist policies, a model of the ways in which a technologically networked world and the "free flow" of communication and democracy create a happy global community (12).

However, "unity in diversity" means different things to different European constituents. Euro-identity makes little if any room for the large number of migrant and diasporic populations who live on the continent. "What does the idea of Europe add up to when so many within feel that they are excluded? European identity, for all its apparent self-confidence, remains a vulnerable and anxious phenomenon, and is increasingly articulated with regressive forms of pan-European white racism" (Morley and Robins 1995, 3). There is a danger that an oppressive European tradition will reestablish itself in the guise of new, reinvented European identities and a touristically united European empire will reassert itself in new ways. Europe is not just a geographical site but also an idea inextricably linked with the myths of Western civilization and grievously shaped by haunting encounters with colonial Others (5).

What new boundaries and divisions might develop between social, cultural and ethnic groupings? What is the relation between the previously dominant Western European culture and the newly stirring nationalist cultures of Eastern Europe? Just as the territories outside the European Community must consider their relationship to this cultural and economic space, so must Europe come to terms with what this "beyond Europe" means for it. (4)

József Böröcz uses even stronger terms to describe the underlying motives of European expansion and the existing divisions between core and peripheral nations. To him, Western Europe's "Eurospeak," or multicultural identity discourse, is full of naïve, confident, but also smug imperial-colonial teleology, indifferent to the world outside, falling back on a "universal" sense of Europeanness. Examining the current remapping of European space in terms of a reiteration of imperial and political ideology and rhetoric, he observes that "Europe" is synecdochically identified with the core EU states, forgetting about the rest of Europe. He classifies the expanding EU as a geopolitically "continuous" empire with shared space and culture between colonizers and colonized, where the flow of goods and people cannot be prohibited but can be severely regulated, and where the colonized is represented less as a slave but as a poor relative, a country bumpkin.

Whereas the EU's founding documents are full of euphemism, euphoria, and idealism about the four freedoms (of services, capital, workforce, and commodities) within the community, there are serious obstacles in place to block or screen the flow of labor from the newly accessed postcommunist states. For instance, even leftist European parties and politicians demand that the Eastern European workforce not be allowed to circulate freely for seven years following accession. Because the previous, Moscow-centered continuous empire was just the most recent among several to dominate eastern and southern states, the shift to the current situation of dependence has been smooth, experienced by most Eastern Europeans with restraint and irony—in stark contrast with Western reactions, which loudly celebrated the "liberation" of Eastern Europe. In reality, however, "The most remarkable aspect of the period following the collapse of socialism was the determination with which the European Union restored economic dependence and uneven exchange; how it exported its governmentality and began—using an overtly colonial tone—to treat 'Eastern' candidates as despised and inferior aliens" (Böröcz 2001).

Whether it is explicitly expressed or only implied, Böröcz adds, postcommunist nations nostalgically yearn for the advantages of a past imperial glory they never had but feel they deserve. Instead, the eastern expansion provides the real Europe new opportunities for schooling, civilizing, and educating rambunctious easterners and southerners while turning a blind eye to or even implicitly supporting everyday practices of Foucauldian governmentality, particularly those that indulge racist

desires. Böröcz calls this a "kindergarten fantasy," one of the most enduring pedagogical tropes of the colonial imagination.

This educational imperative has been present in European tourism
from the beginning. The contemporary patterns of leisure migration,
which emerged in the nineteenth century, developed from the European
Grand Tour of young, well-situated British, French, and German men,
which peaked between the late-sixteenth and late-eighteenth centuries
(Böröcz 1992, 709). This *Tour de France, compagnonnage, Wanderjahr,*
or *Wanderplicht* was an educational experience that served as training
for diplomatic service and craftsmanship. The leisure tourism that arose
with industrialization was new in that it was implanted and embedded
in the structures of an increasingly international industrial capitalism
(714). As Böröcz shows, it is remarkable that the eastern part of Europe,
and thus over half of Europe's population, was all but missing from the
early maps of leisure tourism and migration (715). Communism further
deepened this "tourist gap" within the continent: communist states took
over the control and regulation of internal tourism and carefully policed
their borders, effectively locking the region behind the Iron Curtain.

The hidden imperial history of Western Europe's civilizing educational
mission and the uneven emergence of what Böröcz calls travel-capitalism
puts in a different light the apparent transparence of EuropaGO and
other online games, which allegedly promote innocent touristic grazing.
While the opening in the structures and content of postsocialist educational systems is undoubtedly a welcome development, it is easy to
overlook hierarchies and forms of control imposed by states, the EU, and
media corporations behind the attractive façade of technological euphoria, a rhetoric of inclusion, and the pleasures of electronic edutainment
games through which the subjectivities of the new generation are actively
shaped. In many ways educational trends in global game cultures are
converging, calling for a comparative mapping of globalization and
education if we are to understand the next generation of global gamer
citizens. The differences among various national and regional contexts,
rooted in peculiar historical legacies and formed in local negotiations
among state and regional politicians, corporate executives, theorists,
teachers, parents, media activists, and student consumers themselves are
also highly instructive in this respect. Hungary's national media education curriculum and the print media initiatives that have sprung up
around it are unique in their forward-thinking potential. The peculiarity
of the postcommunist situation is that, unlike in the United States, there

is a great deal of collective investment in the quality of media content and a suspicion about the changing aesthetic of youth media and the commodification of children's culture. At the same time, after five decades of state control over media and education and widespread commitment to Europeanization through technological progress, there has not yet developed a healthy amount of skepticism about intertwined state and corporate ideological and economic interest in education, technologization, and tourism. Theoretically informed comparisons that reach across national borders would undoubtedly yield models for collaboration that combine the most promising features of local media education programs and provide critical tools with which to foreground otherwise invisible local ideological and economic interests.

# 2

## From the Mole to the Dinosaur: Global Nostalgia and the Ambivalences of Late- and Postcommunist Children's Media Culture

### The Arrival of the Dinosaur

There were no dinosaurs during communism. One must wonder why the universal interest in creatures that bear the triple attraction of being "big, fierce, and extinct," according to Stephen Jay Gould's formula (Mitchell 1998, 9), left the cultures of the Soviet empire intact. Dinosaurs have been the subject of human fascination for a hundred and fifty years thanks to the global reach of modern science, commerce, and popular culture. But if children growing up in communist countries had witnessed the craze surrounding the dinosaur in the lives of their American peers, they would have responded much like the imaginary alien visitors would, to whom W. J. T. Mitchell addresses his *The Last Dinosaur Book*, the most informative account of dinosaur iconology to date: "From the point of view of the alien visitors, the ordinary behavior of human beings toward erect reptiles will probably look strange, contradictory, exotic— perhaps even ridiculous. Things that seem obvious to us will have to be explained to them" (Mitchell 1998, 4).

It is telling that one of the few references to dinosaurs and communism comes from two artists who left communist Russia to settle in the United States. Lev Manovich evokes Vitaly Komar and Alexander Malamid's painting *Bolsheviks Returning Home after a Demonstration* (1981–1982) in his discussion of *Jurassic Park* (Steven Spielberg, 1993). In the painting, which is part of the painters' Nostalgic Socialist Realism series, two workers, one carrying a red flag, find a small dinosaur standing in the snow. It is no coincidence that the painting nostalgically evokes Socialist Realism with reference to dinosaurs. Manovich concludes that the aesthetic of *Jurassic Park* is prefigured by Soviet Socialist Realism, whose aim was to create the uplifting impression of a utopian future within the present. However, the very tendentiousness of imposed and rigid standards of representation, the very larger-than-life quality of Socialist Realist artwork lent it a dystopian quality and rendered it already obsolete during socialism (Manovich 2002, 203). As has been abundantly documented in recent films—perhaps most famously in *Good Bye Lenin!* (Wolfgang Becker, 2003)—since 1989 the giant statues that used to mark the Soviet imperial landscape have turned into nostalgic remnants of the past. Many have been sold to Western collectors, while others have been gathered in outdoor statue parks specially designated to be museums of Socialist Realism. The best known of these graveyards is the Memento Park outside Budapest, housing the dinosaurs of socialism, "the gigantic memories of the communist dictatorship"[1] (see figures 2.1 and 2.2).

Manovich singles out *Jurassic Park* as an example of a new, digital aesthetic that refers simultaneously to the future and the past. Rather than being an inferior representation of our reality, the synthetic image, sharp and free of noise, represents the future of sight itself, the perfect, hyperreal, cyborg vision free of the limitations of both the human and the camera eye. However, in the film, the computer image is degraded

**Figure 2.1**
Restorative nostalgia turns reflective: monsters of the past on exhibit in the Communist Statue Park outside Budapest (courtesy of the author).

**Figure 2.2**
Dinosaurs from *Jurassic Park* (Steven Spielberg, 1993).

to blend in with and approximate the older, less perfect film image: edges are softened, the resolution is reduced, grain effect and depth of field are added. This nostalgic yielding of the future to the past is enhanced by the representational content of the film, in which prehistoric giants come to life (Manovich 2002, 202–204).

Angela Ndalianis also references *Jurassic Park* as the central example of a new aesthetic and entertainment form, and economic model, which finds its predecessors in seventeenth-century baroque art's serial forms, its emphasis on spectacle, and its complex sensory experiences. The "neobaroque" convergence of media entertainment forms around the film, including the sequels, video games, and theme park rides, "have increasingly displayed a concern for engulfing and engaging the spectator actively in sensorial and formal games that are concerned with their own media-specific sensory and playful experiences" (Ndalianis 2005, 1–29).

Twenty years after the collapse of the Soviet empire, no one needs to explain dinosaur fascination to Eastern European children. As Svetlana Boym notes, in the late 1990s, the dinosaur was one of the two "fantastic creatures" that dominated the Moscow market (the other was Moscow's patron St. George, the dragon killer) (Boym 2001, 35). While by no means the only cause of postcommunist dinosaur fascination, the release of *Jurassic Park* in 1993 no doubt provided a boost. After decades of being deprived of entertaining spectacle, people flocked to the theaters simultaneously with Western audiences to experience a Hollywood blockbuster, and a landmark in animation technology at that. While ideological and economic obstacles had prevented or delayed the release of many American films in Soviet satellite states during the communist period, it is not likely that state censorship had prohibited dinosaur images even in the darkest times and places of totalitarianism. We will have to look for the reasons elsewhere—in the intimate connections that link the dinosaur with consumer capitalism, nostalgia, and American nationalism.

Svetlana Boym discusses *Jurassic Park* as a centerpiece in her analysis of postcommunist nostalgia (Boym 2001, 33). She detects what she calls "technonostalgia" in the "*Jurassic Park* syndrome," that is, the use of modern science for the recovery of a futuristic and prehistoric world, which escapes from contemporary history and local memories. Instead of provoking ambivalence and a paradoxical interaction of past, present, and future, the technonostalgia embodied by *Jurassic Park* and the syndrome it manifests provides a total restoration of extinct creatures, the final resolution of all conflict, and global exportability. "Dinosaurs are ideal animals for the nostalgia industry because nobody remembers them" (33).

I end chapter 1 with a description of the post–Cold War European cultural landscape, the site of "education post-tourism engaged in performances of Unity-in-Diversity," of a "Grand Tour in an age of Cultural Diversity and Multicultural Disney Theme Parks" (Verstraete 2003, 39). I argue there that the touristic, performative incorporation of the postcommunist East in the EU blurs the history of structural economic and political inequality within Europe, and renders invisible the Iron (or Velvet?) Curtain, which continues to divide the northwestern fortress from the southeastern provinces. This chapter examines the nostalgic turn that has increasingly rendered Eastern European national histories playful, mediated, and most often spectacular, entertainment in the past two decades. Following Boym, I see postcommunist nostalgia as a double-edged ideological sword: insofar as nostalgia is a play with time, it liberates from the tyranny of authoritative national histories and releases a polyphonic reassessment of the past. It may yield alternative histories that have important political consequences for the power games of the present and future. At the same time, nostalgic play with time might erode a sense of a collective narrative altogether. It may yield a fragmented landscape that can be easily recolonized by transnational media corporations or nation-states.

The extended case study at the core of this analysis builds on the previous chapter's discussion of the global generational divide that the postcommunist transitions have amplified. Here I take the analysis of the generational divide further and ask how the globalization of postcommunist media cultures and the nostalgic reassessment of Eastern European histories have transformed the relations between children's and adult cultures, legitimizing such a thing as children's media culture as an area of study in the first place. The three thematic centers around which I track such transformations are the newly arrived figure of the dinosaur; the aesthetics and politics of small creatures in late-communist animation culture, headed by Zdenek Miler's beloved mole, *Krtek*; and the hybrid adult-child culture of the Western in communist film and television.

The fact that dinosaurs are a specifically American invention is a crucial aspect of understanding the post-Soviet Jurassic Park syndrome. "Dinosauromania started as an American obsession; the exploration of nature and achievements in science were later matched by cinematic special effects that together conspired to reanimate the extinct creature" (34). The technopastoral of *Jurassic Park* exemplifies a mythical kind of nostalgia, which draws on the heroic implications of American national identity but is exported all over the world. "What might appear as an expensive children's game, innocuous and universal in the United States, strikes viewers in other parts of the world as an exemplary staging of the American myth, the myth of a new world that forgot its history and recreated prehistory brand-new" (34).

In a similar vein, W. J. T. Mitchell argues that, despite the global reach of dinosauromania, there is something very American about this excessive fascination (Mitchell 1998, 111). Paleontology had been born in Britain and France, but the United States soon became the site of a mad bone rush accompanying various gold rushes to the West, transporting big bones to the East Coast to be exhibited in the great museums of natural science (112). Thomas Jefferson, popularly known as the "mammoth president," was so fascinated with the bones of extinct giants that he set up a bone room in the White House (114). His writings demonstrate a profound connection between his search for big bones and his sense of the natural constitution of the United States, setting the foundation for a four-way link among American national pride, big capital, mass culture, and big bones (120). Dinosaurs are naturally "at home on the range" in the Wild West, where paleontologists worked alongside cowboys, Indians, trappers, traders, outlaws, and miners (Mitchell 1998, 26). They have also been at home in the world of advertisement, an association that goes back to the Sinclair Oil Company's Brontosaurus logo (Mitchell 1998, 168).

As I show, dinosaurs have been conspicuously absent from Eastern European national imaginaries until recently precisely because of their association with violence, commercialism, and the infantilization of cultures, all of which converge in the notion of American imperialism. If the dinosaur is a "universally intelligible symbol" of world conquest and domination and the "prestige symbol of modern nation-states" (Mitchell 1998, 68), it has no role to play in national cultures that are in a permanent state of marginality and inferiority. As an attraction for kids and the masses, it is tailor-made for disaster and action-adventure flicks. "The purism of high modernist abstraction would be utterly contaminated by the intrusion of the dinosaur" (Mitchell 1998, 62).

It is surprising then that Westerns themselves, and a general fascination with the Wild West, were an integral and welcome part of communist cultures and identities. Western films were imported and shown as staples on television in most countries. As I demonstrate in the last part of this chapter, they inspired a succession of imitations and transplants, particularly in animation and children's media. Given the American national roots of both dinosaur and Western mythology, one must ask why communist cultures consistently refused the one and welcomed the other. In the case studies that conclude this chapter, I hope to find an answer to this question by examining what we may consider the specifically Eastern European "indigenous" children's animation that ruled the screens in the absence of dinosaurs. I also discuss the paradoxical communist love affair with the Western with reference to a set of generic imports and adaptations.

Since the early 1990s, dinosaurs, cowboys, and Indians have found a peaceful way to coexist in the all-incorporating postcommunist nostalgia market. Western-themed restaurants, bars, and shops are as ubiquitous in post-Soviet towns as dinosaur toys are on store shelves and mini-Jurassic theme parks on the outskirts of cities. One can consider the transformation of Western imagery into kitsch and the arrival of the dinosaur in postcommunist cultures as hallmarks of the changes in play practices that I examine throughout this book. It is tempting to use the dinosaur image as a way to distinguish between the "before" and the "after" in concepts and practices of collective play. The (post)communist story of the dinosaur should also provide an insight into the ways that the relationship between childhood and adulthood has been transformed in the course of communism's gradual collapse. I begin this book with reference to the ambivalence shared by a generation of people whose childhood and youth are rooted in the extinct world of communism, and whose maturation into adulthood coincided with an accelerated transition toward conditions of global media capitalism. In the introduction, I argue that the concept of "play" is a useful tool to analyze the generational ambivalence toward the transition. On the broadest scale, this chapter is also intended to be a programmatic recommendation for harnessing the ambivalence of such games in order to generate less sweeping theories of global children's media culture.

Here I situate my analysis of the generational shift, and of the transformation of the relationship between children's and adult media cultures, in relation to "nostalgia." Widely identified as a powerful factor in the constitution of postcommunist identities, nostalgia is also intertwined with a cluster of phenomena that recur throughout the chapters, most prominently *consumerism* and *tourism*. These operative terms are useful in demarcating, at least conditionally, communism from capitalism, before and after. As I show in chapter 1, they refer to ludic activities central to the political and economic mechanisms of postmodern media capitalism and postmodern identities. However, they have not been seen to be of much relevance to the operation and retrospective historicization of communist regimes: Communist cultures emphasized production and demonized consumption. They isolated themselves within national and Soviet imperial borders to minimize the mobility of their citizens, only allowing for a limited and controlled internal tourist flow. Even more central to my argument, Soviet regimes had no use for nostalgia. Their careful selection of past events was frozen into an official history and subordinated to a relentless march toward a utopian future.

## Shades of Postcommunist Nostalgia

Postcommunist nostalgia is not simply a necessary symptom of consumerism or the adoption of the "American sublime" (Boym 2001, 35), the willful reduction of collective memories to touristic spectacle. As Boym argues, nostalgia is a distinctly modern disease, a yearning for a different sense of time or a rebellion against history as relentless progress (xv).

It can also be understood as *play* with time, which offers (at least imaginary) release from the modern sense of time, the possibility to return to what D. W. Winnicott calls the "potential space" of play between the individual and the environment in early childhood, where cultural experience begins (Boym 2001, 53). The urgent need to identify individual and collective origins during historical upheavals—and few can rival the end of communism in scale—may take two different routes: one is a creative return to the imaginary space of potential and play, while remaining fully aware that origins are posited, imaginary, and multiple, and total reconstruction is an illusion. Boym calls this "reflective" nostalgia. The other route reduces the creative potential of remembering to an artificially unified, fixed narrative in the service of a political, often nationalistic, agenda. While reflective nostalgia allows for the flexibility to meditate on history and the passage of time, the latter, "restorative," nostalgia wants a perfect snapshot of the past.

Instances of reflective nostalgia, abundant in the post-Soviet world today, seek a playful recovery of socialist memories to withstand the violent "confiscation" of memories by nationalist conservatives (Ugresic 1996). To compensate for the radical and unprecedented disappearance of the world that made up the fabric of identities under communism, reflective nostalgia builds cultural identity out of "a certain social poetics or 'cultural intimacy' that provides a glue in everyday life," recoverable from various shared frameworks of memory (Boym 2001, 50). Such identity involves everyday games of hide-and-seek that only "natives" play, unwritten rules of behavior, jokes understood from half a word, a sense of complicity. Reflective nostalgia "reveals the fact that longing and critical thinking are not opposed to one another, as affective memories do not absolve one from compassion, judgment or critical reflection" (Boym 2001, 50). "Homecoming does not signify a recovery of identity; it does not end the journey in the virtual space of imagination. A modern nostalgic can be homesick and sick of home, at once" (50).

State propaganda and official national memory also use cultural intimacy. Boym insists, however, that it is important to distinguish between political nationalism, based on alleged ethnic homogeneity, and cultural intimacy, based on common social context (Boym 2001, 42). "National memory tends to make a single teleological plot out of shared everyday recollections. The gaps and discontinuities are mended through a coherent and inspiring tale of recovered identity." (53). This formulation recalls Homi Bhabha's deconstruction of national narrative in his "DissemiNation" as a process of narration, reconstructed from the rags and patches of national life and memory, which I discuss in chapter 4 (Bhabha 1994).

Restorative nostalgia tends to channel the play with memory through two main narrative plots: the restoration of origins and conspiracy theory. Ambivalence is written out of its conspiratorial worldview. Conspiracy implies a paranoiac view of the home permanently under siege—as is the case in *Jurassic Park* (Boym 2001, 42). The more rapid the pace of social change, the more conservative and unchangeable the newly "recovered" traditions tend to be and the more selectively the past is presented (41). The Balkan wars have provided the most violent and tragic testimony to the power of restorative nostalgia. But restorative nostalgia, while it always involves a violent rearrangement of history, need not lead to actual bloodshed, at least not in the home. Particularly since the Reagan administration, a U.S.-centered, global military-entertainment complex has wrapped its restorative agenda in the entertaining and spectacular conspiratorial plots of science fiction and action-adventure films to distract attention from actual practices of governmental surveillance and military intervention conducted elsewhere (Rogin 1990). The nostalgic rewriting of history in the guise of entertainment and spectacle has thus taken innocuous forms. *Forrest Gump*'s violent romp across American history seen through the eyes of the white, American man-child whose innocence retroactively tames even the Ku Klux Klan, or Disney's "family entertainment," which retroactively pacifies Indian-settler relations in *Pocahontas* (Kapur 2005, 73–82), are just two conspicuous examples. The *Jurassic Park* syndrome that has swept through the post-Soviet region is primarily a manifestation of such "restorative" nostalgia. It is a product of the global entertainment industry's nostalgia characterized by the excess and boundless availability of desirable souvenirs. This kind of nostalgia manifests itself as a marketing strategy that tricks consumers into missing what they have not lost. Arjun Appadurai calls this "ersatz" or "armchair nostalgia," one without lived experience or collective historical memory (Appadurai 1996, 78).

While by no means intended as empirical evidence, in my own retroactively constructed narrative of the postcommunist transition, watching *Jurassic Park* in 1993 in a Hungarian theater overflowing with people of all ages stands out as an event that marked the beginning of a new era. Although it was one of the few occasions in my memory that the theater had sold out every screening, the novelty was not simply the full house. It seemed that the audience itself was new. There was a pervasive, collective sense of awe in the air that stifled the irony that I had believed was inherent to postcommunist identities. Large groups of adults, along with children, suddenly migrated from their television-ruled living rooms into the public space of the movie theater to submit willingly to the childlike amazement evoked by the animated spectacle of extinct animals. One is tempted to see here evidence to Boym's claim that restorative nostalgia takes itself dead seriously, whereas reflective nostalgia can be ironic and humorous (Boym 2001, 42). But one should be cautious with value judgments. While *Jurassic Park* most likely accelerated a generational shift, it no doubt released existing, dormant sensibilities and unacknowledged class divisions in the public sphere as well. It was only the last, official nail in the coffin of low-budget psychological-allegorical drama and low-key, hand-drawn animated tales. People long deprived of spectacle, tired of the ascetic spirit of politically infused modernist media, had arrived at the theaters famished, just to be devoured by Spielberg's dinosaurs.

In a simplified view, one can see the large-scale transformation in aesthetic sensibilities, encapsulated in the Eastern European arrival and reception of *Jurassic Park*, as a shift from a very "grown-up" children's media culture overwhelmed by adult control and overt political content to an intentionally depoliticized, commercial children's culture that engulfs and infantilizes the realm of adults. The former was the terrain of symbolic negotiation and struggle between the communist state and its oppositional intellectuals, who were trying to find venues of expression under the political radar of censorship. The latter, as I show in chapter 1, is the terrain of transnational media corporations in negotiation with the EU, the state, and native cultural gatekeepers, all of whom are invested in financial and political gain.

This view is echoed by postcommunist intellectuals' and artists' distressed or resigned diagnoses of the transition from "mature" to "immature" cultures. For instance, theorist and critic Péter György gives a sarcastic account of the ways in which "infantile" American popular culture has marginalized the high cultural ghettos of former communist countries. He laments that the "creatures" that U.S. culture has "spawned" have turned Eastern Europe into a "theme/entertainment/ Jurassic Park" (18), and the history of the present into a "never-ending soap opera" (19). Culture has become depthless, essential questions are no longer relevant, and Disney's life lessons have replaced art films, producing cartoon-level identities and narration (György 1997a).

Such an anxiety about the corrupting effects of mass-media culture is profoundly rooted in the history of Eastern European national cultures, bound to poetry as the most authentic expression of the national and regional spirit, as I elaborate in chapter 5. This anxiety draws on Adorno's pessimism about mass culture, and explains the current Eastern European popularity of Neil Postman, evoked in this book's introduction. This pessimism resonates in Lev Manovich's assessment of interactivity as totalitarian, in Jan Svankmajer's damning view of consumerism and the waning respect for childhood, in Balkan artists' attempts to rescue and perpetuate art in the face of the global commercialization of post-Yugoslav conditions (discussed in chapter 5), and in postsocialist educational reforms, discussed in the first chapter. As I write there, Polish-born sociologist Zygmunt Bauman has compared the roles of consumers under the conditions of what he calls "liquid modernity" to the roles of tourists. The "tourist syndrome"—by definition pathologized, much like Boym's *Jurassic Park* syndrome—is a metaphor for contemporary life in Western societies. It implies a preference for substitutes, which mischannel potentially creative impulses into sidetracks or blind alleys. Bauman's chief example is the substitute communities that form around celebrities. They respond to real need, but since nothing real is available in liquid modernity, they settle for substitutes and temporary relations. Substitutes provide instant relief, but they exacerbate the "disease" and make it more difficult to cure. Tourism, an inherently consumerist phenomenon, is such a substitute for the real thing, which would be the proximity of otherness and the recognition of shared humanity (Franklin 2003, 214).

No matter how sympathetic one is, such accounts themselves are colored by unacknowledged restorative nostalgia for a culture of maturity and purity, where the "real thing" allegedly existed and was within reach. As such, they implicitly dismiss the pleasures and yearnings of the audiences that filled the theaters to see *Jurassic Park* as a misguided and fruitless search that can yield only substitutes. Andreas Huyssen points out that critics of late-capitalist amnesia and the global nostalgia business, followers of Theodor Adorno, simply equate commodification with forgetting (Huyssen 2000, 68). Much like Adorno's critique of pop culture, however, such accounts leave out too much. His Marxist categories remain oblivious to issues of media specificity, temporality, memory, and the structures of everyday life. His critique of the culture—or, here, memory—industry is as one-sided as the more uplifting scenario offered by Walter Benjamin, who considers the very media of reproducibility a promise of political mobilization, when they are really an obstacle (Huyssen, 2000, 68–72).

As Huyssen argues, the culture of memory—*Erlebnisgesellschaft*—takes on a more explicitly political inflection in some parts of the world, including Eastern Europe and the former Soviet Union, the Middle East, South Africa, Rwanda, Nigeria, Australia, Japan, China, Korea, or Latin America. In these places, memory is mobilized for varied purposes, from chauvinistic and fundamentalist politics to a search for a true past—an elusive goal—and reconciliation. In Eastern Europe, remembering has not only been politicized but has been almost entirely appropriated by trauma. Entertainment memory has been considered a luxury: frivolous and thus insignificant. However, in the post–Cold War era, we cannot discuss personal, generational, and public memory anymore as separate from the media and their influences. We cannot oppose serious to trivial, lived to imagined memory, Holocaust museum to Disney-fied theme park. There is no correct representation; the question of quality is to be decided case by case. Trauma is marketed just as much as fun is, and often to the same consumers (Huyssen 2000, 66).

The blending of traumatic (historical) and entertaining (nostalgic) memory has accelerated in Eastern Europe in the past twenty years. However, it did not begin in the wake of the fall of the Wall. The intensity of mediated remembering in the post-Wall era provides a critical window for reviewing the rigid separation of official histories and mediated memories during communism. Virtually all accounts of unofficial cultures in late communism need to be revised in light of the popular media's role. While there are sporadic studies about the antiestablishment thrust of rock music and sports,[2] the fabric of cultural intimacy that characterized communism was woven to a great degree by television. In the United States, *I Love Lucy* and other earlier television favorites have become rerun staples, as well as subjects of academic publications, courses, and conferences. However, what would qualify as the popular media culture of communism has been replaced overnight, for the most part, by new global, commercial fair. The entertainment culture of communism—commercials, television variety shows, children's programming—has been gathered by the collective work of individuals and found its way to fan sites, YouTube, and other file-sharing Internet archives. Some of the work is available on dedicated nostalgia TV channels such as the Hungarian-language public satellite Duna ("Danube") Television, established in 1993. Other work, including children's animated series, have been released on VHS and DVD, along with new ancillary products such as stuffed animals, coloring books, and T-shirts.

Reconstituting postcommunist identities from fragmented memories through the work of collective media gathering is in itself a remarkable phenomenon, which makes available a unique archive and immeasurably important resources for theorizing global identity games. Such work calls for the expansion of Boym's description of collective memory as the shared register of everyday life, which constitutes the common framework of individual recollections. To her "folds in the fan of memory" we must add the manifold memories of fans, as theorists of "pop cosmopolitanism" (Jenkins 2006), "consumer citizenship" (Hartley 2004), and "fan democracy" (van Zoonen 2004) encourage us to do. As I argue in the introduction, while these inherently Anglo-American notions do not have the same legacy in postcommunist cultures as they do in postcapitalist consumer democracies, and while they face a great deal of well-founded animosity, to dismiss them as irrelevant would be unrealistic and self-defeating. One simply cannot deny the importance of the fact that audiences left starving by high art have been hungrily consuming *Jurassic Park* and its "spawns" since the early 1990s. One must ask what kinds of entertainment communist audiences had consumed before *Jurassic Park*. György himself reveals the nostalgic parameters of his conception of culture when he expresses a longing for the antiestablishment culture of socialism, which was "young and beautiful," unlike official socialism, which was "ugly and fat, as well as sweaty and plagued by sexual problems" (1997a). In chapter 5, I link this flattering self-image of antiestablishment culture with a rather narcissistic kind of masculinity, rooted in the Romantic cult of the national intellectual, rendered young and beautiful only by its obsessive association with youthful female bodies. The unacknowledged cultural nationalism of such accounts casts the shadow of a doubt over their anti-Americanism and investment in high culture.

Throughout this book, I try to show how such a high modernist conception of culture had marginalized certain groups, who have emerged into representation since the fall of communism by constructing hybrid aesthetics and politics. Such representations draw on a variety of regional, European, and global affiliations while always inevitably confronting the national. Children's media culture has been perhaps the most forgotten aspect of communism, not the least because children cannot speak publicly for themselves. While public resources for the continued production of high-quality television programming have dried up and the area continues to be ignored in studies of Eastern European media cultures, the Disney Channel, the Cartoon Network, Fox Kids, Nickelodeon, and other networks have very much discovered Eastern European children, lending them loud voices to express their desire for programs and products (Lustyik 2006). Unnoticed and overnight, children's media has become one of the most influential dimensions of the future of postcommunist, and by extension, global, media cultures.

### Global Children's Culture in Postcommunism

Most accounts of children's media culture today focus on the United States, Western Europe, and Japan as representatives of an increasingly integrated global digital culture. While gestures are routinely made toward a digital divide, a barrier beyond which the rest of the world resides, the assumption is that technologically advanced cultures represent the inevitable future toward which the rest of the world is moving. As Julian Sefton-Green argues, *children* and *new technology* are terms often yoked together because they embody similar teleological assumptions about growth, progression, and development (Sefton-Green 1998, 2). Theories of children's media culture are typically written from a position that knows no alternatives to a fully commercialized children's media.

For instance, in an otherwise insightful analysis, Mizuko Ito refers to post-Pokemon media mixes such as Yu-Gi-Oh! and Hamtaro to argue that young children in postindustrial societies are growing up in a "convergence culture" of an increasingly interactive and participatory media ecology, where the Internet ties together old and new media. She asks, "What is the nature of childhood imagination when it takes as source material the narratives and characters of commercial culture? What are the modes of social and cultural participation that are enabled or attenuated with the rise of popular children's media? Does engagement with particular media types relate to differences in childhood agency or creativity?" (Ito 2008).

These are fair questions to ask regardless of one's geopolitical reference point. However, most post-Soviet pessimists have vivid memories of an alternative media ecology, where children's culture was a high pedagogical priority for the state and where commercial concerns played a negligible role. These memories constitute a crucial component of individual and collective cultural identities, and influence visions for the future, inherited by the postcommunist generations. In addition, while digital advancement is seen as key to catching up with Europe and the rest of the world, as I elaborate in chapter 1, there is a considerable amount of resistance to the technologization and commercialization of children's media culture across the educational spectrum and the media. Since Eastern European children's media culture has not been legitimized as a research area, empirical data are hardly available. It is safe to speculate, however, that Japanese media mixes are far from colonizing children's fantasies in the region. Ito's argument that the new media ecology mobilizes the imagination of young people in a "more activist way," through the convergence of old and new media forms, personalization, remixing of content, and "hypersociality," sounds like a problematic idea in Eastern Europe, where "activist" and "commercial" continue to have opposing connotations.

How can one find a mutually enriching compromise between these contrasting views, which highlight each other's distinct geopolitical origins? One would have to find some middle ground between the typically Eastern European "adult" cultural pessimism about the commercialization and infantilization of culture, which presumes a children's culture of innocence and purity, and late-capitalist accounts of children's "adult" agency (see Sefton-Green 1998), which cannot conceive of a model outside of media environments created and marketed by giant media corporations, setting the parameters of children's imaginations everywhere on the globe. We need to create accounts that accommodate both, apparently mutually exclusive, paradigms: one that denies the legitimacy and value of commercial culture, and one that cannot think of children's culture outside of commercial frameworks. Ito acknowledges such an objection in a disclaimer, leaving the door open for integration and dialogue:

If, as I have suggested, young people's media cultures are moving towards more mobilized and differentiated modes of participation with an increasingly global collective imagination, then we need to revisit our frameworks for understanding the role of the imagination in everyday life. Assessed by more well-established standards of creativity, the forms of authorship and performance I have described would be deemed derivative and appropriative rather than truly original. It is also crucial that we keep in view the political economic implications of having young people's personal identities and social lives so attuned and dependent on a commercial apparatus of imaginative production. At the same time, we need to take seriously the fact that cultural forms like Yugioh and Hamtaro have become the coin of the realm for the childhood imagination, and recognize them as important sources of knowledge, connoisseurship and cultural capital. (Ito 2008)

One promising way to follow up is the proposition, offered by Marsha Kinder in her book *Playing with Power in Movies, Television, and Video Games*, also evoked by Ito, to focus on and valorize children's agency in their interaction with television and other primarily visual media forms formerly deemed "passive." This is a useful way to foreground the Eurocentric, high-cultural bias toward the written word long held in Eastern Europe (Kinder 1991). Ito, Kinder, as well as Sefton-Green (1998), Helen Nixon (1998), and Anne Haas Dyson (1997) also remind us that current forms of remixing and the mobilization of commercial content may be based on predigital forms of playing.

Late-communist, necessarily predigital children's media can then enter this paradigm—in a way that also revises the paradigm. The emphasis on communication and media networks' ability to mobilize the imagination and emotions in appropriating popular children's culture should be taken to heart as a way to revise the top-down approaches to children and their agency under communism and to legitimate the study of children's media culture in the first place. Notions such as emotional intelligence are just now beginning to surface in the most progressive corners of Eastern European educational institutions. The role of emotions in remixing and appropriating popular culture, foregrounding the agency of young people, was entirely overlooked by the communist state and its apparatuses, as these were invested in the idea that children are powerless and prone to manipulation. Censorship was a highly inadequate mechanism to screen content in this regard, which discounted the vulnerability of media products to appropriation and negotiation.

However, it does not at all follow that the new digital culture would bring along a degree of "activism" or democratic participation just by virtue of being interactive, as Ito argues: "Young people can reshape and customize commercial media as well as exchange and discuss media in peer-to-peer networks through blogs, filesharing, social networking systems and various messaging services." And, "When gaming formats are tied into the imaginary of narrative media such as television and comics, they become vehicles for manifesting these characters and narratives with greater fidelity and effect in everyday life. While the role of the collective imagination in children's culture probably remains as strongly rooted in commercial culture as ever, the ability to personalize, remix and mobilize this imaginative material is substantially augmented by the inclusion of digital media into the mix" (Ito 2008). Even though children's emotions might be mobilized by interacting via commercial digital networks, the content and purpose of such an engagement cannot be trivialized, as they tend to be by enthusiastic accounts. Buying and selling, a training for life in a capitalist economy driven by consumerism and consumption, as well as an explorative, virtual tourism seem to provide the ideological infrastructure of interactive social networking technologies for children. And again, how do we incorporate in this account the legacy of a culture where children's imaginations are not "as strongly rooted in commercial culture as ever," and where commercial culture is a fairly recent economic, social, and political arrival, which has met significant resistance? From a postcommunist point of view, creating consumption-driven networks of communication and exchange is a very limited position.

I want to return to the concept of nostalgia to work toward integrating postcommunist and late-capitalist frameworks. Nostalgia is a product of modernism (Boym 2001) and an essential component of postmodern media culture (Huyssen 2000; Jameson 1991). In the postcommunist region, as I said earlier, nostalgia has a more specific function: it has become a crucial vehicle of releasing long-suppressed emotions and fantasies and processing communist memories, which mingle and interact with the more global, consumerist fantasies introduced by global media culture, which create what Appadurai famously called "communities of sentiment" (Appadurai 1996, 6–8).

Digital technologies have been instrumental in this process of virtual self-preservation and reinvention throughout Eastern Europe. They help to bridge the divide between the lost before and the new after. The shared memory material thus recovered in journalism, television shows, social networking sites, discussion lists, blogs, and in everyday conversation continues the intimate collective conversations that characterized socialism, while incorporating contemporary media influences. Communist public discourse was strictly national. It created secret national societies conspiring against Soviet authorities, which included virtually everyone, even the party leadership, in the most liberal of communist countries. However, postcommunist nostalgia discourse brings to the surface those mediated memory connections that had fallen outside the borders of public-national discourse: the influence of broadcast signals received across borders, which allowed Albanians and Yugoslavs to watch Italian TV, Hungarians to receive Austrian TV, and East Germans to watch West German TV in a divided Berlin. It includes communist TV commercials and consumer products, many of which have survived the changes because of a nostalgic longing for continuity; memories of regional internal tourism such as trips to the Croatian seaside or Black

Sea resorts—once a symbol of shame in the absence of Western travel but now a fond and quaint memory; pioneer camps to which specific neighborhoods of schoolchildren were generally assigned, thus creating postcommunist memory communities according to geographical location; and commercial media imports such as the first jeans, *Star Wars* memorabilia, and various commodities made in Soviet-ruled countries. All such memories transcend and question national lines of affinity and community.

Some of the most fondly cherished memories concern popular children's songs, television shows, and films. Whereas the smells, tastes, and sights of communism are recoverable only through individual corporeal memories, most children's films and television programs have been kept in circulation by the nostalgia wave as an alternative to global commercial media for children. The launching of Minimax, a regional children's television network in 1999, provided a crucial boost and infrastructure for this mission. Minimax was created to provide European programming in Central and Eastern Europe, with a special emphasis on shows from the region, both old and new (Lustyik 2006, 127). Many of the popular children's media products made under communism never crossed borders; they were certainly not exported to the West. They were made for and enjoyed primarily by national audiences—and enjoyed a great deal more than high cultural opuses. But many others, primarily children's television programs, were produced in regional or European collaboration and distributed and viewed in most Soviet satellite countries. A shared television infrastructure and flow of content was enhanced with the establishment of Intersputnik in 1971, one of the first satellite communications services on the globe, shared among the Soviet Union, Poland, Czechoslovakia, East Germany, Hungary, Romania, Bulgaria, Mongolia and Cuba. The role of technology in circulating and censoring content, as well as issues of audiences, reception, and pleasure, have been as intensely neglected in studies of Eastern European film until now as indigenous art films were by their own national audiences.

**Mole versus Dinosaur: Late-Communist Children's Media**

While ethnographic studies of children's media habits in communist countries in the 1970s and 1980s are not available, I have yet to talk to an Eastern European over five who is not familiar with *Krtek* (the "Little Mole"), created by Czech animator Zdenek Miler in 1956, with an uninterrupted production of episodes from 1963 to 2000 (see figure 2.3).

**Figure 2.3**
Krtek, the Little Mole, and his friends (Zdenek Miler, 1983).

The protagonist won himself enormous popularity in most Eastern European countries, as well as Germany, Austria, and China. *Krtek* yields 225 hits on YouTube; and a simple Google search turns up fan sites in German, Japanese, and most Eastern European languages. Thanks to the regional Minimax network, along with the ancillary marketing of stuffed animals, books, DVDs, posters, toys, and T-shirts, one bumps into *Krtek* virtually anywhere in the region. A short case study of late-communist children's television centered on this popular series should shed comparative light on the reasons for the long absence and recent arrival of the dinosaur, the role of children's media in postcommunist nostalgia, and the potential importance of both for theorizing children's media in a global context today.

Films made for children during the communist period showed great aesthetic diversity and innovation. Animation received a potent boost from the 1960s onward, when adult animation became a site of stylistic and ideological experimentation, concentrated around major animation studios in Prague, Krakow, Budapest, and Zagreb (Lendvai 1998; Holloway 1983). But most of the short and, later, feature-length films produced during communism were populated by creatures much smaller than dinosaurs: animals from nearby forests and waters, such as rabbits, hedgehogs, frogs, and foxes, or creatures from folktales and national legends. As Svetlana Boym notes, "After the dictatorship the subversive cultural tendency is to miniaturize, not aggrandize." In the Soviet Union, after the collapse of Stalinism, children's monsters were miniature, not gigantic (Boym 2001, 39). The spectacle of the dinosaur—even of Barney—would be utterly inconceivable in such a universe.

Mitchell cites *Jurassic Park* to discuss the function of the dinosaur image in terms of scale: it is a film in which "mass media, massive animals, mass destruction, mass consumption, and mass resurrection from the dead . . . all converge in the 'animation' of the dinosaur" (Mitchell 1998, 63). By contrast, it is hard to imagine a successful animated character on American children's screens as unspectacular as Little Mole and his friends, Rabbit and Hedgehog. These cartoons are characteristically economical, in aesthetics and content alike. Miler wanted his *Krtek* tales to cross borders with ease. For this reason, after the first, narrated episode, he eclipsed dialogue altogether, including only exclamations and other noises. The simple stop-motion, hand-drawn cartoons call for an old-fashioned spectatorial sensibility and evoke a slower, smaller, more contemplative world. The characters' power does not come from smart talk, physical abilities, frenzied Pixar motion, or simple "cuteness." Rather, paradigmatically, one roots for them because of their ability to survive despite the odds. Their little lives in the shadows of greater enemies, such as people and machines, are precarious. But they appreciate the smallest pleasures, taking disappointment with patience and good humor. They are not troubled by oversized ambitions, the perpetual promise of growing big or making it big. Unlike Disney or most other American cartoons, which usually single out a character as the center of identification and afford it the dominant point of view, *Krtek* is more of a narrative tool to deliver an allegorical message about the entire community.

In the first and probably most memorable episode, "Jak krtek ke kalhotkám přišel" ("How the Mole Got His Pants"), released in 1956, the Little Mole, setting the horizon of the socialist citizen's wishes appropriately humble, yearns for overalls with big pockets. The entire forest comes to his aid, each animal lending useful skills that turn flax into fabric, which is then cut and sewn into an attractive pair of overalls. The satisfaction is immense as the mole parades around in his homemade clothes. The episode provides a characteristic and, in retrospect, ironic lesson in sustainability, given the zeal with which public opinion and, to some extent, policy in the United States has recently begun to urge a shift to sustainable means of production and consumption, imposing this newly found wisdom on the newly "wasteful" Third World. While communist regimes hardly proved to be sustainable in an economic sense, the approach to the environment as an essential resource for survival is a message to be taken to heart by the late-capitalist West as well as by postcommunist Eastern Europe, increasingly permeated by the imported consumer ideology that condones and even encourages waste.

Other episodes are even more openly critical of Stalinist bureaucratic modernity and mass consumerism alike, prefiguring the current global worry about the ecological impact of mass consumerism. The episode "Mole in the Dream" evokes the dystopia of the loss of electricity. A man survives the winter in his snowed-in house only with the help of the unbreakable endurance and spirit of Mole and his little friends, the real Eastern Europeans. Yet another episode, "Mole in the City," foreshadows environmental disaster: It begins with an army of machines relentlessly leveling the entire forest to make room for a row of soulless, identical housing blocks. All that is left is a tree stump, on which Mole, Rabbit, and Hedgehog huddle together. The bureaucrats try to compensate for the animals' loss by assigning them an inflatable forest in an office. The three friends happily settle even for this until they accidentally puncture it. They are politically powerless against socialist bureaucracy and, like the actual people of Eastern Europe, have to make the best of grotesquely inadequate living conditions.

If, as Adorno argues, dinosaurs stand for the monstrous, totalitarian state apparatus and patriarchy (Mitchell 1998, 19), the bulldozers, mechanized tools of the mass destruction of the environment, as well as their operators, embodied by the chief bureaucrat on top of the food chain, fulfill the role of dinosaurs. Unlike the monsters of *Jurassic Park*, however, the menace of bulldozers and bureaucrats is all too real and thus fails to fascinate. The child viewer of these fairy tales is expected to identify with the displaced and oppressed underground animal's point of view. The monsters are represented as purely external, alien, imposed. This is different from the point of view constructed by *Jurassic Park* and other dinosaur tales, which actively invite identification with the dinosaur at the same time as they evoke a sense of ecological horror and guilt over causing extinction, which is inscribed in American children's positions within the global economy (Willis 1999, 193).

*Krtek* could be most didactically contrasted to a popular dinosaur series for young children, a kind of "*Jurassic Park* Jr.," produced by Steven Spielberg: *The Land Before Time*. The fluidly animated, anthropomorphic vegetarian dinosaur kids of *The Land Before Time* are in perpetual danger from the elements and the real baddies, the meat-eaters. The center of the youth gang and the point of identification is the big-eyed orphan boy sauropod, Little Foot. In part VI: *The Secret of Saurus Rock* (Charles Grosvenor, 1998), Little Foot finds a father-figure role model in the Lone Dinosaur, a warrior longneck with a scar, who comes to the community's rescue in a heroic battle against predators, says little, and then wonders off into the sunset. Little Foot's and, by implication, the spectator boys' desire is to grow up to be a tough, masculine hero just like The Lone Dinosaur, whose life is unfettered by longings and belongings and entirely devoted to fulfilling his duty of fighting evil (see figure 2.4).

The dinosaur's intimate connection with American national mythology, and the overlapping histories of bone and gold rushes in the heroic period of Western expansion on which Western narratives draw, make *The Secret of Saurus Rock*, a dinosaur Western, a perfectly logical hybrid. Given this convergence in the support of a specifically American

**Figure 2.4**
The Lone Dinosaur of the *Land Before Time*, part VI, "The Secret of Saurus Rock" (Charles Grosvenor, 1998).

kind of nationalism, a penchant for violence, and the assertion of tough masculinity, one might assume that Westerns were just as unwelcome in communist Eastern Europe as dinosaurs were. Just the opposite is true, however.

In the last section of this chapter, I highlight some of the most interesting results of domesticating Westerns in late-communist cultures. *Krtek*, the border-crossing Eastern European animated series for children who are expected to develop a mature political consciousness, is in some ways the opposite of the big, fierce, and extinct qualities of the dinosaur, designed to impress adults into an emotional and cognitive state associated with childhood. Contrasting the culture of the mole with the culture of the dinosaur allows us to begin to address important historical differences that inform Eastern European media for children, to be taken into account when formulating a theoretical approach to global children's media.

True to this book's commitment to ambivalence, I now show at least one way in which late-communist cultures were not essentially different from capitalist ones when it came to phantasmatic engagements with popular media material, defying the sharp and hierarchical differences between children's and adult, as well as high and low, cultures. This is another way to underscore the suprising hybridity of late-communist popular cultures, and their subsequent potential for generating postcommunist reflective-nostalgic fantasies. While *Krtek* and many other animated tales were made specifically for a young audience, American Western films, shown on television across the region, constituted a bridge between adult and children's media cultures. Far from being innocent entertainment, however, imported and locally produced Westerns performed a complicated function for local national identities: they created avenues to articulate and experience the officially silenced relations toward Europe and its imperial others in former colonies (uncomfortably identifying with both), and a similarly ambivalent relationship with America and its admired and despised national culture—a series of identifications that Christian Feest, in the German context, calls "cultural transvestism" (Feest 2002, 31). Eastern European Westerns appropriated in ambivalent ways the aesthetic and ideological features of a genre that is at once "quintessentially American," according to Bazin, and well adaptable to depictions of grand struggles elsewhere. The Western's simple narrative and ideological structure also makes it rather cartoonish, lending itself to animation.

## Performing the Western in the East

The fascination with the American West and its near-mythical inhabitants has a long European history. In the Europe of the late nineteenth
and early twentieth centuries, Western stories and films constituted part
of a large colonial intertext, along with imperial adventure tales that
depicted white men's encounters with the exotic and savage people and
animals of Africa, Asia, and Latin America. These colonial representations were building blocks that allowed imperial Europe to constitute
itself "on the backs of equally constructed others" (Stam and Spence
1976, 636). Ella Shohat and Robert Stam argue that the cinema, and
later television, continued the project of nationalism that Benedict Anderson attributes to print capitalism. "The cinema, the world's storyteller
par excellence, was ideally suited to relay projected narratives of nations
and empires" (Shohat and Stam 1996, 153). In addition to securing white
supremacist viewing positions, as Shohat and Stam argue (153), the
colonial adventure story of imperial cinema provided a psychic playground for the enlarged boy subject, "for the play of the virile spectatorial imagination."

The Western, a genre within what we can call imperial cinema, has
been a significant, if rarely acknowledged element of European cultural
nationalisms, which are discussed in chapter 5. As I mention there, Joep
Leerssen has recently argued that we should see European nationalisms
as primarily cultural, and study European nationalism in a cross-national,
comparative perspective. He points out that, from the very early days of
nationalism, intellectuals across the continent worked in dense patterns
of mutual influence and exchange (Leerssen 2006, 565). This implies
that the widespread fascination with the discoveries in the New World,
the expansion to the Wild West, and encounters between Europeans
and Native Americans should also be considered in a cross-cultural
European, if not global, context. This also means that Eastern European
engagements with these American adventure stories should not be
exempted from the same postcolonial and gendered critique to which the
Western genre has been subjected in the United States and imperial
adventure stories have been in Western Europe.

Postcommunist intellectuals are rightly frustrated by the general infantilization of culture—about the "cartoon-level narratives and identities"
to which Disney, the commercialization of television, the use of digital
edutainment techniques at school and of computer games after school
have reduced practically all spheres of daily life. Their nostalgia for the

abstract aesthetic and allegorical charge of *Krtek* and other "valuable" kinds of children's entertainment is understandable. At the same time, there is a general amnesia about an entire register of communist and precommunist popular cultures that blatantly and uncritically incorporates racist and imperialistic ideologies. The cultural transvestism facilitated by Westerns shows only the tip of the iceberg in this regard. The unexamined Orientalism of much of what is considered "folk" children's culture in Hungary, for instance—including songs, legends, stories, and nursery rhymes, the earliest bits of language through which young citizens are interpellated—is saturated with racist depictions of Turks and, by extension, Muslims, inherited from the Ottoman Empire. As I show in chapter 3, everyday language abounds in racist stereotypes of the Roma.

One can claim that embracing the Western's cartoon-level identities is part and parcel of such nationalistic and imperialistic identity games. Jyotsna Kapur argues that Disney's *Pocahontas*, along with many other popular representations of Indians in American (and, by extension, global) children's culture exemplifies the commodification of history within what Jameson calls the "postmodern condition." According to Jürgen Habermas, this condition is characterized by a loss of history and utopian ideals, where the past is conjured up as a series of costumes or styles—"for instance, as a kind of game between cowboys and Indians—with no allusion to the material conflicts that characterize earlier times and ours" (Kapur 2005, 74). Kapur faults consumer culture for the "cannibalization of history," for "reducing [history] to a costume party." As a result, the dead are erased from memory not because of a totalitarian regime but by the mind-numbing tyranny of the market's demand that things should not be taken too seriously (75). Disney used the concept of children's play in this way to defend itself from accusations of falsifying history on multiple accounts in its seriously airbrushed and romanticized version of the encounter between the Indian maiden Pocahontas and the white soldier John Smith. Play equals entertainment here, which teaches children "an early lesson in accepting the tyrannical demand of the entertainment industry that we must enter its halls with our brains turned off" (82).

To use the concept of children's play to defend the film is to agree to Disney's reinvention of play as entertainment and thus reduce it from a site of utopian thinking to a site of consuming market-produced commodities. This is a serious reduction of the symbolic value of childhood. Of course seriousness is hardly a desirable quality in the idealized consumer in late capitalism. In an economy run on debt, the adult consumer too is drawn in the image of the child—impulsive, seeking immediate gratification, and playfully consuming toys such as computers and cars. . . . It thus makes a pygmy of the adult at the same time as it empties childhood of its distinction as a place from which another world can be imagined. (Kapur 2005, 82)

While dinosaurs had been identified with American imperialism and commodity culture and had thus been repudiated in the Soviet region, the fascination with the noble savage that infuses Westerns has fueled the emulation of the white supremacist ideals of European imperialism. This is the other side of the coin of high cultural pessimism about the U.S.-led commodification of children's and adult culture: the high-brow, Euronostalgic criticism leaves intact the imperialist playground, the psychic lebensraum of the masculine and white supremacist imagination, which Eastern European cultures have preserved long after post-imperial Western Europe embarked on the self-critical road to political correctness.

Christian Feest locates a massive minor literature of Indian fascination in Europe. He counts about a thousand titles published in the German language alone between 1875 and 1900. Karl May's Indian stories, favorites across Eastern and Central Europe, would be unthinkable without this large and unexplored intertext (Feest 2002). In the central and eastern parts of Europe, where modern empires remained rather static and uninterested in imperial ventures outside the continent, Western stories about the frontier played a special role in solidifying nationalistic sentiment. During the socialist period, when the same populations were pushed outside the continent and locked into an ideological ghetto, Westerns functioned as screens onto which to project compensatory desires for full Europeanness, manifest in the images of untainted white-ness and impeccable masculinity. James Fenimore Cooper's and Karl May's novels, supported by state book publishing industries, introduced young pioneers to Westerns and perpetuated an unchecked fascination with the binary universe of the Wild West.

Another important reason why Westerns were able to nourish identi-fication with the American West in the face of the widespread official rhetoric of anticapitalism, as well as identification with local national-isms in the face of official rhetoric about international communist broth-erhood, was that Westerns were not supposed to be taken as seriously as contemporary adult American film dramas were. May's and Cooper's novels were distributed as children's or juvenile literature along with similar classic boys' adventure stories by national and regional authors (e.g., Ferenc Molnár's *Pál Street Boys*, an international favorite among boy-bonding stories), adolescent adventure tales about boys conquering nature, overtly propagandistic novels and films about heroic boy groups, often in wartime contexts (e.g., Arkady Gaidar's *Timur i evo komanda (Timur and His Platoon)*, 1940), war films and partisan films (e.g., the Yugoslav epic *Walter Defends Sarajevo*, 1972), male-bonding TV series set in wartime (e.g., the Polish favorite *Czterej Pancerni I Pies (The Tank Crew of Four and a Dog)*, 1966), and historical novels and films that evoke selected and glorified events from the national and European past, particularly from the Ottoman occupation (e.g., Géza Gárdonyi's classic Hungarian novel *Egri csillagok (The Stars of Eger)*, 1899). American Western films constituted a part of the loose genre of indigenous edutainment films and TV programs about male historical figures fighting and conquering, in front of which the entire family could curl up.

Children's media, especially animated films, often drew on the mythical themes of the Western: In an episode of the TV series *Bolek and Lolek* (Wladyslaw Nehrebecki, 1964–1986), the eponymous pair of popular Polish cartoon boys stop in the Wild West between a trip to the Moon, an adventure in Argentina, a hike on the cliffs of the Kilimanjaro, time travel to the "Golden City of the Inca," and the exploration of the North Pole (see figure 2.5). Since from an Eastern European vantage point every location is equally mythical, devoid of the baggage of

**Figure 2.5**
*Bolek and Lolek*, "Bolek i Lolek na dzikim Zachodzie," ("Bolek and Lolek in the Wild West," Stanislaw Dulz, 1986).

the actual histories of imperialism, they can be cowboys in Texas as easily as visitors to an ancient Mayan city. At the beginning of each episode, the boys spin a globe to decide where to go, literally holding the world in their hands.

The aesthetic of the hand-drawn, abstract, allegorical world of socialist children's animation is very different from the CGI hyperverisimilitude of *Jurassic Park*. However, the wish-fulfilling acts of the masculine exploration and conquering of other places and species that is most evident in Eastern European Westerns is imbued with nostalgia not unlike *Jurassic Park*'s magic re-creation of extinct, near-mythic animals. This longing is different from the nostalgic relationship to a lost imperial glory in *Indochine*, *The Jewel in the Crown*, and other Western European "heritage" productions. Rather, Eastern European Westerns reveal a deferred nostalgia for an imperial heritage that cultures of the region could claim only by implication rather than by actual historical heritage, by crossing the fantasmatic cultural bridge from the Other to the Real Europe. The generic schema of the Western provides a perfect blueprint for performing Eastern Europe's ambivalent, peripheral, semicolonial relationship to Europe: a cultural transvestism where the East is both cowboy and Indian, colonizer and colonized.

While *Bolek and Lolek* was made specifically for children, and is successfully marketed as children's fare to this day, animation itself was not primarily a children's medium. As even *Krtek* shows, much of the animation produced in the Soviet region carried an allegorical dimension of anticommunist dissent, especially following the failed anti-Soviet uprisings in 1956 and 1968, when censorship forced many filmmakers into the "safer" fields of animation. Jirí Trnka, the founding figure of the Kratky Studio for animation in Prague, followed a long tradition of politically charged puppetry, a tool of protest and revolt since the seventeenth century (Holloway 1983, 228). In 1949, he created the popular puppet satire *The Song of the Prairie* based on Jirí Brdecka's *Lemonade Joe* stories. These stories entered a regional circulation, also influencing the Yugoslav cartoon *Cowboy Jimmie* (Dusan Vukotic, 1957) and the Polish animated short *The Little Western* (*Maly Western*, Witold Giersz, 1961), and were later adapted into the Czechoslovak feature film *Lemonade Joe* (*Limonadovy Joe*, Oldrich Lipsky, 1964).

*The Little Western* continues to play with the archetypal elements of the Western, mixing them with those of other adventure genres: the treasure motif, for instance, mingles the Gold Rush with pirate tales. Transplanting elements of the Western into animation in Eastern Europe created something markedly different from the main course of both American children's animation and the Western in America. When the shadow puppet cowboy lifts the water to find the treasure buried underneath, or when he borrows paint from the figure of a fellow puppet to draw a rope, there is no mistaking the intention to demystify frontier heroism and use the genre simultaneously to comment on the horizon of possibilities on an Eastern European, communist scale. The very attribute "Maly" ("Little") issues this ironic commentary: the Western is the genre of the grand—vast open landscapes, untamed wilderness, and spectacularly dressed and poised manly men with big weapons engaged in fights to the death for magnificent ideals. All this takes place in the name of the budding country's God-given manifest destiny, which justifies even genocide and the destruction of the environment. It seems that the stripped-down encounter that the Western stages between Man and Nature lends itself well to a similarly elemental fascination with movement, the chief feature of animation. The victory over wild animals in the course of bull fights and horse taming, which recur in the world of Witold Giersz, is mirrored by the taming of the animator's material, staging a chain of self-conscious reflections on man's intellectual struggle with the elements within the grotesquely reduced and regulated landscape of socialist cultures.

The covert discourses of the American Western, hidden just barely under the water, to borrow the pictorial metaphor from *Maly Western*, inverted the genre from the 1960s onward to generate ironic, comic, self-reflective, revisionist Westerns such as *Unforgiven, Blazing Saddles, Dead Man*, or *The Ballad of Little Joe*, or Westerns geographically distanced from American nationalism such as Sergio Leone's spaghetti series. Eastern European manifestations of the genre have typically sustained an element of performativity, evident in playful imaginative transgressions of realism, overt parody, or allegorical deployment. This is unmistakable in Trnka's puppet film *Song of the Prairie*, and even more so in Oldrich Lipsky's 1964 feature film *Limonadovy Joe, or a Horse Opera*. Both films were scripted by writer Jirí Brdecka. They both take place among the cacti and rocks of the southwestern desert and pay tribute to a number of Western films, but their characters also resemble those of European fairy tales: the lady for whose favors two antagonists vie—the good and clean cowboy-prince on a white horse, whose entrances are accompanied by lengthy songs, and the diabolical magician, dressed in black, who commands a gang of shifty-looking Mexican bandits.

In actual Westerns there is no room for effeminacy; whether the cowboy is with or against the law, he is expected to be unshaven, sweaty, leather-covered, and laconical, with a strictly controlled economy of movement and certainly no show of emotion. Limonadovy Joe, the blond protagonist of the 1964 film, blindingly white from boots to hat, is made to appear even more puppetlike than the earlier puppet film's exuberant hero. But while the cowboy is so emotionless and expressionless that he needs to be constantly beaten up and injured to prove he is alive, Limonadovy Joe's appearance remains impeccable. In what is probably the most out-of-place shot in a Western, it is the camera that takes on the task of proving that he is made of flesh: Joe is first introduced by a disrespectful close-up on the mouth and teeth, which borders on the pornographic as well as the medical. Even more jarring is the cut to the slightly wider shot on the mouth and jaw framed by the strap of Joe's hat, which creates the impression of a woman's bonneted chin.

Joe breaks as easily into big smiles as into song and is as friendly with people as a traveling salesman—which he turns out to be in the film, further feminizing his character. Since he sells "Kolaloka Lemonade" (hence his nickname), he quickly joins forces with the two Goodmans, young Winifred and her father, who are on a mission against excessive whisky consumption. Their antagonists are, naturally, the Badmans: Doug and his brother Horace, aka Hogo Fogo, the dark-complexioned, wicked magician. In one scene, Hogo Fogo appears in blackface to deceive Joe, which simultaneously accentuates and mocks the racial underpinnings of the dialectic between hero and antihero.

Joe is played by Karel Fiala, a Czechoslovak operetta star. Olga Schoberová, who plays Winifred, also appeared in the West German Westerns *Gold-Diggers of Arkansas* and *Black Eagles of Santa Fe*, both filmed in Czechoslovakia (before becoming a *Playboy* covergirl [Hames 2002]). Peter Hames claims that *Limonadovy Joe* is "a tribute to an era of innocence" before directors like Anthony Mann, Sergio Leone, and Sam Peckinpah "turned Westerns into something altogether more disturbing" (Hames 2002). But, again, I think the nostalgia of the film is much more complex and self-aware than this would suggest. Rather than holding on to an era of innocence lost in the real West, the film is simultaneous with, if not prefiguring, the deconstructive turn in the Western's history, building on a rich history of ironic humor in Czech culture and of genre subversions in Eastern European animation. Fiala's Joe is more like an Eastern European intellectual's wish-fulfilling fantasy, an East-West hybrid: a cowboy with an artistic vein, who is master of his gun

**Figure 2.6**
Karel Fiala as the smiling cowboy in *Limonadovy Joe* (Oldrich Lipsky, 1964).

and is followed around by pining girls, but for whom "honor" is not contingent on duels to the death. The cowboy's mission to enforce frontier law is perfectly consistent with the job of a traveling lemonade salesman (see figure 2.6).

The film's narrative is woven across a conspicuous grid of Manichaean symbolism. Joe's blinding whiteness and the Goodmans' naïve goodness are as extreme as the dark magic and shady intentions of the Badmans and the whiskey consumption of their men. To the extent that "narrative models in films are not simply reflective microcosms of historical processes; they are also experiential grids or templates through which history can be written and national identity created" (Shohat and Stam 1996), we should read this foregrounding of binary symbolism as a comedic effort to demystify the rigid framework of official Soviet ideology in the 1960s. This is achieved, perhaps inadvertently, by ridiculing the rigid racist and sexist framework of the Western genre. The mockery of tough masculinity and of the moral superiority of whiteness reaches a hilarious climax, where the hero, instead of riding off into the sunset alone after killing the criminal, unites with the two Badmans, as well as the bad girl, Tornado Lou, in one big family. They all turn out to be siblings separated after birth and raised separately. The deus ex machina fusion is celebrated with a new, similarly hybrid drink, Whiskykola, which can be enjoyed by both alcoholics and teetotalers.

While Eastern European transplants of the Western invariably engage in self-reflective national transvestism, most fall short of the sophisticated satire of *Limonadovy Joe*, a cult classic. Most Eastern Europeans are much more likely to be familiar with the twelve DEFA (Deutsche Film-Aktiengesellschaft) Westerns produced between 1965 and 1983 in the Babelsberg studios, as well as on location in Yugoslavia, Czechoslovakia, Romania, Bulgaria, the Soviet Union, and Cuba. These East German Westerns, or *Indianerfilme*, were produced, distributed, exhibited, and enjoyed regionally (Gemünden 2002, 241–242). They may also be the oddest Westerns in film history. They were made with the approval and funding of communist states, who set out to appropriate an inherently capitalist, American genre to support the ideological mission of the socialist state and to appease socialist citizens yearning for entertainment. Unlike Hollywood Westerns, or West German adaptations of Karl May's sensationalist novels made by Harald Reinl during the same period, DEFA Westerns provided politically correct entertainment: they took a historical-materialist view of history and a semiscientific, anthropologically inclined view of the Wild West. They also shifted the focus from the cowboy, the universal hero of the animated films I discussed earlier, to the Indian (Gemünden 2002, 245).

East German Westerns were conceived as enlightened entertainment, as the state's way to regain the interest of East German citizens alienated by the didactic film dramas of the 1950s. They acknowledged the long history of German fascination with the Western but were meant to distance the communist public from Karl May's uncritical celebration of the Wild West and its noble savage. Despite producer Günter Karl's intention to create an anticapitalist Western, however, the deep synergy among all nationalisms—which conditions national unity on processes of international and intranational othering and provides the basic representative infrastructure of the Western genre—reasserted itself. Soliciting identification with the freedom struggles of humanized noble savages such as Chingachgook, in fact, followed from and perpetuated the long-standing exoticization of American Indians, whose potential point of view continued to be mediated through the white sidekicks who joined the Indian struggle for independence (all related to May's legendary character, Old Shatterhand). The public seized the opportunity for an allegorical reading: the potential, autonomous Native American history was replaced by German national history, and the depiction of Indian struggles gave expression to a rejuvenated desire for autonomous national culture in a divided Germany (Gemünden 2002, 246).

**Figure 2.7**
Gojko Mitic, the "Indian" hero of the DEFA Westerns.

Indianerfilme became screens onto which to project a mix of phantasmatic identifications. The central figure of these identifications was the dashing and desirable actor Gojko Mitic from Yugoslavia, an honorary East German, whose exotic Balkan roots stood in for the exotic Indian as the most authentic substitute possible. His image united Yugoslav partisan, model German, American, displaced Jew, and Native American hero (see figure 2.7).

Mitic's Balkanness at once ensured a desirable distance between Indians and German national culture (confirmed by the taboo on miscegenation in the DEFA narratives) and allowed various desires for deferred imperial others to be articulated. In GDR Westerns, Gojko Mitic acts as resistance fighter and antifascist guerrilla, provides a role model for young citizens, and relieves older ones of the responsibility for genocide committed in the name of Germany (Gemünden 2002, 250–251). Mitic himself had worked on West German and Italian Westerns before moving to East Berlin and choosing to be a star Indian. Throughout the socialist period, he remained a universal role model for children, a pacifist (on- and offscreen), an antialcoholic, and a teen idol across the region.

Eastern and Southern European identities, not quite European, neither colonized nor colonizer but shifting ambivalently between the two, are able to inhabit the opposite positions of the Western—cowboy and Indian—with particular flexibility and vigor. The various national versions converge in a regional pattern that derives from the discursive practices of Orientalism and imperialism. During communism, the inherent nationalism of the Western provided an "innocent" blueprint for sustaining and confirming the validity of ethnoracial hierarchies without having to address or take responsibility for them. Deploying the Western always implied a pedagogical intention on the part of the paternalistic communist state to entertain and educate its childlike public at the same time. The purpose of such an education was to naturalize the Manichaean moral options available to patriotic communist citizens: a choice between good and bad, white and black, male heroism and effeminacy, with us or against us. The alleged childlike innocence of such collective identity games has helped to naturalize the restorative nostalgia that culminated in violent conflicts in the postcommunist region. However, the ideological contradictions of the Western's generic schema continually reasserted themselves in native Westerns. They mobilized a network of discourses around Eastern Europe's ambivalent relationship to Europe and turned Westerns into diverse performances of nationalism that exceeded and often undermined the narrow pedagogical intentions of the state.

## Nostalgic Resources for the Future

Since the fall of the Wall, East German Westerns, along with many children's television programs, have turned into objects of nostalgia virtually overnight. The Indianerfilme returned to German and other local television channels and reappeared in fan books as part of *Ostalgie* (Gemünden 2002, 247). It is now primarily advertising that perpetuates the popularity of Westerns and of the myth of the frontier, forever erasing the violent history that American Westerns themselves have consistently critiqued for the past thirty years or so.

At the same time, the Western has also become available for a more radical subcultural deconstruction of the racist and heterosexist infrastructure of nationalism than the all-male art world of the socialist period could possibly conceive of. In chapter 4, I discuss one example of such an appropriation, the short video *Puszta Cowboy* (2004), "the first Hungarian Lesbian-Transgender-Paprika Western, complete with horses, gunfight, goulash, and traditional Hungarian csárdás-dancing" made by the Budapest-based Lesbian Film Collective, a group of semiprofessional lesbian filmmakers. It is only from the present postcommunist vantage point, when identities are beginning to become unhinged from the absolute allegorical grip of nationalism, that one can read *Limonadovy Joe*—no doubt against the filmmakers' intention—as a carnival of gender and racial transvestism, which finally marks Eastern European whiteness, the need to contain women in binary categories, and the symbolic emasculation of Eastern European men.

What imported and adapted Westerns shared with *Krtek* and other locally produced children's media fare was that they did not qualify as (mature, adult, educating) art. From a postcommunist perspective, this is not so much a limitation as an opportunity for research that will revise Cold War paradigms and draw important theoretical conclusions for a globally networked media future. While "art" has been tirelessly censored, monitored, appreciated, and showcased in the East and in the West, "communist entertainment," especially its least valued form, animated children's entertainment, has remained ignored by official and Western academic attention. Since the end of communism, however, the psychological-allegorical art film has rapidly dwindled in relevance, while communist entertainment has been recovered through processes of reflective nostalgia. Studying and understanding the continuity between communist and postcommunist media entertainment, with all its ambivalences, holds out the important possibility to revisit what is increasingly taken to be the dominant, if not the only, consumerist paradigm for the future of global media culture.

# 3

# Euro-Visions: Musical Play and Ethnic Entertainment in the New Europe

We are the Gypsies of this world, brother.
We've lived in peace here for a long time
Without any wealth, without a country.
We've come from India, but we're at home everywhere.

The Roma know how much they can love,
Everybody knows how much we like to play,
We respect each other and we respect everyone,
But it's no use if no one respects us.

The stars dance only with us,
Nothing you can do against our joy,
We love Hungarians and all other peoples,
Let's live together in this world in peace.
—LL Junior, "We, the Roma," my translation

## The "Musical Gypsy" on the World Music Stage

The "Gypsy's" inherent musicality has long been established in popular representations. More recently, however, the figure of the "musical Gypsy" has taken on a new, overtly politicized role in emerging Roma identity politics in postcommunist Europe. A number of young Roma musicians have drawn on Afro-Caribbean music, particularly hip-hop, to reclaim the degrading, romanticizing stereotypes in which Roma identity and music have been glued together, and turn such stereotypes into a critical tool against nationalistic discrimination and European exclusion. At the same time, as I argue in this chapter, the new avenues of transnational mobility and global media access do not automatically lead to a political intervention in the relations between national or European majorities and Roma minorities. While Roma musicians' engagement with other racialized, hybrid musical flows does constitute a qualitatively new form of political expression, the dangers of commercial co-optation by the world music market, entrapment in inherently racist national languages and surveillance by the nation-state, continue to lurk.

Furthermore, as I argue in the second half of the chapter, any assessment that focuses on "the Roma" runs the risk of creating a monolithic concept, whose real-life referents are multilingual groups scattered across countries, with diverse local affiliations and internal divisions. When analyzing the recent rise of the "Roma," a transnational group, on the wings of transnational musical entertainment, ethnographic approaches clearly need to be complemented by interdisciplinary theorizing that allows for overlapping and flexible conceptual categories. Accordingly, my discussion of Roma musical performances on the national, European, and world stage is always counterbalanced by a poststructuralist understanding of identity inspired by transnational and postcolonial theories of gender and sexuality. Only such an approach can enable us to explain how hip-hop, a traveling, derived, hybrid musical form, can authenticate local ethnic masculinities that have come to stand for battled ethnic and national communities at the expense of women and sexual minorities within the community. While the chapter is primarily focused on Roma examples, these are situated in relation to a wider pattern of localizing global pop music in Europe and the Middle East.

## The Roma in Fortress Europe

The tenuous rise of Roma musical entertainers in the New Europe is set against a distressing background of poverty and continued racist discrimination. A recent issue of the European Roma Rights Center's quarterly journal dedicates itself to the theme of Fortress Europe, which, in his editorial introduction, Claude Cahn calls "the most visible, systemic evil in Europe today" (Cahn 2002, 6). He recalls the very first, September 1996, issue of the *Roma Rights Quarterly*, titled "Divide and Deport," which examined the restrictive laws and policies aimed at or resulting in the exclusion of Roma and other noncitizens from Austria and Germany. Cahn assesses the major developments that influenced European policies toward the Roma between 1996 and 2002, including the antiforeigner sentiment catalyzed by the events of September 11, 2001, and the Treaty of Amsterdam in 1999, which passed responsibility for asylum and migration issues onto the European Union. He identifies Central and Eastern Europe as the site of ongoing trouble, ill-prepared for the obligations to integrate EU rules and standards in the absence of legal immigration or refuge protection. "In addition," he continues,

Western Europe has increasingly treated the states of Central and Eastern Europe as a borderland zone into which unwanted migrants and refugees can be expelled without explicit, egregious violations of international law taking place. A new harsh regime ordered in place by cynical Western Eurocrats, displacing the harsh old regime in countries in which governments have done little to nothing to roll back the rising tide of xenophobia and racism: This is Central and Eastern Europe today. (Cahn 2002, 6)

In light of the cases of police abuse, illegal expulsion, racist violence, lack of access to health care, gravely inadequate housing, illegal evictions, and educational discrimination, which the rest of the journal proceeds to discuss—no doubt the tip of the iceberg compared with the number of cases that had not received any legal attention—it would be hard to disagree with the ERRC's statement that "the Roma (Gypsies) remain to date the most deprived ethnic group of Europe" (back cover of *Roma Rights Quarterly*, no. 2, 2002). However, while NGOs, governmental organizations, and social scientific studies have tirelessly called attention to the nationalistic scapegoating of and violence against the Roma in post–Cold War Europe, it would be hasty to dismiss all recent changes as negative, and it would be counterproductive to ground Roma identities solely in victimization.

A more complex model of postcommunist developments is offered by sociologists Gail Kligman, Iván Szelényi, and János Ladányi, who conceptualize the changing situation of European, particularly Central and Eastern European Roma in terms of an *underclass* (Kligman, Szelényi, and Ladányi 2002). The notion of underclass is usually associated with urban Black ghettos, which represented the growing segment of the population who remained stuck at the bottom of the socioeconomic hierarchy after the postwar deindustrialization and restructuring of affluent Western economies. Neoconservative theories from the late 1960s onward tried to essentialize the "culture of poverty" in underclass ghettos, pointing to race as their defining feature, and ultimately blaming the victim for the reproduction of poverty. In the 1970s, however, the sociologist William Julius Wilson, in his book *The Declining Significance of Race*, returned the underclass formation to its structural roots and contested the equation of underclass with Blacks. He explained that the significance of race (but not racism), in fact, had declined in relation to economic restructuring. Blacks were differentially affected by deindustrialization. Some benefited from economic opportunities and formed part of a new Black middle class. Those employed in the sectors hardest hit by deindustrialization, however, remained in the increasingly segregated inner-city ghettos, locked into extreme poverty (Wilson 1980).

The underclass formation, Kligman, Szelényi, and Ladányi explain, helps analogically to describe the changing situation of the Roma in the course of the postcommunist transformations. Most Roma are increasingly excluded and segregated as a result of deindustrialization, decollectivization, and the outburst of purifying Eurocentric nationalisms. Some of them, however, have seized economic opportunities and are upwardly mobile. "[I]t is this fundamental dynamic of increasing socioeconomic exclusion on the one hand, and socio-economic improvement on the other, that makes it possible to speak of underclass formation" (Kligman, Szelényi, and Ladányi 2002, 113).

While the underclass dialectic is a useful model because it interrupts monolithically negative ideas about the Roma rooted in discrimination, racism, and poverty, it remains somewhat too dialectical and homogenizing. If we reach across disciplinary fences and take into account the extent to which global media culture has penetrated and transformed postcommunist economies, societies, and identities, we will see multiple, fluid connections not only between the upwardly mobile and ghetto-bound parts of the Romany populations but also between Roma and non-Roma within each nation, and within Europe as a whole.

The pan-European attention that has turned anti-Roma discrimination from an institutionalized, naturalized fact—the private business of communist states—into a major condition of desired EU accession[1] has also brought the "Roma issue" into daily media prominence. This has fueled anti-Roma fury but has also increased collective sensitivity to stereotypes. Even more important, some of the same qualities that had for centuries served to demonize and homogenize the Roma as deviant, shiftless, lazy, naturally unfit to be hardworking citizens of the territorial nation-state, are revalorized by the transnational, mobile, hybrid, intersecting scapes of transnational media capitalism.[2] The task is then to develop an approach to the postcommunist "Roma problem" in Europe that is able to take into account the influence of transnational mass media culture without ignoring the unique histories of Eastern European nationalisms (see Shohat and Stam 1996, 145).

## The Time of Some Gypsies

Global popular culture voraciously incorporates ethnic differences in the unabashed pursuit of selling and consuming nonstop entertainment.[3] This process has two sides: It can be seen as liberating and democratic, empowering minorities whose voices and images would be missing or stereotyped otherwise. At the same time, it implies the appropriation of such voices and images by corporate multiculturalism and its cultures of simulation, which retrivializes racial difference on a commercial basis (see Gilroy 1998). In Eastern European national regimes, global popular culture is generally seen by political and cultural opinion makers as threatening—ostensibly because it undermines "authentic" national literacy grounded in the Eurocentric cult of modernist high culture. While the growing resistance to the new triumph of commercialism is a justifiable and necessary reaction (Iordanova 1999), it has an unacknowledged side, bound up with the neocolonial mobilization of nationalism by comprador state and intellectual elites: the fear of racial contamination (as well as gendered and sexualized plurality) by a kind of play that is multicolored and hybrid.

One can see that the Roma are twice abjected in this negotiation between nation-states and corporate agents of globalization and Europeanization: First, they are perceived as unable and unwilling to assimilate to the national project, and are thus universally judged to be an impediment to full and furious EU accession. One can also see that excluding the Roma from the national body altogether will not help state governments fix the national self-image. Rather, it is precisely this negative collective self-image, the result of long-term economic inferiority to the West,[4] which has been projected onto the visibly different and initially nomadic Roma, obeying the trickle-down logic of colonialism that compels the colonized to perpetuate internalized colonial exclusions.[5] Second, the Roma are also demonized because of their inherently transnational identity affiliations, which turn them into convenient suspects for allying themselves with the dreaded forces of globalization. This is then compounded by traditional representations that reduce the Roma to (musical) play and inferior, "mobile" ethics, employed as a proof of inadequate rationality rather than metaphorical evidence of politically progressive identity-in-play.

Maintaining a fear of cultural imperialism helps support the state's own hegemonic tendencies toward its minorities, conforming to a global pattern Arjun Appadurai describes (Appadurai 1994, 326). Eastern European nation-states' reinvention of the "cultural imperialism" paradigm in the most simplified format that the term suggests—despite ample evidence that the multidirectionality of the global cultural landscape far exceeds this designation—itself follows a long European tradition. Also, it is continuous with the communist regimes' propaganda warfare to belittle most things Western and magnify most everything national. Finally, it denies both the fact that, to varying degrees, Eastern European cultures have been Westernized and Americanized since before 1989 (see Arpad 1995, 9; Barber-Kersovan 2001) and the eager collaboration in which Eastern European states do engage with global corporations, including media conglomerates, when their interests so dictate (see Sparks 2000; Downey 1998).

Some instances of this ludic, global "mediation" between Eastern European nations and their scapegoated Roma others is quite worrisome for reproducing the violent opposition between a homogeneously conceived Roma population and proper national citizens: The practice of "Roming" in Slovakia, for instance, refers to the playful circulation of cell phone text messages that offer a certain number of calling minutes for every ten murdered Roma (Vasecka 2001). The computer game Oláh Action was downloaded by about four thousand people in Hungary in the course of the thirty-two hours that it was accessible on the Internet in February 2005. The task of the game was to exterminate the Roma from Hungary, county by county, with a choice of weapons. When a county turned Roma-free, its map turned white.[6]

Other examples of Roma media play are more ambiguous: Roma faces have become more common and more varied on Eastern European television screens over the past ten years, and not only on crime reports and cabarets—most programming has shown increasing sensitivity to the politics of stereotypes. The fate of the satirical television show *My Big Fat Roma Wedding*, which aired on the Hungarian commercial TV channel RTL Klub in 2002, is instructive. The creators intended to capitalize on spectators' global film experiences by adopting the title and plot of the blockbuster *My Big Fat Greek Wedding* in order to unite the nation in laughter at the expense of Gypsies, as numerous TV shows had done with impunity before. However, the program provoked the first universal media uproar over Romany representation in national history. Romany and non-Romany organizations alike contested the gross stereotypes of the Roma as lazy, uneducated musicians and dancers, making it clear that the nation can no longer have unlimited fun with its dancing slaves, and that the Roma themselves wish to take some ownership of their representations as entertainers. The makers of the show defended themselves by arguing that their parody had come from old cabarets and Gypsy jokes and their purpose was "only entertainment." They further appealed to artistic freedom—in other words, the excessive moral liberties that artists enjoy—adding that their representation was purely fictional, rather than sociological; if it was objectionable, then so should be Kusturica's film *Time of the Gypsies*.[7] The time of the Gypsies, however, is also a time when the political empowerment of Romany minorities is conditioned on the politicization of entertainment and representation.

Another way of putting the mistake the creators of the show made is that they misunderstood their audience. They neglected to consider the extent to which the global media had already transformed identities that had been primarily national before 1989, introducing a new sort of postmodernism that is able to wrest alternative pleasures from the control of high modernist culture but that also brings along greater exposure to the multiculturalism of global media.[8] Playfulness, which used to be the exclusive property of state elites and postmodern intellectuals, has become the property of the media business, in which the rules of profit compete with those of "national ethics." These compromises, this shared turf between transnational media corporations and the nation-state, provide an ambivalent situation for the Roma, who are poised between empowerment and exploitation by both sides.

## Play in the Postcommunist Ghetto: *The District*

The most radical way in which global entertainment culture has mediated the postsocialist situation of Romany minorities in Eastern Europe is by turning the ghetto, the place of the urban ethnic underclass, the very site of Roma segregation, into the site of profitable entertainment. A term loaded with traumatic historical connotations, *ghetto* immediately evokes the Roma Holocaust, an often-neglected effect of Nazi persecution during World War II. The wars of Yugoslav succession brought the term back into circulation in Eastern Europe in the 1990s. Large-scale post–Cold War migrations led to the establishment of "Roma ghettos" in Western Europe.[9] In the east, the atrocities committed against Roma minorities have been particularly disturbing. Some have caused international outrage, including the brutal beating to death of a Romany woman in front of her children in Slovakia, the infamous wall that the

Czech city of Ústí Nad Laben built to segregate Romany homes (Johnson 2000), or the Hungarian high school that organized a separate graduation ceremony for its Romany students (Kerényi 1999). While hate speech directed against Roma had been acceptable and naturalized even before 1989, since then many "decent" Eastern European citizens have seriously considered the establishment of apartheid, and members of the Slovak parliament proposed setting up Native American–type reservations (Vasecka 2001).

The extreme measures of exclusion only continue what had been happening in Eastern Europe during the communist period with tacit state approval and even encouragement: the "caring" communist state masqueraded as the benefactor of backward and unwilling Roma groups. Until the 1960s, Hungarian Roma were issued identity cards of a distinct color. Roma children have often been automatically considered mentally disabled and sent to "Gypsy schools" throughout the region (Kerényi 1999). Assigning Roma families inferior housing in government complexes, the state's direct effort at forced integration, also led to the formation of Roma ghettos. As Renata Salecl argues, while on the level of ideological meaning nationalism and communism were opposed, the former being anticommunist and the latter declaring itself to be internationalist in orientation, on the level of fantasy, they shared a solid ground in homophobia, anti-Semitism, xenophobia, and sexism. After 1989, the takeover of governments that represented the right-leaning Eastern European moral majority reduced the distance between manifest ideological meaning and underlying racist and sexist fantasies (Salecl 1994, 20–30).

In an ironic convergence, the exclusion of the Roma from European nation-states and the emergence of Romany play on the stage of global media, particularly world music, have recently come together in the representational space of the ghetto. I examine the implications of this spatial convergence in some detail by taking as my case study the recent animated feature *Nyócker* (2004)—literally, *"Eightdistrict,"* also translated as *"The District"*—produced in Hungary in a collaboration of Romany and non-Romany artists.

*Nyócker*, one of the richest testimonies to the re-eroticization of the emerging Eastern European ghetto, references its setting in its very title and generic designation: "animated ghetto film." "Nyócker" is spoken slang for "nyolcadik kerület," or "the eighth district" of Budapest, also known as Józsefváros, originally named after the Habsburg Emperor

Joseph II, king of Hungary. The setting is a very real center of urban poverty, prostitution, drug traffic, and, most important, a high concentration of Roma inhabitants. The urban postsocialist ghetto's typical underclass characters inhabit the film—a white entrepreneur-pimp with the group of prostitutes he operates, the accented Chinese restaurant owner and his martial arts–obsessed son, the alcoholic but charming Jewish plastic surgeon and his geeky son, members of the Ukrainian Mafia, corrupt and dumb policemen, and, most prominent, members of an extended Roma family. These realistic, although at the same time stereotypically cartoonish characters are thrown into what appears to be a Shakespearean romance. The Romeo-protagonist, that is, the Roma teenager Richard (Ricsi), is infatuated with his white Hungarian classmate Julika. But the ongoing feud between the two families, which breaks down along the color line, prevents their happiness. The group of inner-city teenagers led by Ricsi conspires to make the two fathers happier so that they will approve of the union. The way to achieve this, as Ricsi is advised by an old drunkard uncle, is by making money. At this point, the already rather ironic and flimsy story takes a metaphysical-carnivalistic turn. Here is how the official Web site of the film sums up what follows:

Poverty, prostitutes, pimps, gravitation, space and time don't matter. The kids become friends and, with the help of a brilliant idea, fly back in time to draw oil out of the corpses of dead mammoths. The earth under the district turns into a giant oil field; and the kids become rich overnight. It is a thriving business.

Special-edition Rambo DVD, five-star school cafeteria, golden Rolex on their wrists, Szinyei-Merse's *Picnic* [famous painting] for an art assignment. The parents get suspicious. What's worse, the entire world gets suspicious. The huge amount of oil out of nowhere upsets the machine; and the world powers launch an investigation.

The circle is drawing tighter around the district.
What will happen to the dream?
And what will happen to love?
One thing is sure: the Nyócker will remain Nyócker forever.

(http://www.nyocker.hu)

Indeed, the conventional love-conquers-parents narrative throws off the shackles of time—the first decade of the new millennium—and space—an urban ghetto in an increasingly transnational postcommunist city—and combines the cliché of prehistoric time travel from science fiction with a satire of concurrent global political events that involve

Osama bin Laden, the Pope, and a mercilessly ridiculed George W. Bush. At the end of the film, to take care of the district and its oil once and for all, the cartographically challenged Bush bombs Bucharest instead of Budapest.

*The District*'s postmodern, hybrid style incorporates a combination of global media models, from MTV music videos to television news, from Japanese anime to Monty Python's two-dimensional animation, from themes of prehistoric sci-fi fantasies and adventure films to the stock characters of teen flicks—an entertainment mélange that strikes viewers as farcical. This combination of elements results in an explosive ventilation of suppressed and repressed energies, whose symbolic locus is precisely the urban ghetto, an increasingly multicultural, material space of racial exclusion, material deprivation, unemployment, and immigration. Three of the most important strategies the film uses to introduce new, cool Romany identities are its music, its use of language, and its innovative animation technique.

The filmmakers deliberately drew on the Eighth District's association with Roma rap by recruiting several Roma musicians for the project, including rapper LL Junior, who lends his face and voice to the protagonist, Ricsi. It was the infiltration of Eastern Europe by world music, particularly by MTV, that had first shored up Roma musical talent and turned the eighth district, by analogy, into the local Harlem. Several local Romany bands from the neighborhood became popular in the late 1990s by playing Roma rap, including Fekete Vonat (or "Black Train," named after the commuter train that shuttles Roma workers between Budapest and eastern Hungary). They have employed the hybrid sounds and languages of global music to rap about love along with racial politics—a term artificially neutralized by the "ethnic" policies of the nurturing communist nation-state—and to turn the poor district into a metaphorical space of budding Romany identity politics in the language of music (Fáy 1999).

The use of language is the most immediate source of humor in *The District*. Both spoken language and song lyrics mock the state-controlled media's and educational institutions' insistence on the purity of Hungarian, the official language of the nation-state, cherished as a chief survival avenue since Johann Gottfried von Herder's ominous prediction of the death of small nations in the eighteenth century. Similar to other small Eastern European nations, the Hungarian nation "lives in its language"— to borrow the title of Peter Sherwood's investigation of the thorough political interdependence of language and nationalism in Hungary

(Sherwood 1996. At the same time, the film consistently ridicules the invasion of global consumerism in a series of linguistic and visual puns, such as "McKivánsz," that is, "You Want Me"—the name of a fast-food outlet prominently displayed in various scenes of the film. *The District's* antipurist linguistic strategy rejects the idealized national homogeneity that earlier forms of antistate resistance assumed: it speaks in a mix of languages including Russian, Hungarian, German, English, and Romany, mocking and subverting the ethical and political registers to which each had been assigned earlier. English, the language of American media imperialism, MTV, and the African-American ghetto consistently contaminates Hungarian. Most subversively, the Romany language, formerly obliterated from venues of national media and politics, is represented as the local equivalent of Black English, the youth language of the new millennium. In *The District*, even non-Roma characters mix Romany expressions in their language. By elevating Romany to the level of "language" in the first place, equal in value to Hungarian but with a "cool" difference, the film confronts Hungarian speakers with the fact that many Romany expressions had been a part of spoken and even written Hungarian for generations. It is just that their etymological origins remained effaced in an effort to insist on an absurd model of unidirectional influences, where only the national majority language and culture impacts the racialized minority. The latter's only enlightened option is assimilation.

*The District* turns this model upside down not simply by associating the Romany language with youthful cool but also by its thematic introduction as a language of diplomacy and trade within the narrative: Ricsi, the gang leader, makes sure that the polyglot robot that their Jewish "Einstein" constructs to handle international oil negotiations is programmed to speak Romany along with English, German, French, Arabic, and other world languages. In another scene, the teens, led by Ricsi, go back to prehistoric times to bring oil into the future-present. Most of them wander around in the new location disoriented, utterly confused from the time travel. While Ricsi's white antagonist, Simi Csorba, makes inane remarks, Ricsi engages in negotiation in the Romany language with a local, a prehistoric woman, who wears his actual Gypsy fortune-teller aunt's face. This is a powerful statement about the transnational reach of the Romany network: it playfully asserts that Romany roots go farther back than the tenuous, imagined historical roots of nations. This is also demonstrated by an earlier brief interruption of the time travel at a place where wild horsemen rushed around, representing the cherished forefathers of the Hungarian nation. The scene also evokes the quick adaptability and negotiating abilities of the Romany—traits that have been widely known in the negative only: the Roma will cheat you. Here they take a reverse twist to indicate valuable life skills essential for access to and success on a global capitalist marketplace.

### National Cinema with Roma Protagonists

One of the keys to *The District*'s novelty as a postsocialist allegory of glocal ethnicities—also its most frequently noted aspect—is its innovative animated form. Without the substantial state support and large studios of the past, a handful of ambitious and talented young men including Romany scriptwriters Jakab László Orsós and Damage combined hand-drawn, two-dimensional stop-motion animation with digital animation of a limited technological scale. In effect, two-dimensional characters move around in the realistic, three-dimensional space of the eighth district. In addition, many of the characters carry photographed heads of the dubbing actors or other well-known media personalities on their awkward two-dimensional bodies. The film's satirical-allegorical effect derives largely from the jarring distance between photographic realism and jerky two-dimensional animation.

The projection of stereotypical, hand-drawn characters with photographed, masklike heads into a recognizable cityscape within a fantastic plot that requires quick editing, split screens, and other familiar techniques of global television and film foregrounds its own performative function at any moment of the film. The mockery is directed against the state's political and cultural elites, constructing spectatorial solidarity in a knowing, cynical repudiation of both communism and capitalism offered on the terms of the nation-state. While the plot is fantastic and barely coherent, the musical numbers provide interpretive clues. The theme song, "Forog a pénz" ("The Money Rolls"), raps,

District's a mate, one of a kind,
You took a knock and lost your mind.
See this tale of the town unfold,
A house of cards in a land of gold.
You can't get lost, diggin' around,
If ya got the cash, you're safe and sound.
The cops down there don't fuck about,
Pay them off or just get out.
We all know where we belong,
Pimpin' and trickin' all day long.

Some new guy wants to get to the top
Don't cost much to give it a pop.
The gov'ment throws all sorts in 'ere,
Chinese, Arab, Gypsy, queer.
Everything looks grey and brown,
Take one card out and the lot falls down.
Cash makes a dash from hand to hand,
All addin' up in a promised land.
The shit we go through ev'ry day,
It's a bitch of a game, you wanna play.

(http://www.nyocker.hu)

In other words, the ghetto film allegorically constructs the micromodel of the dirty card game that the state plays in the real eighth district. This hybrid, ethnicized, "trash" place is like a castle made of cards: temporary, unstable, without a solid foundation—an image that, by extension, stands for Hungary as a whole.

At the same time, the film's publicity campaign emphasized continuities with previous currents of Hungarian animation. It turned seeing the film into a moral duty by reminding viewers of the fact that the Hungarian Motion Picture Foundation, the agency responsible for distributing state funds devoted to the national film industry, and which funded half of the film's meager production budget, is contracted to be reimbursed unless the film sells eighty thousand tickets in the theaters. Eighty thousand became a magic number, wedding the heroic times of communist production with a marketing trick. The film's online forum engaged viewers in a patriotic race to save "national animation" and support "our film" by going to see it, multiple times if possible, and recruit other viewers to do so as well. This enthusiasm, fully exploited by the filmmakers, is also rooted in the nostalgic shadow of a collective opposition to the heavily centralized institutions of cultural control under socialism, whose place is here metonymically filled by the Hungarian Motion Picture Foundation.

The latest Hungarian animated feature derives much of its appeal from capitalizing on postcommunist, post-EU-accession Romany empowerment. The film's rap duels between "gadje" and "Roma" are testimonies to this new, cool "black" power (see figure 3.1). The lyrics from the song "Vigyázz!" ("Watch Out!") leave no doubt that Ricsi, personified by rapper LL Junior, is the guy to identify with.

Tell me what you want from me and I won't hurt you
But if you pick on me, you'd better be tough!

**Figure 3.1**
Ricsi Lakatos and his multiethnic gang from *Nyócker* ("*The District*," Áron
Gauder, 2004).

Here is the Gypsy force, the power is mine,
We'll find out who will win out.

In the district I am the coolest kid, watch out!

. . .

The Gypsies are the blacks of Europe
They will rule the district!

Following Ricsi's lead, the kids turn their oil discovery into a thriving
international business. The money starts pouring in. After the two
fathers are let in, they even put aside their rivalry and become business
partners. The discovery of "black gold"—an ethnically suggestive phrase
that resonates with other senses of discovering marketable Romany
resources—becomes a global media sensation and an earth-shattering
economic event, forcing Wall Street financiers into suicide and turning
even the ailing Pope John Paul II into an investor. The Hungarian prime
minister visits the neighborhood with his delegation to meet the two
business partners. The event is presented as if through a documentary
camera, with the politicians' faces blocked out, emphasizing both the
reality potential of the scene and the representation's sarcastic, allegorical
quality. The meeting takes place in a public area, with pro-EU demon-
strators in the background noisily waving their blue signs. This provides
an ironic background to a scene in which the chief politician of a new

member state pays his respects to the economically powerful, notwith-standing the fact that the latter are embodied by Lóránt Lakatos, "life artist," and Károly Csorba, "entrepreneur," as the Roma bar owner and the white pimp introduce themselves.

During these introductions, the prime minister's assistant whispers into his boss's ear Lakatos's and Csorba's criminal records, including the fact that Lakatos "wants street signs in Romany." One can also hear someone in the prime minister's group say aloud, "Gypsy and white trash together.[10] Which one do you think stinks worse?" Csorba and Lakatos overhear this remark and react in a satisfyingly violent outburst of ethnic-class solidarity that involves the kids, the prostitutes, and the Romany, Chinese, Arab, and Jewish locals. They force the official delegation of suited men and reporters to flee onto an arriving tram, where the ultimate humilia-tion is waiting for them: the bloodthirsty controller, the king of public transportation—that is, the real world, from which politicians are widely considered to be removed.

The protagonists of this new, glocal narrative are people who are only rhetorically included in the national collective, those the national elites would rather leave behind in the east in the course of their relentless march to the west: the criminal and the drunk, the foreign-speaking and the foreign-looking—in other words, the Gypsies of the nation. From the film's allegorical perspective, it is the contaminating element, the Roma in particular, who stand for the transitional nation, retroactively making visible the whiteness and nationalism of the voices who had previously represented it.

But before one jumps into celebrating the progressive transnational potential of the new national animated film, one needs to consider that it also, by necessity, plays by the rules of the very global entertainment market that provides it with political and aesthetic inspiration. These rules do not allow more involvement in local politics than is sufficient to make the film a local and translocal sensation, to lend it trendiness and sexiness. Ultimately, the film's critical voice remains noncommittal, self-underminingly playful and postmodern, at times even cynical, poking fun at stereotypes without a consistent political project. For instance, after the united forces of the neighborhood triumphantly fight back the sleazy state politicians, the two fathers turn to each other: "Now what? Let's drink." With that, they retire to Lakatos's pub to swear friendship and quench their revolutionary zeal with many glasses of liquor. Later, they revive from drunken stupor to find out that the oil wells have dried up. This puts an abrupt end to friendship, collaboration, and ethnic solidarity, and throws Nyócker/Hungary immediately back into its original state of urban warfare.

It would be far-fetched to claim that the Roma's ethnic prominence in the film's taboo-breaking, demystifying thrust, or the new, youthful cool associated with Roma rap, contribute to establishing a more dignified collective Roma identity. But at the very least, the film complicates notions of ethnic representation by foregrounding, deploring, exoticizing, and then mocking stereotypes all at the same time. It explicitly undermines the fragile unity that the postcommunist state is trying to solidify between state and nation by extending the nation beyond its state borders and exposing the way in which transnational capital manipulates nationalism more efficiently than top-down appeals to purity of language and love of country.

### Ghetto Play without Women

While *The District* undoubtedly represents a new voice in the politics of Romany representation, in one aspect, such representation remains remarkably conservative. While the film issues a democratic address, this address remains steeped in masculine, nationalistic principles. Even if one resists reducing representational critique to an "images of" approach, it is hard not to notice that when women in the film do not fade into the background or are not absent altogether, they are arranged into age-old and rather crudely reproduced stereotypes, which are offered without any hint of the self-conscious mockery that accompanies ethnic stereotypes of men. The theme song, "Forog a pénz" ("The Money Rolls"), establishes the district's trademark prostitutes as practically part of the neighborhood's architecture, willingly and naturally ensuring the inhabitants' proper masculine psychosomatic health. The cynical mantra of the film comes from Ricsi's uncle Guszti, who advises his love-struck nephew, Ricsi, to make lots of money to get girls, or, as he puts it "pussy." "Pénz és pina" or "money and pussy" is what *everyone*—and there is no doubt about the film's selective gendered address in this choice, also posed to the viewers as a poll on the film's Web site—ultimately needs in order to be happy. Love will follow once you have the other two, according to Uncle Guszti.

While prostitutes are at least believable in a story about the eighth district, the complete absence of mothers is less easily explained. Single fathers are not a common feature of Hungarian society in general, and particularly not of lower-class and immigrant families. The filmmakers do not appear to consider it necessary to explain where the mothers are. One suspects that mother characters would be unnecessary baggage in a social satire focused on ethnic strife and politics—a playing field reserved for brothers and fathers.

From a gendered perspective, the film's musical register is equally ambivalent. While *The District*'s valorization of Roma rap undermines the nation-state's ethnic hierarchy, it fails to criticize the gendered hierarchy of state-sanctioned anticommunist rock. This is not surprising in itself, as it is characteristic of the very global trend on which Roma rap draws. In this view, *The District* in particular and other popular forms of Roma music in general never depart from the "cock rock" of anticommunist rock movements. The only female performers who contribute their musical talents to the film are the sister rap duo Ludditák (Luddites), two college students who carved out a loyal underground following who appreciate their untranslatable, sarcastic language games, often employed in the service of gendered, if not feminist, social critique. Their lyrics offer a humorous and sophisticated critical mirror of transitional Hungary, with a sensitive eye to the differences between urban and provincial transformations, reflecting on their own transition from a small village to the capital. They are especially keen on mocking pretentious masculine or macho attitudes, and rejecting the media-fabricated, seductive body image doubly imposed on young women by an advertising-driven image culture and local patriarchal tradition. For instance, their song "I'm So Pretty" announces (in my own literal translation),

You're killing me by saying
I'm not pretty like Britney Spears.
But your ideal won't do it for me.
I'm an MC girl, an MC girl.

You want a tip-top girl,
I want the hip-hop noise.
Your figure is like King Kong's, man,
Your brain is like a Ping-Pong ball.
Screw it, I won't be ascetic because of you.
You dumped me like a rocket
But who cares, when your idol,
Your ideal is too lame for me . . .[11]

Hungarian pop music criticism, a male-dominated territory that selectively welcomes male Roma rappers, is either openly hostile or sarcastic toward the Luddites, at best condescendingly allowing the "girls" into an underground subpocket of the national music scene. "A girl should not rap," as one interview sums up what there is to know about them ("Sokan azt mondják" 2004). As if internalizing the widely held opinion that they are impostors, the Luddites often talk about their own music in self-deprecating terms. At the same time, they also try to complicate this view by referring to ideas of gender without identifying them as such, however tentatively, as in this conversation:

We've just completed a rap number, together with four other girls. Our contribution addresses the opinion that girls should not rap but stick to singing instead. This is a typical stereotype, that a woman should be beautiful, kind, smiling, and if she's even a little different, we'll deny her femininity. But I don't understand why you couldn't talk in masculine style just because you're a girl. Feminine and masculine styles are not bound to whether one is a boy or a girl. You have your style and your biological sex, and there isn't a necessary correlation between the two. ("Sokan" 2004)

The argument against nationalized authenticity grounded in the male body couldn't be made more clear here. The Luddites' own tough and combative lyrics announce the legitimacy of a new, less male-defined body image and persona, and may even empower a lesbian aesthetic, much more in line with gendered punk music than with "cock rock." It is shocking, then, that after the producer of *The District*, Erik Novák, proudly takes credit on the online discussion forum for recruiting the Luddites for the project, in the first images of the film we recognize the girls' faces on top of hooker characters' bodies. The prostitutes' bodies combine Barbie with pornographically large-breasted computer-game characters. The Luddites' musical and linguistic talents are put to use only in a single short rap number, in which they exhaustedly bemoan the hardships of a prostitute's work, striking various seductive poses.

It appears that while the film has successfully complicated the relations of media representation through which Romany identities are inevitably filtered, the new space it opens for ethnic negotiations not only remains a masculine space but also might actually be conditioned on shutting out women. The players who animate the new national allegory are multi-cultured, multicolored, and transnational. They participate in new, perhaps even more democratic alignments against state politics and the consumer culture of global capitalism. However, gender and sexuality remain very much fixed in the essentialist categories promoted by the nation-state and exploited by the global hip-hop industry. On the one hand, the filmmakers criticize the state for its ethnic divide-and-conquer approach; on the other, they adopt the same divisive nationalistic strategies when it comes to gender and sexuality. This implies a strategic separation of state from nation, assuming that the former is rotten but that the latter still refers to a collective affiliation in which ethnic difference matters a whole lot more than gender difference. Whereas *The District* uproots and throws into play ideas of Romany authenticity and national primordialism, in the very same gesture, it imprisons women in discursive, representational ghettos.[12]

## Hip-Hop Nation and Gender Politics

We have run into a paradox: On the one hand, global pop music, particularly hip-hop, legitimizes a space for ethnic identity games that may finally revise the damning, age-old, essentialist portrait of the Musical Gypsy. On the other hand, the emerging "new" Roma artist, admittedly a hybrid construction heavily drawing on Afro-Caribbean and Mediterranean motifs, is eager to reclaim a sense of authenticity that is conditioned on an essentialist gender divide. As a minority star, the Musical Gypsy automatically stands in for the entire disenfranchised community, whose hierarchical sexist and heteronormative structure is left intact or even reinforced through the appeal to Roma authenticity. A feminist lens immediately reveals an old pattern, familiar from the histories of post-revolutionary and postcolonial nations: the new community is constituted on the backs of and through the continued exclusion of women and sexual minorities, whose "cause" is constantly deferred and delegitimized. What appears to maintain the authenticity of transnational hip-hop is precisely the hyperbolic performance of racialized, heterosexual manhood. Most of the critical, scholarly, administrative, and political attention that has been lavished on the cause of "the Roma" since the end of the Cold War has entirely ignored gendered and sexualized hierarchies that permeate Roma identities. The Roma continue to be represented as a singular, ethnically defined group, whose homogeneity is broken up only by national, linguistic, and occasionally class differences traditionally studied by anthropologists.

What is most surprising is that it is the sexual politics of the inherently fluid and performative flows of pop music that justify the claim to Romany authenticity. This is a transnational paradox, characteristic of the global travel of hip-hop on the whole. In the United States, the sexism and the homophobia that underscore performances of a combative, "real" black masculinity have recently opened up hip-hop to criticism. For instance, *Hip-Hop: Beyond Beats and Rhymes* (2006), a documentary made by former college quarterback and self-identified hip-hop fan Byron Hurt, interweaves direct commentary by the filmmaker with interviews with African-American rappers such as Mos Def, Fat Joe, Chuck D, Jadakiss, as well as with critics, activists, and young rap consumers. The picture is bleak: the current state of hip-hop in the United States is devoid of the initial, justified antiestablishment anger and resistant spirit that propelled this musical form from inner-city ghettoes onto MTV. Instead, rich "white guys in suits," as a critic puts it in the film, the executives of the globally interconnected music industry, have consolidated a self-hating, violent, and disturbingly misogynistic rap culture, which is designed to appeal to a large white audience. Because this is the most lucrative package in which hip-hop sells, the rappers featured in the film, exhibiting attitudes from denial through irony to cynicism, see no other way but to continue supplying the mainstream with what it rewards.

Such a model serves as inspiration and justification for hip-hop performers around the world to become the authentic voices of their nations or other marginalized communities. For instance, the documentary *Saz* ( Israel, 2005), by director Gil Karni, features Palestinian-Israeli rapper Samekh Zakhut, whose declared mission is to enlist hip-hop in the service of Palestinian nationalism. Hip-hop is to be reunited here with its original mission as a politicized artistic tool with which to negotiate—or, in this case, violently stage—social conflict. Only the ongoing debate between Samekh, who sees the Arab minority in Israel as increasingly marginalized, and his communist grandfather, who argues in favor of peaceful coexistence, introduces some ambiguity into the film's apparent justification of Samekh's anger. During the one-year period when the camera follows the rapper, he becomes increasingly successful. The film wraps up as he is boasting to his grandfather of a likely record deal that would shoot him onto the Euro-American market. The audience is left wondering what will happen to his commitment to the cause of Palestinian nationalism. Both the feminist critique and questions about the corrupting strategies of the music industry seem alien to *Saz*—something that can be safely generalized across worldwide adaptations of African-American hip-hop. The political negotiations in which Samekh's tendentious music engages, although overtly masculinist and militarized, are performed exclusively between an oppressive nation-state and the oppressed diasporic national community for which he volunteers to speak.

It is perplexing that such performances, unlike those of African-American rappers, are seen as exempt from gendered critique, even though feminism has had so much to say both about the structural gender and sexual inequalities inherent to nationalism and the fragmentation of identity politics into the commercialized matter of individual choices. The work of postcolonial and transnational feminists has produced a body of writing that critiques the violence involved in the act of speaking for the subaltern, even if the speaker has the best intentions (Spivak 1994, Chow 2001), as well as the control over women by nationalistic discourses and technologies strategically employed by both the nation-state and transnational business corporations (Grewal and Kaplan 1994; Marciniak 2006). The alleged authenticity of political statements by hip-hop artists such as Samekh should logically be undermined by their derivative, staged, and commercialized participation in performing world music. In particular, there is something profoundly contradictory in the alliance between hip-hop and territorial nationalism. A migratory, hybrid musical form is employed to confirm primordial boundaries and blood ties. This connection works against what many take to be the logic of world music, hip-hop in particular.

In her discussion of hip-hop/flamenco hybrid music, Susanne Stemmler appeals to the notion of the "transnational" to dissolve the contradiction. She argues that the inherent hybridity, openness, and performative irony that hip-hop and flamenco share is amplified in their combination and creates a new space for social and political critique (Stemmler 2007). Hip-hop, in this account, is not only a highly politicized news channel connecting the transnational communities of the "Black Atlantic" but is also a musical form that functions as an easily accessible open source. It provides a virtual home of shared experiences, a space of connectedness and belonging to a transnational community sometimes called "hip-hop nation." In this sense, "home seems to be a habitual practice of mobility, itself a symbolic habitat, a way of life" (Stemmler 2007). According to Stemmler, hip-hop and flamenco are both sound cultures that act against the territorializing impulses of the nation-state.

While this is a contagiously optimistic account, I argue, with reference to transnational rappers such as Zakhut, that it overlooks the gendered, sexualized, and racialized dimensions of hip-hop's transnational migration. In the case studies I discuss, one can trace an unspoken, reterritorializing effort by ethnic or minority rappers who, similar to most African-American rappers, stake out their turf in the essentialist language of rather old-fashioned sexism and homophobia. Such blatant sexism goes hand in hand with territorial nationalism or militarism, undermining the celebratory ideal of a global hip-hop nation. Even when rappers do not speak for a nation, as in the case of Roma artists, discourses of nationalism permeate the construction of "authentic" racialized bodies on the global music marketplace.

The celebratory logic of world music often simply equates hybridity with resistance and labels a feminist critique frivolous. But a critical feminist approach is crucial to sorting out how Afro-American and Afro-Caribbean masculinities, constructed as objects of exoticizing emulation by transnational record and media companies, come to reproduce nationalistic ideology and underscore latent nationalistic purposes.

### Visions of Europe in Minority Performances

An extreme example is Kobi Shimoni, the "Israeli Eminem," who also calls himself "Subliminal" to mystify his own hybrid persona. He rose to wide popularity after the Palestinian-Israeli peace talks failed in 2000 and violence escalated in Israel. His music represents a sharp departure from traditional Israeli music, which has been "a mix of Hebrew-language rock and Mediterranean crooning" (Mitnick 2003). Subliminal blends American hip-hop styles with traditional Hebrew and Persian music samples "layered with fat basslines and catchy choruses," evoking a Jewish history and tradition with Middle Eastern overtones. But the lyrics reveal a perspective that is identified as "patriotic" at best and violently anti-Palestinian at worst, announcing the claims of a divisive territorial nationalism in the "tough" macho language of L.A. "thug" rappers. Shimoni and his band all come from military backgrounds. The military also provides their widest fan base ("Q's Interview" 2005). The rapper says he sells "pride and a dose of reality" through his songs, which he considers his weapons. In the song "Divide and Conquer," he sings: "Dear God, I wish you could come down because I'm being persecuted. My enemies are united. They want to destroy me. We're nurturing and arming those who hate us. Enough!"

It appears that the name "Subliminal" refers less to the subtlety than to the ambiguity of Shimoni's and his sidekick's, Yoav Eliasi aka "Shadow," patriotic politics. They are directly supported and sponsored by the Israeli government. The rapper sells more than patriotic pride: he has a lucrative clothing line, under the logo TACT or Tel Aviv City Team. All of the items, from caps to baggy pants, are decorated with a Star of

David, which he claims to have rendered trendy, along with a stitching that reads, "The Architects of Israeli Hip Hop." The cover of Shimoni's second album, *The Light and the Shadow*, portrays a muddy fist menacingly clutching a silver Star of David pendant. In the song "Bottomless Pit," violence appears self-serving, divorced from the national cause, as he warns an unnamed enemy: "Anybody who messes with me ends up in a coffin."

A similar, highly politicized set of identity negotiations between the white national majority and, in this case, the immigrant Muslim minority has been carried out by Ali B, perhaps the most popular rapper in the Netherlands. Unlike Shimoni, however, who gives voice to majority nationalism, Dutch-Moroccan Ali B has been welcomed by both Moroccan/Arab and Dutch constituencies. As I show, Ali B's position as an ethnic minority pop star reveals a pattern that is analogically relevant for understanding the position of young Roma artists in Eastern Europe. His career has risen amid increasing national tension over post–Cold War immigration, the European Union's eastward enlargement, and the unresolved situation of guest workers who have settled in the Netherlands over the decades. Taxed religious and ethnic relations burst through the surface of the traditional Dutch national self-image of tolerance in November 2004, when controversial director Theo van Gogh was murdered by another Dutch-Moroccan, Mohammed B. Ali B, who raps mostly in Dutch but straddles both cultures, is seen in the Netherlands as a figure of great political relevance. His hybridity makes him both flexible enough to represent the Moroccan community and easy to appropriate as the poster boy for Dutch multiculturalism, used to keep in check resistance to the very process of fortifying borders and clamping down on immigration that his figure as an "alien" foregrounds. The music and entertainment media industry have been glad to tap into the interest created by yet another exotic identity mix, whose "authenticity" is enhanced by his controversial political position.[13]

In both cases, it is in the rappers' performance of African-American hip-hop masculinity that their authenticity and power for political mobilizing lie. While their cultural politics is exploited by both the nation-state and the commercial media industry, their national political clout is formidable. This is particularly obvious in the case of Ali B, who is a frequent celebrity guest and topic of discussion in mainstream Dutch media. In his seductive music videos, such as "Till Morning" and "Ghetto," he is typically featured as a ghetto rapper surrounded by a multiracial cast of dancers and singers. The lyrics of the songs address the sense of abjection that pervades the Muslim immigrant ghetto in a mix of languages. "Ghetto's" chorus goes,

This goes out to my Tatas in the [ghetto]
My Toerkoes in the [ghetto]
My Mokros in the ghetto [ghetto]
This goes out to the Antis in the [ghetto]
Malukus in the [ghetto]
The Joegos in the [ghetto]
[Ghetto living]

These streets remind me of quicksand
When you're on it you'll keep goin' down
And there's no one to hold on to
And there's no one to pull you out
You keep on fallin'
And no one can hear you callin'
So you end up self-destructing
On the corner with the tuli on the waist line just got outta the bing doin' state time
Teeth marks on my back from the canine
Dark memories of when there was no sunshine
'Cause they said that I wouldn't make it
I remember like yesterday
Holdin' on to what God gave me.[14]

The video clip of the song "Zomervibe" ("Summer Vibe") shows a less threatening but even more seductive side of Ali B's, and, by extension, the Moroccan immigrant's, seductive masculinity: It showcases the half-naked rapper on a luxury boat in a bright Mediterranean setting, surrounded by pining white women, basking in the glory of his celebrity life. It is likely that such images of successful, powerful immigrants mitigate and positively alter the perception of the stereotypical violent Muslim to which the Moroccan minority tends to be assigned in Dutch mainstream culture. However, the same concerns emerge here, perhaps even more forcefully, that *Hip-Hop: Beyond Beats and Rhymes* raised: to the extent that hip-hop is a predominantly male and heterosexist genre, it seems that the empowering potential inscribed in its cultural politics remains limited to men who are or aspire to be rightful representatives of their communities. The lines of opposition and resistance presuppose and confirm a national, by definition male-populated field of action. One suspects that hip-hop's sexual politics consolidates an alliance between the men of national majorities and minorities. This unspoken alliance is grounded in and serves binary gendered and sexual inequalities in which women and homosexuals have a choice between staying silent or engaging in the game like men.

Todd Boyd writes, "Ultimately, hip hop's concern with cultural identity has been about affirming authenticity, in what would otherwise be considered a postmodern, technologically driven, media-dominated, artificial world. To 'keep it real' means to remain true to what is assumed to be the dictates of one's cultural identity" (Boyd 2004, 23–24). As Boyd readily admits, this quest for authenticity "often translates to one's perception in the marketplace" and one's relationship to capital (24).

The tension around authenticity that is at the heart of the global migration of hip-hop is also captured by Stuart Hall in his description of cultural identities in his native Caribbean as a play of difference within identity. His analysis provides a model that helps to foreground the contradiction embedded in each of these global musicians' performances—that between their own transnational, hybrid cultural and economic constitution and their supposedly pure representative politics, which enables them to sing for an allegedly homogeneous national or minority group.

According to Hall, in a situation captured by Derrida's "differance" on a theoretical plane, the "authentic" state of being from the Caribbean is continually destabilized by the historical, colonial ruptures and discontinuities that constitute Caribbean identities. While "being" of a certain essence is always "becoming"—just like, in the deconstructionist model, absolute difference is always a sliding difference, on its way to new meanings without completely erasing traces of other meanings—imposing a single imaginary coherence on an area so obviously fraught with dispersal and fragmentation would be very hard. It is this evidence of imagined roots and positioned identities that makes Hall turn to "play" to evoke instability and permanent unsettlement, differences inscribed *between*, rather than *within*, identities. Besides the full palette of skin hues, he argues, the complexity of this cultural play can be most powerfully experienced in the play of Caribbean music (Hall 1990).

## World Music, Post-Wall Europe, and Romany Authenticity

Hall's point about cultural identities and musical performance has a more universal potential, which can serve analogically to contest the essentialist unity that nation-states impose on the identities they claim to contain within their state borders. It is also a useful lens through which to examine the alleged "authenticity" of world music's politics vis-à-vis nationalism. The relationship between the two senses of play Hall discusses—diasporic dispersal and unsettlement, on the one hand, and musical play, on the other—is especially relevant for the Roma.

As I argued earlier, the Roma's associations with musical entertainment and their ability to adapt different musical traditions have recently been revalorized as serious assets on the global media market that has invaded Eastern European cultures since the end of the Cold War, as well as resources for a newly emerging Roma politics of identity. The decline of socialism and the arrival of global television, particularly MTV, in Eastern Europe also brought about a generational and ethnic shift in musical sensibilities. Rock continued to be harnessed in the service of nationalist sentiment, most notably in the Serb turbo/folk/rock scene that had led up to and thrived during the post-Yugoslav wars. But to many in the younger generation, the violent purity and whiteness of such music pales in comparison with the cool and erotic energies of the African-American ghetto. As the success of *The District* demonstrates, Eastern European Roma have now come center stage as the local embodiments of the spirit of ghetto music. While Roma musicians have always maintained extended international networks regardless of the musical genre they pursued, during socialism, their activities were monitored and regulated by nation-states. The state provided contracts and visas for foreign venues, and took credit for the achievements of "their good" Roma (Kállai 2000).

Since the fall of the Wall, the European popular music market has turned toward postsocialist Eastern Europe and the Balkans in search of novelty and originality.[15] There is no shortage of neologisms that describe the varieties of world music transplanted into and growing out of East European soil: Along with Gypsy techno and Roma rap, one hears of speed-folk, Transylvania-pop, Balkanrock, and so on. Romany musicians have taken advantage of Western interest, easier travel, and international family networks to build transnational careers.[16] But it was the infiltration of Eastern Europe by world music, particularly by MTV, that had first shored up Roma musical talent and turned the Eastern European ghetto, the place of the urban ethnic underclass and the site of Roma segregation of exclusion, into a resource for politicized pop music.

It seems quite likely that hip-hop has introduced Roma voices that had not been heard before into national cultures. The image and sound flows of hip-hop help Roma rappers transform their own ethnicities by reappropriating the image of the Gypsy musician formerly tamed by the state in the service of a transnational identity politics. There are many examples of such success stories. Similar to Fekete Vonat ("Black Train"),

**Figure 3.2**
Gipsy.cz.

mentioned earlier, the Czech Roma band Syndrom Snopp, led by the Roma rapper Gipsy—who often also calls himself *Cerny pes*, or "Black Dog"—distinguishes itself from mainstream Czech hip-hop bands by its radical critique of racial hatred and commercialism.[17] The band Gipsy. cz, also from the Czech Republic, has recently made it onto the World Music Chart's European Top Ten (see figure 3.2). Led by rapper Gipsy (Radoslav Banga), the band of Roma musicians performs in Romany, English, and Czech and mixes Romany music sounds with various pop styles. Gipsy.cz's first CD, *Romano Hip Hop*, released in 2006, has been distributed throughout Europe by Indies Scope Records. The title song was named song of the year by the readers of the popular Czech music magazine *Filter*.[18]

At the same time, when one takes a closer look at the ways in which most Roma rappers try to carve out new spaces of identity in Eastern Europe, their efforts seem to leave them suspended between global media and nation-state more often than allowing them to critique both. For instance, following Black Train's success with local Roma and non-Roma audiences, as well as abroad, the band signed a three-album contract with the Hungarian EMI in 1997. When making the third of these albums, however, a changed Hungarian EMI leadership refused to allow the band to record songs in Romany. A statement from the parent company, EMI London, summed up the situation succinctly: "It's not good business to be racist."[19]

**Figure 3.3**
LL Junior.

LL Junior, founding member of Fekete Vonat and the voice of Ricsi Lakatos in *The District*, is one of the most popular Roma pop musicians in Hungary (see figure 3.3). His offerings, for the most part, are romantic songs, which infuse traditional Roma tunes with Afro-Caribbean influences. Most of his music videos are in Romany, some with Hungarian subtitles. In the video of the Romany-language song "Korkorro," he appears as a Latin lover, in white slacks, a sleeveless shirt, suspenders, and a hat, pining for a dark-haired girl in a red dress. The dance numbers that pepper the courting narrative increase the exotic lure of the Gypsy lover and flamenco dancer almost to the point of camp. This is a marked departure from the image of the Roma buffoon, or "dancing slave," in which Roma musical performances had been contained during the communist decades. While Junior taps into discourses of Gypsy romanticism, he remixes them—along with the music—to reassert a kind of racialized virility that is an object of transnational envy rather than national subjection. On YouTube, the narrative comments from viewers are partly in Romany, confirming the existence of a transnational Romany audience. Unsurprisingly, the Hungarian comments are intensely racist, infused with homophobic overtones. A few additional comments are in Spanish and English. For the most part, the latter express shock over the intensity of racism evidenced by viewers who identify themselves as Hungarian.

As Black Train's and LL Junior's mixed success stories show, the new opportunities for travel, marketing, and distribution outside the channels controlled by the state constitute a transnational opening for Roma musicians. However, national languages and racist discourses continue to influence the distribution and reception of Roma music. As a result, Roma musicians invariably need to make allowances in order to be heard in their own countries. The local versions of the popular musical talent show *Pop Idol* have provided rich case studies of the ambivalent relationship between Roma musicians and their nation-states. As I argue elsewhere, they provide the best illustration of the minefields that Roma entertainers, easily exploited by both commercial media and state politicians for the economic and political capital they represent, have to negotiate (Imre 2006). Romany singer Vlastimil Horvath won the 2005 season of *SuperStar* in the Czech Republic[20] at the same time as Caramel, aka Ferenc Molnár, won *Megasztár* in Hungary. While these national winners' ethnicity was at the center of public debates speculating about whether the rise of Roma stars will elevate the status of the entire minority, the singers themselves have been eager to renounce the burden of representation (Sümegi 2005).[21]

In a pattern reminiscent of the situation of Dutch-Moroccan Ali B in the Netherlands, embracing selected Roma musicians has long been a strategy employed by the state and the moral majority to hand-pick and isolate from their communities "model" representatives of the minority, most of whom will remain all the more excluded from the national community. György Kerényi, longtime manager of the minority station Rádió C in Hungary, reminds us that urban Gypsy musicians have always been a token part of the Budapest bohemian intellectual world (Sümegi 2005). Such tactics continue in the postcommunist state's and the national media's management of Roma pop stars.

Ibolya Oláh, who finished a close second in the 2004 season of *Megasztár*, was officially chosen to represent Hungarian culture in the European Parliament in Brussels, where she performed a patriotic song in the spring of 2005. Unlike Gipsy or even LL Junior, whose hybridized Roma images are carefully calculated and cultivated, the YouTube presences of Oláh and Caramel reveal nothing about their ethnic origins. In the eyes of the global media world, these national media stars are represented as simply "Hungarian." Oláh, an orphan girl with a spine-chilling, powerful voice, marched forward in the 2004 *Megasztár* race performing two kinds of music: One of her sources was popular songs from the Hungarian classical pop repertoire of the explicitly nationalistic variety, such as Péter

Máté's "Hazám" ("My Country"). The lyrics speak the sentimental language of patriotism from the position of the white male intellectual. They open with the metaphor of paternal lineage to confirm the genetic bond between family and country, *patria* and *patriarch*: "I can hear my father's voice. You may not like this, but this is my country." In Hungarian, the word used in the song for "country," *haza*, merges "home" and "country" in one. The Gypsy woman, by definition excluded from both categories, is symbolically included on stage while performing the role of the model exception that confirms the rule about the bad minority. Oláh's other choices consisted of international hits, mostly by African-American singers, such as Queen Latifah's song from the musical *Chicago*, "When You're Good to Mama." Oláh's ethnic difference became acceptable on the national talent show when removed by a degree of separation and colored by the image of the nurturing, mythical black mother.

The embodiment of the doubly excluded, the Gypsy woman, has been fixed in subsequent appearances to demonstrate the state's programmatic multicultural outreach and European generosity toward minorities: her performance of the song "Magyarország" ("Hungary"), has been employed to enhance the patriotic television spectacle during the coverage of national celebrations twice in 2005: on New Year's Eve and on the state holiday of August 20, the birthday of King Stephen, legendary founder of the Kingdom of Hungary.

Caramel's image and music have been similarly whitewashed and nationalized, with the singer's voluntary participation. His hit song and video clip, "Párórára" ("For a Few Hours"), features Caramel sitting on the grass in a baseball hat, baggy pants, and a long shirt, absorbed in the timeless existentialist art of observing people rushing by. Caramel moved audiences during the 2005 season of *Megasztár* with his performance of "Egy Elfelejtett szó" ("A Forgotten Word"), rendered classic by the Hungarian 1980s rock band LGT. The song was a cult item of the "rock revolution" that sustained youthful national opposition to the communist state and has become a nostalgic brick in the construction of postcommunist national unity. The irony that the Roma were generally assumed to be the recipients of state favors and therefore allies of the party leadership is erased in this performance along with Caramel's ethnic minority status. The singer's more recent rap song "Mennem Kell" ("I've Got to Go") features the voice of a confident and well-to-do star on the rise. The clip shows Caramel, who is hardly an athletic type, emerging from an elegantly disheveled bed shared with a sleeping blond bombshell. The song announces that the world is waiting for him and therefore he cannot be tied down by a woman. We see him enjoy the blowing wind and his new mobility while driving a Mercedes-Benz (emphatically emphasized by a gratuitous shot of the car's hood).

As Todd Boyd argues, hip-hop revisits the dilemma of assimilation in the United States—that of pushing for integration but constantly asking at what cost (Boyd 2004, 22). Roma musicians face a similar dilemma, but, it appears, with even more limited choices. The continued racism of the postcommunist state and moral majority and the co-opting seductions of the transnational media market leave a very narrow space in which to assert a positive Roma difference. Oláh thus can be employed by the state as an object of token exchange between Hungarian and Roma minorities as well as between the state and the European Union. Caramel, whose success is intimately tied to his rise on a national reality show, plays out the scenario of upward mobility that renders him indistinguishable from Hungarians and unthreatening in the patriarchal rivalry between the majority and the minority.

The *Eurovision* song contests of recent years have provided a European playing field for nations of the new Europe to perform nonnormative ethnic and sexual identities, whose excess is essential for defining the borders of the "normal" nation. *Eurovision*, organized by the European Broadcasting Union (EBU) and sponsored primarily by Britain, Spain, Germany, and France, was a contest among Western European nations until 1993, when Eastern Europeans were first included. Eastern European performers won their first contest in 2001, and have continued to triumph ever since. Roma musicians have played an important role in these victories, representing specific nations.

In 2006, one of the memorable contenders was Bulgarian chalga (pop-folk) singer Azis, or Vasil Troyanov Boyanov, a gay Roma drag queen with a bleached beard and mustache, who often performs heterosexual roles in videos. He is a superstar with a trans-Balkan appeal, whose career highlights have included running for Parliament as a representative of the Evroroma (Euroroma) party in 2005 and participation along with his husband in the Bulgarian *VIP Big Brother*. The 2007 competition's runner-up was Ukrainian Verka Serduchka, another man in drag, with a characteristically flamboyant, special-effects-ridden performance. Serbian singer Marija Serifovic, an open lesbian, won the competition with her song, "Molitva" ("Prayer"), launching ecstatic national celebrations in Serbia and once again uniting Yugoslavia, torn to pieces by the recent ethnic war, in triumph over the West. Similar to Oláh's nationalization, Serifovic has been intensely deployed in the service of national and

**Figure 3.4**
Marija Serifovic, winner of *Eurovision* 2007, next to the Serbian flag.

party politics. On December 24, 2007, she sang "Molitva" at a campaign rally for the Serbian Radical Party, commenting that her song is a prayer for a new, different Serbia (see figure 3.4).

The most extreme example of the dangers of double co-optation, by both state discourses and commercial media, is Roma singer Gyözö Gáspár, leader of the band Romantic. Gáspár's music and declared intentions are barely concerned with identity politics. He wants his band to be the nation's favorite, simply to be embraced by Hungarians and the Roma alike. It is no surprise that the first prime-time television show starring a Roma in the region revolves around the nonoffensive, slightly overweight Gáspár: *The Gyözike Show*, in production since 2005 on the commercial channel RTL Klub, is a reality docusoap, which records the daily life of Gáspár and his family. While the fact that a Romany man and his family occupy a precious prime-time television slot and attract a large non-Roma audience is a significant development, the family's life in the expensive villa they inhabit more closely resembles *The Beverly Hillbillies*. The décor is in bad taste, family members constantly shout at one another in the stereotypical Roma dialect familiar from cabaret scenes, and most of Gáspár's efforts to assert himself backfire in one ridiculous way or another. The program seems to confirm nothing but Gypsies' inability to function as hardworking citizens. It displays the results of putting childish Roma entertainers in the china shop of an expensive house, comically performing a lifestyle that they will never be sophisticated enough to appreciate. The "real Roma" that this reality show delivers appear to be hopelessly hovering among various stereotypes. On the show, in live concerts and in his Web presence, Gáspár seems eager to please by offering himself up for easy consumption and by dedicating his own life and music to consumption. Perhaps the most explicit of these consumptive performances is the song "Fogyni volna jó" or "It Would Be Great to Lose Weight." The song's message amounts to this: "It would be nice to lose weight but I like bacon and sausage too much." Gáspár's physical appearance certainly underscores this message, providing for a depoliticized common ground with many out-of-shape Hungarians.

Popular music's global migration opens up and renders problematic its twin claims of authenticity and political resistance. In particular, when hip-hop becomes a global open resource, unmoored from its Afro-American home, its effort to "keep it real" is thrown into relief as a specifically American construction. To reconstruct hip-hop's authenticity, musicians need to reinvent and insist on the naturalness of the exotic, racialized male body borrowed from African-American performances, which are themselves enhanced and manipulated by the record industry for mainstream consumption. This act of reinvention rests on problematic imperialistic assumptions and is easily exploited by or willingly collaborates with the nation-state's desire to pose as natural. The examples of rappers from Zakhut and Shimoni through Ali B, and Roma rappers Gipsy, LL Junior, Caramel, and, most co-opted and least seductive of all, Gáspár, show rather ambivalent efforts at minority empowerment in relation to the nation-state and consumer culture. To account for this ambivalence, it is not sufficient either to fall back on celebration or to cynically dismiss local manifestations of global popular music as always already co-opted. To analyze the enduring patriarchal strategies of nationalism and the nation-state, one needs to engage postcolonial and transnational feminist approaches. Such an examination should also ask whether African-American hip-hop's "authenticity" itself is conditioned on the unspoken, taken-for-granted national privilege of Americanness and thus on an oppositional binary relationship between American and "other" nationalisms.

The current European prominence of the "Roma issue" has finally brought "race" into representation in postcommunist Eastern Europe.

However, racial politics is transforming itself in the same breath into a politics of new ethnicities,[22] crossed by age, economic and cultural class, gender, and sexuality. When it comes to assessing the changing situation of Eastern European Roma, then, traditional ethnography and other social scientific methods alone are ill-equipped to take into proper consideration the social and political role of mediated fantasies and emotions. The larger aim of this chapter is to argue for the need to connect media and cultural studies and social sciences in discussing postcommunist, post–Cold War transformations of ethnicity. Any approach that sets out to "solve the Roma problem" necessarily limits itself to the perspective of modern (Eastern) European nationalisms. The perspective I adopt in this chapter is not contingent on authentic membership in one or the other kind of community. While it rejects the binary categories of postcommunist state nationalisms, it is not a "Roma" perspective, with which I cannot claim to be able to identify. It is, rather, rooted in the acknowledgment that the distinction between Roma identities and "proper" Eastern and Central European identities is the discursive and institutionalized product of Eurocentric nationalisms, contingent on the perpetual performance of its own legitimation, not the least by rejecting relational and hybrid models of identity.

At the current stage of post-Wall European transformations, it seems not only productive but also inevitable to rethink nationalisms through the lens of Romany identities that are enabled and rewarded by global entertainment media and world music, and to reflect on the coexistence of this play—often in the same actual place and representational space—with brutal discrimination against Roma populations. To what extent and in what ways the former trend can engage with and transform the latter remains the most important question to speculate about.

# 4

# Affective Nationalism and Allegorical Lesbian Media Performances

## Lesbian Play and Emasculated Nationalisms

Among the many fascinating pieces of information one finds on the Web site of Labrisz, the only registered lesbian organization in Hungary, there is a report on the sixteenth *Cineffable* Lesbian Film Festival, held each year in Paris. Two core members of the small filmmaking-activist collective who call themselves the Budapest Lesbian Film Collective had attended the 2004 festival, where they showcased their short film, *Puszta Cowboy*. Katrin Kremmler, the director of the film, shares their inspiring festival experiences in the report: She writes that they saw many good films, met numerous like-minded, creative women from all over Europe, and returned energized to initiate and transplant new kinds of collaborations with people from various countries for whom lesbian activism and filmmaking are inseparable. The report concludes with these words:

> I think we represented Labrisz/Hungary well. We feel really enthused by all the interest and encounters; we invited everyone here, and can warmly recommend *Cineffable* to all of you! At times we tend to think here that we are behind, that nothing happens in Hungary, and so on. . . . But at places like *Cineffable* one can see that this is not exactly true. People appreciate what we do and create here; they just know very little about it. We should try and organize a small, one-day lesbian festival, or "film day," to start with. They also started out small sixteen years ago! (Kremmler 2004)

There is a strange echo to the national "we" when lesbian feminists use it. It is particularly loud in postcommunist Eastern Europe. It has been well established that the "we" of nationalism implies a homosocial form of male bonding that includes women only symbolically, most prominently in the trope of the mother, the embodiment of ideal femininity (Parker et al. 1992, 6). In times of national instability, nationalist discourses are especially eager to reassert the "natural" division of labor between the sexes and relegate women to traditional, reproductive roles. The postcommunist transitions have involved the often violent realigning of national borders; shifting conceptualizations of ethnic and racial identities in the course of migration and ethnic warfare; the thorough transformation of political systems and regimes; a large-scale opening toward the global market of commerce, ideas, and images; and the staggered process of accession to the European Union. Such changes have put great pressure on the patriarchal scaffolding of nationalism, invariably resulting in a sense of the nation's "emasculation," anxieties about the "disappearance" of "real" men and women, and widespread antifeminist backlash across the region (see Graff 2005; Eisenstein 1993; Occhipinti 1996).

In Hungary—not unlike in other small posttotalitarian nation-states—the response to the embattled nation's perceived emasculation has been the defensive "normalization" of gender relations. It is a place where a leading political party proudly embraces the slogan "For a Normal Hungary." As is the case elsewhere in the region, the right-leaning moral and political coalition has been trying to rebuild the eroding narrative fortress of nationalism under the triple umbrella of "God, Nation, and Family" and pin the nation's future on the increasing production of wholesome new citizens. Besides conjuring up the fearful image of a monstrous "alien" nation overpopulated by the Roma and immigrants from undesirable places, mainstream media and the policies of the nation-state are particularly intolerant toward sexualities perceived as nonreproductive.

"If the right working of the nation is the right working of masculinity," and threats to the nation are experienced as "emasculating" (Brinker-Gabler and Smith 1997, 15), women are saddled with the extraordinary symbolic burden of reinforcing traditional ideals in such a transitional situation. The nonheterosexual woman, who cannot be forced into the binary paths of heterosexual reproduction, is thus poised to disrupt the discursive economy of nationalism. Lesbianism is still beyond the naming capacities of the Hungarian language, even more so than male homosexuality. Representations of lesbianism in national discourses have remained largely offstage in what Teresa de Lauretis describes as "socio-sexual (in)difference" (Parker et al. 1992, 7) or appropriated by mainstream porn. The majority of lesbians in Hungary are exiles, leading secret double lives likely to be tainted by self-hate (Sándor 1999).

All this makes it curious indeed that the members of the Budapest Lesbian Film Collective identify with the national "we," in which the lesbian collective Labrisz and the Hungarian nation are somehow continuous. The situation is further complicated by the fact that the two women who represented Hungary at *Cineffable* are citizens of Germany and France, respectively, speak Hungarian as a second (or third) language and consider Budapest their home of choice rather than birth. Are they naïve or ignorant as to how the nation's moral majority feels about their kind? The film they showed at the festival suggests otherwise. *Puszta Cowboy* is a parodic genre-mix, which replaces the muscular peasant boy turned national hero in the center of the Hungarian national epic on which the film is based with a transgendered protagonist, directing its mockery at the heteronormative structure of nationalism. Then, is it an elitist, idealistic transcendence of the walls of nationalism by those who possess the luxury of European mobility? This is not the case either. As I elaborate, their work testifies that these women's relationship to the Hungarian nation-state and its moral majority lacks all illusions; it is one of daily negotiation and sober resistance.

Then, how can a pair of oppositional, excluded, accented lesbian feminists embrace a "normal," phobic nation and its nationalism? As a feminist, let alone a lesbian feminist, does one not need to choose between a commitment to the flexibility of gender roles and the dubious pleasures of nationalist affiliation, a false consciousness whereby one embraces what one is structurally excluded by? Feminists around the world have been increasingly investing in developing transnational alliances to theorize and find a way around this shared dilemma. Inderpal Grewal and Caren Kaplan argue that feminists should find paradigms that can provide alternatives to nationalism, and that examine and critique the ways in which crucial terms become circulated and co-opted by national culture in the course of intercultural translations (Grewal and Kaplan 1994, 2). Transnational feminists have demonstrated a complex awareness of and engagement with the power of the nation in its diverse local manifestations (Burton et al. 2001, 23). This engagement involves both an ongoing critique of the nation and democracy as the primary categories of analysis and the recognition that these concepts may be mobilized as a means of resisting an equally or even more powerful global capital (Burton et al. 2001, 31).

However, Labrisz's and the Budapest Lesbian Film Collective's political orientation cannot simply be labeled transnationalist. Rather, their identification as lesbians who represent Hungary reveals a paradigmatic and, I believe, productive ambivalence toward nationalism and the nation-state in the work of emerging Hungarian and, by extension, Eastern

European lesbian and feminist groups. To analyze and understand this ambivalence is useful in answering increasingly crucial questions about the place of nationalism in relation to feminist, lesbian, and queer identities and theorizing insofar as those can be neatly separated at all. Is nationalism not what it seems? Can it be constructed, adopted contingently and selectively, and negotiated so that it becomes not only enjoyable for women but also transnational, cosmopolitan, and salvageable for feminism? Are feminism and nationalism somehow compatible, able to share an affective and political space within subjectivities that is not simply borne out of the poststructuralist necessity to go through the power structures that one cannot escape? How is such an ambivalence represented and made sustainable by lesbians in Eastern Europe today?

Such questions are at once specific to the emergence of lesbian representation and visual activism in Eastern Europe, processes further embedded in the context of a post–Cold War, rapidly transforming Europe, and have wider implications for imagining, doing, and rethinking the relationship between feminist theory and activism on a transnational scale. What does nationalism mean in the creative, theoretically informed activism of an international group of lesbian feminist filmmakers who are still largely unrepresentable in Hungary? And what does this paradoxical but symbiotic relationship mean for feminist, lesbian, and queer theories, which have paid little attention to the ambivalences of nationalist affiliation?

While I only have room to work through a single case study here, my intention is to describe a geographical and cultural pattern, whose complexity compels the observer to allow different strands of feminist thought to bear upon one another in the process. Particularly important for understanding the situation and aspirations of Eastern European lesbians, feminists, and lesbian feminists are poststructuralist theories of the performative aspect of gendered identity as these theories cross studies of nationalism and postcoloniality These two directions are often seen as in conflict or in a power struggle within global feminism: poststructuralist theories are seen as more relevant for the Western world, as evolving in a semiorganic manner from previous waves of Western feminist movements. Postcolonial studies of nationalism are seen as relevant mostly for Third World and other non-Western cultures, where theories of gender are secondary to the real-life issues of survival and political equality that women still face today. While such a hierarchical duality is clearly untenable in a post–Cold War, post–September 11 world, neither model can be dismissed, particularly when it comes to assessing the emergence of "Second World" feminisms. "Second World" feminisms are equally informed by both the essentialist, allegorizing force of postcolonial nationalisms—which freezes differences among and within nationalized subjects into the homogeneity of the national collective—and by the political need to conceive of identities as fluid, processual, and performative. This necessity to work out a compromise between these two models of identity plays a significant role in the ambivalence that Labrisz and other lesbian and feminist groups sustain toward the nation and nationalism.

Therefore, I begin by examining these two ways of conceiving identity with particular attention to their relevance for the patterns of feminist theory and activism that characterize postcommunist Europe. First, I situate such patterns in relation to the playful visual features that have characterized Western queer activism since the late 1980s and early 1990s. Such activism evolved in intimate connection with poststructuralist feminist theorizing centering on performativity and play closely identified with Judith Butler's enormously influential paradigm. Then, I ask what happens to lesbian representation when it is subjected to the merciless allegorization at the heart of postcolonial national historiography. I offer a comparative analysis that juxtaposes three film texts, from Argentina, India, and Hungary, respectively, which try to work out a compromise between gender performativity and national allegory in remarkably similar ways. Finally, I return to the postcommunist emergence of lesbians and lesbian discourses from the closet to examine how they necessarily draw on both models at the same time to represent themselves in transnational, performative allegories that are somehow still bound by specific nationalisms and national cultures. Homi Bhabha's account of the ambivalence between the performative and pedagogical functions of nationalism complement Teresa de Lauretis's incorporation of the concept of allegory into her gendered poststructuralist framework in attempting such a synthesis. Bhabha's model is not specific to gendered and sexualized identities, while de Lauretis's model has no specific concern with nationalism and national identities.

Ultimately, I would like to contribute to the ongoing work of rethinking lesbian representation, queer theory, and theories of visuality and gender as they cross studies of nationalism, postcoloniality, and globalization. As Judith Butler puts it, sexual difference *within* homosexuality has yet to be theorized in its complexity, as the vocabulary of describing play, crossing, and the destabilization of masculine and feminine identifications within homosexuality has only begun to emerge (1993, 240).

"The inquiry into both homosexuality and gender will need to cede the priority of both terms in the service of a more complex mapping of power that interrogates the formation of each in specified racial regimes and geopolitical spatializations" (1993, 241).

## Lesbian Play and Poststructuralist Theories

Since the late 1980s, queer theorizing and lesbian political activism have been injecting new energy into an increasingly fragmented feminist movement by mobilizing a set of concepts clustered around "play": performance, theatricality, humor, and excess. This productive convergence between queer theory and lesbian activism around concepts and practices of play and performance has been thoroughly informed by feminism's ongoing concern with the visual and the visible, particularly in psychoanalytic models of identity formation and spectatorship, which are closely tied to discussions about pleasure, pornography, and representation. As Ann Cvetkovich explains, feminist artist-activists such as Barbara Kruger and Cindy Sherman revalued popular media, fashion, and consumer culture as political resources and redefined the link between theory and activism (Cvetkovich 2001, 283–286). Following the initiative of the group ACT UP, which consciously employed style as a tool of lesbian activism, the first manifesto of the collective Lesbian Avengers identified activism as fun and drew on mainstream media tactics to make lesbian identities visible by organizing demonstrations, parties, and "Dyke Marches" in large U.S. cities (290–291). In a similar vein, visual collectives such as DAM! (Dyke Action Machine!) began to use conventions of corporate advertising during the "gay '90s" to install lesbians within the public sphere, reminding consumers that political and visual power are continuous and that activism and advertising are both grounded in the fiction of diversity and inclusion while harnessing fantasy for political goals (297).

Judith Butler suggests that it is not only unproductive but also impossible to oppose the theatrical to the political within contemporary queer politics. Performativity and play are crucial to the very process of gender constitution in her paradigm: "Gender is neither a purely psychic truth, conceived as 'internal' and 'hidden,' nor is it reducible to a surface appearance; on the contrary, its undecidability is to be traced as the play *between* psyche and appearance (where the latter domain includes what appears in *words*)" (Butler 1993, 234). Since this is a "play" regulated by heterosexist constraints, "the subject who is 'queered' into public discourse through homophobic interpellations *takes up* or *cites* that very term as the discursive basis for an opposition. This kind of citation will emerge as *theatrical* to the extent that it *mimes and renders hyperbolic* the discursive convention that it also *reverses*" (232, emphasis in original).

In an era when identities increasingly pass through processes of media entertainment, the conscious, politicized foregrounding of the play and theatricality of gender constitution appears to be an effective strategy to battle the essentialized polar opposites through which homophobia operates. Cross-dressing, drag balls, marches and parades, die-ins by ACT UP, kiss-ins by Queer Nation, and other events in which theater converges with activism produce "theatrical rage" and reiterate the injuries of homophobia "precisely through 'acting out.'" The goal is not simply to recite those injuries, but to deploy "a hyperbolic display of death and injury to overwhelm the epistemic resistance to AIDS and to the graphics of suffering, or a hyperbolic display of kissing to shatter the epistemic blindness to an increasingly graphic and public homosexuality" (Butler 1993, 233).

However, despite a shared global media culture in which images and fantasies travel at digital speed, queer and feminist studies continue to conceive of the "playful turn" in lesbian visual activism, celebrity culture, and films as specific to First World metropolitan and academic centers. Notwithstanding the occasional interpretive "queering" of postcolonial national or regional cinemas or of particular films from Third World contexts, the kinds of performativity that have bridged mainstream consumer culture and lesbian activism to create some of the most fruitful examples of feminist intervention have been understood as Western phenomena. This situation conjures up an uneven global map, with a few bright spots of ludic lesbian visibility, with the rest shrouded in oppression. While the map no doubt reflects an existing distribution of justice and liberties, to some extent it might also be the result of critical and theoretical blind spots, due to limited or unidirectional channels of intercultural distribution, exhibition, communication, and translation. In particular, it seems that the implicit hierarchy between activism (as primary, more effective, and more important) and studies of representation (as derivative, secondary, even parasitic), which has been historically important for feminism but has become ultimately problematic by the 1990s, survives on a spatial scale.[1] While B. Ruby Rich's caution that feminist work on film is moving away from its early political commitment to issues of "life" and "the combative"—that is, an analysis of and weapon against patriarchal capitalism—toward the "merely representational" (Rich 1985, 343) was entirely valid in 1979, it has by now become untenable as feminists have realized that the representational is an indispensable political tool.

When it comes to Third World or non-Western cultures, lesbian representation, as well as feminist and queer theory in general, tend to yield priority to "women's issues," which are seen as more urgent and legitimate within their oppressive national contexts: to the representation of women on a strictly political basis, presupposing the primacy of an essentialist identity politics. As a result, when lesbianism is distinguished from women's problems or, at best, feminist issues in non-Western contexts at all, its activist kind is singled out, severed from representational aesthetics and popular culture, let alone feminist theory. Such an approach does not only overlook the crucial role of the performative rather than combative creation of visibility for lesbians in these cultures but may also unwittingly collaborate with nation-states' essentialist reliance on a binary gender division.

The recent wars of Yugoslav succession reignited the conflict between feminists of a transnational orientation, who wish to construct a common ground across differences, and feminists of a radical, activist brand, whose goal it is to liberate women from patriarchal violence. Feminist narratives of rape became instrumentalized in nationalistic constructions of Serbian or Croatian ethnic identities, preventing coalitions among feminist groups who otherwise shared an antiwar stand. What Djurdja Knezevic calls "affective nationalism" of a specifically Eastern and Southern European kind energized "patriotic feminist" organizations in Croatia, among them lesbian groups such as Kareta (Knezevic 2004). These groups condemned the war but insisted on measuring and comparing on a national basis the victimhood assigned to women through rape, torture, and humiliation. They refused to communicate with antinationalist feminists in Serbia and elsewhere. The activism of Croatian patriotic feminists is an extreme expression of the ambivalence that characterizes postcommunist feminist and lesbian emergence. Importantly, it converged with the activism of Western liberal feminists who, headed by Catharine MacKinnon herself, saw the solution in giving voice and legal protection to women regarded as voiceless, passive victims (Batinic 2001).

"Performativity" implies the productive acknowledgment of one's implication in what one opposes. It is the turning of power against itself to produce alternative modalities of power in order "to establish a kind of political contestation that is not a 'pure' opposition, a 'transcendence' of contemporary relations of power, but a difficult labor of forging a future from resources inevitably impure" (Butler 1993, 241). I suggest that, to varying extents, the performativity and play of identity constitution, which lesbian representation inevitably foregrounds, may create a common ground for assessing and theorizing the geographical and cultural multiplicity of lesbian representations. In cultures and regions where lesbianism has limited or no visibility due to extreme religious or nationalistic hostility, it is not necessarily true that serious political activism and essentialist identity politics are more effective than forms of performative activism and the playful subversion of representations sanctioned by local versions of heteronormative ideology.

In a recent infamous feminist debate, Gayatri Spivak refused Martha Nussbaum's "matronizing reference" to poor rural Indian women who, according to Nussbaum, have no use for the kind of "symbolic" feminism espoused by Butler and her followers. On the contrary, Spivak writes, "gender practice in the rural poor is quite often in the performative mode, carving out power within a more general scene of pleasure in subjection" (Spivak 1999). In a similar vein, in post-Soviet Eastern Europe, lesbian theorizing and activism do not follow the evolutionary path that Western sisters have treaded since the 1970s. Rather, one can detect a kind of development where local theorists and activists pick and choose from the entire set of coexisting theoretical models developed over decades and employ performative forms of activism to bring gender and lesbianism into visibility (Györgyi 2001; Kalocsai 1998; Graff 2005).

Beáta Sándor, Hungarian lesbian activist and Labrisz's legal representative asks, "Why is it not enough for minorities to have equal rights?" Poststructuralist feminist theories constitute Sándor's starting point. Her goal is to develop a lesbian standpoint epistemology. "How is it possible to create new subject positions so that not only recognizing but also creating strategies for transforming existing institutions and practices can be a project? Feminist politics are crucial in determining which existing theories might be useful in the effort for such a change" (Sándor 1999). Her goal, shared with many Eastern European feminists, is to challenge the language of biological femaleness—to question naturalizing expressions that efface language as a site of political struggle, which are often legitimized with reference to social scientific, empirical data. Sándor explains that, as a particular effect of the belated emergence of feminism in the region, Eastern European feminists have simultaneous access to all "waves" of feminism. As a result, theoretical discourses seem to initiate, rather than follow, (pre)political organizing.

> We need theoretical discussions of the relation between language, subjectivity, social organization and power, partly to understand the primary questions why women tolerate social relations which subordinate their interests to those of men, what makes it particularly difficult for women to organize and structure their identities outside the constraints of heterosexuality, and what the mechanisms are whereby women and men adopt particular discursive positions as representative of their interests. (Sándor 1999)

In a similar vein, Romanian feminist anthropologist and activist Enikö Magyari-Vincze compares the "state" of the Romanian feminist movement to a growing island among, and influenced by, different waves of feminism that originated elsewhere but are developing into something new and as yet unpredictable (Györgyi 2001). Polish feminist academic and activist Agnieszka Graff uses a strikingly similar metaphor to describe the postcommunist development of Polish feminism. In her article "Lost Between the Waves?" she argues that Polish feminism employs the tools favored by third-wave feminism—irony, camp, play, cross-dressing, carnival, poststructuralist theory, and a concern with images and representation—to achieve goals typical of the second wave, such as reproductive rights, equal pay, and political representation. She also proposes that such a refusal of the chronology of "waves" may lead to something unfamiliar in Polish gender politics and the feminist movement in general (Graff 2005).

However, it is noticeable that all of these feminist activist-intellectuals theorize what are conspicuously similar patterns of emergence primarily with reference to their own national contexts. To me, this signals less a limitation of vision but a recognition on their part of the continuing power of the nation-state and of nationalist discourses to filter and transform globally circulating ideas and provide a shared affective ground that cannot simply be replaced by the transnational. I argue that even for cosmopolitan feminists who are critical of gendered and sexualized discourses in the national media and in the practices of national governments, the identification with nationalism remains a force that cannot be ignored. While nationalism is something to be discursively and continually performed, it also provides a culturally specific blueprint for gender identification itself. This allegorizing force of the national has been theorized in terms of a wider postcolonial pattern.

## National Allegory and Female Sexuality: *Fire; I, the Worst of All;* and *Another Way*

Fredric Jameson, in a text that launched a widespread discussion in postcolonial studies in 1986, argued for the specificity of "third world" literary (and, by extension, cinematic) texts with regard to the ratio and the relationship between the personal and the political. In an admittedly cursory comparison, he claimed that instead of the radical gap that exists in the First World between the private and the public, the poetic and the political, sexuality and the sphere of politics and economics, in Third World national cultures, the libidinal and the political are inseparably tied together—a bond that makes all Third World cultural products inevitably allegorical (Jameson 1986, 77).

Jameson's "provocation" has catalyzed a wide debate about postcolonial allegory, which has become acknowledged as "an especially charged site for the discursive manifestations of what is at heart a form of cultural struggle" in a world of postcoloniality (Slemon 1987, 11–12) and has led to explorations of similarity and exchange between "third" and "first world" allegories (Shohat and Stam 1994, 271). Since then, it has become evident not only that postcolonial allegories represent a variety of forms and purposes but also that there has been an aesthetic shift from the teleological, Marxist-inflected allegories of earlier, immediate postindependence phases of nationhood to a more self-deconstructive, postmodernist use of allegory (Shohat and Stam 1994, 271). In postindependence national cultures, allegory was initially called upon to legitimate the sacredness and unity of new nations. However, as Reda Bensmaia argues, drawing on Homi Bhabha's work, the division between the pedagogical and performative functions of allegory has become increasingly apparent in more recent postcolonial texts, which acknowledge the crisis of the hermeneutic stability of national history and national allegory. As a result, it is no longer possible to read Third World allegories as "self-righteous and predetermined discourses on good and evil, on the pure and the impure, on true and false identity, on the glorious past scorned by colonialism . . ." (Bensmaia 1999, 2).

Although Jameson is not directly concerned with issues of gender, his own notion of the "political unconscious" offers a way to deconstruct the collective, allegorical force of the national. A concept that marries Marxism and psychoanalysis, it is based on the Marxist assumption that every text is, in the last analysis, political; and the distinction between cultural texts that are social and political and those that are not is "worse than an error" (1981, 20). Jameson works from the Althusserian tenet that history is not a text, not a narrative, but an absent cause, and like the Lacanian Real, inaccessible, except in a form mediated by the political unconscious (35). Instead of "weak" interpretations, or the kind of ethical criticism that perpetuates certain moral codes without questioning them on the authority of some metaphysical thought, he proposes "strong" interpretation, or rewriting, which presupposes the political unconscious of the text and takes into account a process of mystification and repression at work (59).

This possibility is inscribed in the very paradoxical structure of allegory as a trope, genre, and interpretive method. As Jonathan Culler, Paul de Man, and other poststructuralist thinkers have argued, much like representation itself, allegory carries an inherent structural contradiction within its binary structure: it is grounded in metaphysical essentialism, something ideal and atemporal, which nevertheless unfolds in language and time through a linear progression of signification (Madsen 1996, 140–145). The post-Romantic use of allegory, which Culler and de Man theorize, calls attention to this duality and denaturalizes the illusory identification of self and Other. It reflects the demise of the interpreter's faith in the transcendental authority of any sacred book or interpretation, evoking the crisis of hermeneutic legitimation in the twentieth century (Hendershot 1995, 11). The contemporary, postmodern, and postcolonial use of allegory fully exploits this self-deconstructive quality and allows play at the heart of signification and thus of identity to reassert itself.

As Rey Chow writes, women "have all along been objectified as the very devices of representation, as the signs that bear specific moral or artistic significance in a world created by men," that is, as functions of exchange that establish relations among men (Chow 2001, 40). The more insecure a nation-state or other perceived basis for nationalist affiliation, the more forcefully gender and sexuality are called upon to justify and naturalize the hierarchical ethical divide implied in the binary structure of re-presentation, "a moral opposition between implicit notions of absence and presence, primariness and secondariness, originality and derivation, authenticity and fakeness, and so forth, that are attributed respectively to the two parts involved" (38). The allegorical tendency of nationalistic discourse continues to be a strong force within postcolonial nations, which makes many women prioritize their national identities above all other affiliations. Representations of lesbianism, however, necessarily foreground the self-deconstructive aspect of allegorization. Because of its dual character—pedagogical and performative, simultaneously lending itself to essentialist and poststructuralist conceptions of identity and nation—the concept of allegory itself can be seen as a link between postcolonial and feminist theories' concerns with binary discursive mechanisms. In both areas, allegory has been deployed to establish a connection between essentialist and poststructuralist models of identity and representation. The very concept that helps us understand important differences between First and Third or Second World representations of lesbianism also helps to emphasize the continuity among them.

This can be achieved by subjecting to a "strong reading" lesbian representations that are embedded in national allegories within postcolonial contexts. In Jameson's terms, the task is to rewrite the texts in such a way that they would be seen as restructurations of prior historical or ideological subtexts, which would then uncover their internal contradictions (Jameson 1981, 81). Teresa de Lauretis arrives at a similar conclusion. Her feminist reappropriation of de Man's poststructuralist deployment of allegory also incorporates Jameson's call for interpretive work to uncover master narratives in the text's political unconscious and resonates with the work of other feminist theorists of lesbian identity such as Diana Fuss and Judith Butler, who argue that psychoanalysis is a crucial tool for keeping the constitutive force of desire in sight (de Lauretis 1987, 110–111). However, feminist theorists committed to "queering" deconstructive and poststructuralist approaches to allegory tend to focus on films and other visual practices that have emerged side by side with or embedded in Western feminist movements and theories. Such practices are equipped with tools of radical deconstruction to carve out a theoretical and activist space for the female subject for whom conventions of looking and seeing within Hollywood cinema constitute more relevant "master narratives" than does national allegory.

Let me illustrate the kind of "strong reading" that unites Jameson's and de Lauretis's discussions of allegory with reference to three films about lesbians made in postcolonial national contexts. *Yo, lo peor de todas* ("I, the Worst of All," 1990, Argentina), a historical costume drama directed by Maria Luisa Bemberg, focuses on the figure of the legendary Mexican nun-poet Sor Juana Inés de la Cruz and her passionate relationship with the wife of the Spanish viceroy, Maria Luisa, in the context of the colonization of Mexico by Spain and the Inquisition in the seventeenth century. Indian-born Canadian Deepa Mehta's melodramatic *Fire* (1996, India/Canada) centers on the sexual and emotional bond that develops between two neglected and abused wives trapped in a traditional Hindu family in contemporary Delhi. The Hungarian film *Another Way* (1982), a historical drama made by director Károly Makk and cowritten by lesbian writer Erzsébet Galgóczi, is about a tragic affair between lesbian journalist Éva and her married female colleague Lívia, which takes place in 1958 Budapest, two years after the failed uprising against the Soviet-communist invasion.

Unlike in most Western films about lesbians, the nation looms as the center of narrative coherence in all three films. All three allegorize female homosexuality, refusing even to speak its name and effacing its representations by directing attention to larger, "universal" issues that are putting collective pressure on the nation, such as colonial oppression, religious fundamentalism, or women's equality in the public sphere. The relationships that secretly develop in the shadow of oppression are inherently tragic—symbolic of the individual's fate in hopeless collective situations. As each director insists, their lesbians are postcolonial allegories. Nevertheless, their representations of lesbian desire, however effaced, caused controversy in the films' national environments, provoking condemnation and even banning by the defensive nation-state (in the case of *Fire*) but also galvanizing lesbian activism (in the cases of *Fire* and *Another Way*).

In all three cases, however, if we subject the films to a feminist "strong reading" of desire, one can discover instances of play and performance both in the texts themselves and in their interaction with their respective contexts of reception, which undermine and transcend the strict allegorical straitjacket of national seriousness into which the lesbian representations are forced, and mobilize the performative, self-deconstructive aspect of allegory. The moments of play, humor, and irony—"homotextuality," to borrow Judith Mayne's term for lesbian disturbances in spectacle and the structure of the look (Mayne 1990, 26–27)—appear in the film texts in different disguises: as excessive symmetry of visual details, which reflects ironically on allegories of gender and nationalism; as theatrical acting and exuberant, "feminine" décor; or as a recurring thematic reference to cross-dressing, dancing, and other forms of play. As a result, in different ways, the representation of lesbianism visualizes and critiques the arbitrary foundations of the nation and its supportive fundamentalist ideologies, grounded as those are in the ostensibly neutral binary divisions inherent to representation itself. In none of these cases can the lesbian representation be contained as a teleological national allegory.

Both of *Fire*'s protagonists are married women (see figure 4.1). However, the husband whom the younger Sita is arranged to marry at the

**Figure 4.1**
The beautiful lovers of *Fire* (Deepa Mehta, 1996).

beginning of the film unabashedly prefers his Chinese lover, and the older Radha's husband is devoted to the religious guidance of a swami, who is helping him purge himself of worldly desires. The neglected women experience joy and happiness together until they are finally betrayed by a jealous manservant. In the eventual confrontation with her husband, Radha's clothes catch on fire. After her husband chooses to remove his helpless mother from the fire instead of helping Radha, she leaves the house with Sita to begin a—no doubt uncertain—life together. The film's title refers to the last, climactic event. Radha's burning sari presents an ironic, reversed performance of the myth of Sita, Lord Rama's wife, the epitome of the image of the obedient and loyal wife in Hindu mythology, who had to walk through trial by fire (*agni-pariksha*) to prove her fidelity to her husband (see Syed 2002; Kapur 1999; Katrak 1992; Panesar 1999).

While the film follows the conventions of a stifling social melodrama, which takes place almost entirely in the cramped spaces of the shared family home, its spectacle—the two gorgeous women themselves, the color and composition harmonies of the clothes and furniture, Radha's memory sequences and the manservant's elaborate, Bollywood-style sexual fantasies—subtly introduces an element of camp. Explicit instances of humor and play repeatedly puncture the seriousness of the familial and religious limits imposed on the women: In Sita's first solitary moment after she arrives in her new husband's home, she tries on a pair of men's jeans and dances in front of a mirror to a pop tune. At the height of the women's newfound happiness, they perform another dance together, this time dressed as a heterosexual couple. This queer, performative tone is further amplified by the insertion of a rather inorganic scene-within-the-scene, a visualization of the servant Mundu's narcissistic fantasy, in which his secret infatuation with Radha is reciprocated, and in which all the family members appear in various kinds of drag, performing roles assigned by Mundu's desire for power and love.

The framing look is importantly transnational, informed by the director's diasporic perspective and revealing the extent to which the oppressive religious nationalism urged by the Hindu Right, which officially banned the film's exhibition in India after its release, was already a desperate performance of authority, fighting a losing battle against the forces of globalization to secure a strictly national space purified by nationalism. This is also evident in the younger brother Jatin's transnational affair with a Chinese woman, and in the presence of the porn video outlet the brothers operate, literally on the side of their respectable family restaurant business. As Ratna Kapur argues, *Fire* needs to be located in the broader cultural wars that have been exploding across the country, setting up Indian culture in opposition to an "outsider," "the West" (Kapur 1999).

Thomas Waugh goes so far as to say the censorship battle between the film and the anxious Hindu Right, represented by the then-leading Shiv Sena Party, the self-appointed moral and cultural guardians of the nation, was itself a desperate performance of politics, a "censorship brouhaha" similar to those that surrounded other diasporic films such as *Bandit Queen* or *Kama Sutra*, inefficient in the face of a long tradition of queer representations. The attacks on such films are reminders that state censorship can hardly keep pace with, let alone contain, the proliferating sexual discourses in films such as these, much less in Bollywood and regional popular cinemas. Waugh explains that Indian cinema has traditionally been very open to same-sex desire—regardless of the fact that it has never been so named—within institutions of publicity, stardom, fan culture, and reception, as well as within narrative worlds where the borders around homosociality have been quite ambiguous. While the queer cinema scene in India is not as prominent as it is in Taiwan or the Philippines, in the past decade, the "liberalization" of the Indian economy and the transnationalization of the media have increased the cross-border importation of erotic commodities (Waugh 2001, 280–281). Deepa Mehta herself declares that she wanted to capture a society in transition, where cultural transformation is being fostered from the outside by globalization (Kapur 1999).

The Hindu Right's quest to "protect" Indian tradition from contamination is deeply grounded in local tradition. It constitutes a patriarchal and religious convergence with Gandhi's appeal to "female" virtues such as chastity, purity, self-sacrifice, and suffering, embodied by the figure of the ever-suffering, virtuous Sita (Katrak 1992, 398–399). The dimension of Hindu mythology that recognizes the spiritual in the physical also socializes women to subsume sexuality in the spiritual realm, leaving behind desire and pleasure. According to Gandhi, women could be pure and noble only if they renounced sex altogether; and they are to assume a public role only for the national cause (Katrak 1992, 401). But the historical roots of this oppressive ideal also represent points of convergence between Gandhian and nineteenth-century British colonial attitudes, both of which reinforced women's subordinate position in patriarchal family structures.[2]

*Fire*'s power to perform the heteronormativity of nationalism to itself and imagine alternative arrangements among the sexes was harnessed by lesbian activist organizations based in India, such as the Campaign for Lesbian Rights, which was instrumental in organizing broad-based protests against the Shiv Sena's attacks on the film. *Fire*, a feature film, became a key point of reference for activists, the subject of reports and discussions, in which the two senses of representation—aesthetic and political—crossed and supported each other. As part of the activist effort that developed from the defense of the film, the activists of the organization Lesbian Emergence wrote two Hindi street plays and a version of the Rajasthani folktale *Teeja-Beeja*, which narrates the story of love between two women. They also distributed leaflets and educational materials in order to debunk negative myths about and increase the visibility of lesbianism.[3]

Luisa Maria Bemberg's film *I, the Worst of All* revolves around Sor Juana Inés de la Cruz and her relationship with the vicereine of Spain, Maria Luisa. Upon their arrival in "Nueva España," the viceroy and his wife decide to "adopt" the erudite and beautiful nun. This involves providing ideological protection from the religious excesses of the misogynist archbishop, the representative of the Inquisition. Years later, when the viceroy and his wife are called back to Spain, pressures from the Inquisition and the vicereine's absence destroy Sor Juana emotionally.

At the end of the film, after being forced to renounce her books and other possessions, she dies caring for people decimated by the cholera.

The film does not speculate about whether Sor Juana is a lesbian and if so, what kind she is. Like Sita and Radha, she is rather a woman who cannot find happiness in the severely constrained roles assigned to women in a colonized society—a context that no doubt stands as an allegory of conditions created by postcolonial nationalisms in South America. In this case, the Spanish Inquisition in colonial Mexico provides a backdrop of repression and stagnation not unlike the Rosas dictatorship, the military regimes of the 1930s, or the Dirty War of the 1970s. Such a broad allegorical interpretation is reinforced by the transnational aspect of the production: Bemberg, a director from Argentina, insisted on making a film about a Mexican subject and shooting it in Mexico—a plan that eventually failed for financial and political reasons (Williams 2002, 137).

While the Indian women run away from their family prison of unhappiness perpetuated by religious fundamentalism, Sor Juana joins the convent because, as a woman of humble origin, she is forced out of the public world of intellect where she rightly perceives her place to be. In both cases, it appears that more freedom might make these women make different, perhaps heterosexual choices. There is no taken-for-granted, let alone natural, lesbian identity in either film; rather, women seem obliged to take on men's roles because men themselves cannot adequately perform them. While Radha is unable to bear children, which is seen in the film as something that contributes to her husband's religious sexual abstinence and her own openness to embracing the joy Sita has to offer, the vicereine, who sees motherhood as women's most natural and noble mission, bears a child while in Mexico after repeated miscarriages. In his discussion of the role of lesbianism in the film, Bruce Williams argues that lesbian desire is integral to the text, but is obscured or tamed by the film's ostensible aim to depict women seeking to assert their autonomy at key moments of an oppressive national history and by Bemberg's own comments, which open up the film's significance to a universal, atemporal rejection of repression, fanaticism, and fundamentalism, downplaying lesbianism as friendship (Williams 2002, 139).

But the gendered colonial dynamic is subversively performed and allegorized within the relationship of the two women themselves. Sor Juana is visually and verbally identified in their interaction as an allegory of Mexico, while the vicereine is symbolic of Spain. Their communication is determined by colonial dominance and submission, which, however, is performed by the wrong subjects. During the vicereine's last visit to the convent, she asks Juana to remove her veil—an act that compels a joint postcolonial and queer reading of drag. She insists on seeing the "real" Juana under the habit. When Juana resists, the vicereine employs her colonial authority and "commands" her to expose herself to her dominant gaze. But this familiar dialectic of domination-submission is wrested from its colonial moorings in the course of its all-female performance and yields the most intimate and erotic moment of the film, the first and only kiss between the two women. "This Juana is mine. Only mine," the vicereine declares, to Juana's silent ecstasy (see figure 4.2). Shortly thereafter, when the viceroy is dismissed from his post as colonial administrator, he visits the convent to say good-bye to Juana

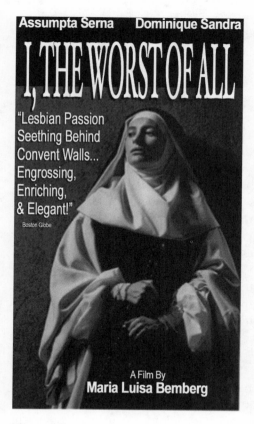

**Figure 4.2**
The poster from *I, the Worst of All* titillates viewers with the forbidden spectacle of "Lesbian passion seething behind convent walls" (Maria Luisa Bemberg, 1990).

on his wife's behalf. As he and Juana sit across the bars that separate her from visitors, he explains that returning to Spain is very painful for his wife because "she fell in love with Mexico." "And Mexico will miss her," Juana responds, devastated. "It will sink into a lake."

The gendered binary scaffolding of colonial desire crumbles when women on the two sides of the colonial divide use the very allegorical language that renders them tools of symbolic traffic among men and assert their own desire for each other as active agents. Such binary divisions are turned theatrical, performative in several other subtle ways. The first encounter among Sor Juana, the viceroy, and the vicereine takes place in the convent after the first of several performances of Juana's plays. Amid the applause, the viceroy turns to his wife: "How does her poem go, the one that makes fun of men?" The vicereine begins reciting, while Juana approaches unnoticed, adding the last lines of the poem. "I was eager to meet you," the vicereine greets her. "There must be few cultured women in Mexico." "Or elsewhere, madam," Juana reverses her inadvertent condescension. "Shall we adopt her, Maria Luisa?," the viceroy joins the erotically charged conversation, turning it into a love triangle, in which it is the women who use the man in the middle to flirt with each other. The desire between the women turns each utterance into a performance queered away from its proper function: the viceroy proves his worldly sophistication by citing a poem that makes fun of men, written by a nun; the first exchange between the colonizer woman and the colonized female subject is wrapped in flirtation, which makes the viceroy's allusion to the colonial subject's need to be saved and protected by the colonizer carnivalesque. No wonder the outraged archbishop whispers to a priest upon witnessing all this, "This is not a convent, this is a bordello."

Indeed, the archbishop's narrative function is to make visible and attempt to reestablish the "proper" allegorical workings of gender constitution, religion, and colonization. He is in the business of dividing and separating, of rendering distinct and discrete. The first thing he demands of the nuns during their introductory meeting is that they veil themselves. He wants more "discretion" in the convent and battles "laxity" on every front, including the regulation of Sor Juana's desires and creative output. In an initiative that requires "utmost discretion," he creates a rift among the nuns by bribing some of them with additional internal power in exchange for enforcing his rules. "Secrecy is the key to the Church's ascendancy," he utters in justification of the surveillance and control mechanisms he installs.

However, in this historical costume drama, "historical" and "costume" push against each other as forcefully they do in *Orlando* and other feminist reappropriations of the genre. The setting and mise-en-scène are allegorical, stylized, abstract, and often ahistorical. The tone of theatricality is set in the very first scene, introduced by the intertitle "Mexico, 17th century/Méjico, Siglo XVII." The brightly lit composition in the foreground, placed in front of a stationary camera against a completely dark background, is perfectly symmetrical. A long table divides the frame horizontally, on which stand two straight, tall glasses. A stagelike rectangular structure in the background creates additional parallel horizontal lines, while tall candleholders add vertical ones. The bars of the dim window on the back wall repeat the crossing lines and introduce the motif of prison bars, which divide and connect, both literally and figuratively, colonial subjects, sexes, and genders throughout the film. Two hands reach into the artificially lit center of the frame from left and right in synchronized movement and remove the glasses. A cut to a longer shot reveals the new viceroy and archbishop of "New Spain" sitting at the table facing each other and foreshadows the power struggle that develops between them. Two allegorical figures, they identify themselves as the representatives of state and church authority, "Caesar and God," respectively.

Their struggle is for the right kind of colonization, fought over the bodies and souls of the colonized. As the archbishop puts it, "Our responsibility, yours and mine, sire, is to save this new Spain, this innocent people, which Heaven sent to us." Their ensuing sparse, evenly paced dialogue outlines their ideological differences about how to perform the task. The chiaroscuro lighting, the symmetrical structure of the setting, and the rhythmical lifting of the glasses that accompany the measured dialogue provide a dialectical pattern, which is repeated at all levels of the film. It boils over only in the final confrontation between the two of them toward the end of the film, when they openly clash in an argument to decide under whose "jurisdiction" or "protection" Sor Juana's poetry and desires fall, which consistently subvert the gendered economy of colonization.

Cross-dressing, once again, is represented as a manifestation of this subversion: The vicereine does not only unveil but also dresses Juana, giving her a spectacular headdress made out of the plumes of the quetzal, the "Mexican bird," which Juana puts on immediately, accompanied by a playful curtsy that carries out and simultaneously undermines her performance as a colonized love object. Another instance of cross-dressing takes place in Juana's imagination as she sits by the bedside of her dying mother, realizing that her aversion to marriage and other forms of proper femininity had caused a never-healing rift between the two of them. She then sees herself as a young girl, dressed in male drag to be able to go to university but facing her mother's derision and rejection. Juana's memory-double playfully whispers to her: "Since I couldn't dress as a man, I dressed as a nun."

The Hungarian *Another Way*, the only film made in the Soviet-controlled region during communism that openly depicts lesbianism, is similar to *Fire* and *I, the Worst of All* in that the film's own discursive strategies, the creators themselves, and the critical community all converged in interpreting the lesbian protagonists as mere allegories of larger national and universal issues. Felice Newman, one of the English translators of the novel *Törvényen belül* (1980) ("Within the Law," English title *Another Love,* 1991) from which novelist Erzsébet Galgóczi and director Károly Makk developed the film, writes: "In how many novels written in the 'free' and 'liberated' West does a lesbian character represent the soul of the nation? . . . In Galgóczi's view, Hungary is a nation caught in an Orwellian squeeze. And Éva is Hungary's national spirit. *Another Love* is Erzsébet Galgóczi's State of the Union address, and she has chosen a fiercely independent (albeit emotionally battered) lesbian to carry the message. . . . Such guts, Galgóczi!" (Newman 1991, 17).

The misunderstanding here is profound. No Eastern European writer can "choose" a lesbian character within cultures where there is no such thing as a lesbian. Galgóczi, who was a closeted lesbian until the untimely end of her troubled life, struck out in this one novel to bring her own unrepresentable subjectivity into representation. But the only way she could do so was by pulling the smoke screen of national allegory in front of the highly autobiographical story of the tragic lesbian.

This strategy worked for the film version, too. At the 1982 Cannes Festival, Polish actress Jadwiga Jankowska-Cieslak, who played the role of Éva—in the absence of Hungarian actresses who would have taken on such a role—won the award for best actress. The film received the FIPRESCI Award "for its clarity," for the "originality of its libertarian message," and for its struggle for "individual freedom." European reviews praised it for the "extraordinary richness with which Makk and Galgóczi linked two disparate themes: the human right to another kind of love, namely lesbian love, and the search for political freedom" (Zsugán 1982, 16). American film critics and academics have been just as uncritically thrilled, ignoring the contradiction that a lesbian should allegorically stand for the cause of the nation, in whose official discourses lesbianism is inconceivable.[4]

What makes this contradiction possible to miss is precisely that the film's aesthetic successfully sublimates the lesbian theme in the realm of political allegory and suppresses a potentially lesbian look. Éva is the only "real" lesbian in the three films—still without a name, but with a certain harassed lesbian self-awareness. "She is that way," declares a male character in the film, indicating that her sexuality does not fall within the normative categories of language. She "suffers from two perversions," as the director puts it in an interview: she "loves her own sex," and is "unable to lie" (Szilágyi 1982, 12). Her sexual "perversion" is never directly identified in the film, yet the circumscriptions, empty pronouns, and pronominal adjectives that refer to lesbianism point to a collective understanding of the secret (Moss 1995, 245). This "understanding" crystallizes in the stereotype of the male-identified and mannish lesbian, who cannot resist the seductions of traditional femininity and competes with men for women.

Tragic lesbian love is a feasible allegory for signifying the failure of heroism in the face of complicity and oppression because Éva, an Eastern European lesbian, is constructed as an anomaly, an aberration, a contradiction in terms, as someone not viable other than a trope from the start. Shortly after she begins her job on the staff of the Budapest daily *Igazság* (*Truth*) as a reporter in 1958, she falls in love with a married colleague, Lívia, a markedly feminine blonde (Polish actress Grazyna Szapolowska). Lívia, much like Radha in *Fire*, seeks an outlet from her eventless and emotionally deprived life at the side of her military officer husband and finds it in the new erotic energy that Éva radiates. After several dates and much emotional agony, she yields to the sexual temptation. Following their single sexual encounter, however, everything comes crashing down on the lovers: Lívia's jealous husband shoots his wife so that she becomes wheelchair-bound and bitter toward Éva, a living memorial of regret and just punishment, whose greatest fear is that nobody will want to impregnate her. Éva, whose reporting about communist atrocities has made her situation simultaneously impossible at the newspaper, gives in to despair. The scene that opens and closes the film (whose plot is told in retrospective narration) finds her at the Austro-Hungarian border, hinting at the possibility that she may have intended to emigrate illegally. But she does not hide from the border guards when they try to stop her, and is shot dead.

Unlike in *Fire* or even in *I, the Worst of All*, the camera refuses to eroticize contact between the women, including the sex scene, and medicalizes the crippled, naked, infertile body of Lívia in the narrative introduction, which warns us of the consequence of "perversion" before the story begins. The film starts out with Éva's removal from the plot and ends the same way, teaching a lesson to those (like Lívia) who diverge from the correct path of livable choices. A sigh of relief accompanies Éva's exit, as she is not a point of identification to begin with. She is useful only to the extent that her sacrifice can posthumously be converted into political capital. At the same time, comrade Erdös, the editor-in-chief who had supported her all along, emerges as a feasible ethical alternative to Éva's radicalism in the film: a hero of survival and quiet resistance.

## The Budapest Lesbian Film Collective

Despite Makk's and Galgóczi's efforts to allegorize lesbianism, the pressure put on national allegory's apparently self-contained referential system by the representation of lesbian desire released allegory's ghostly, inherently self-reflective side. Although the performative dimension in *Another Way* that lesbianism opens up within national allegory is not as explicit as it is in *Fire* and *I, the Worst of All*, a retrospective, collective "strong reading" has highlighted the ways in which Éva's refusal to choose between available feminine and masculine identities makes national allegory unravel. Both the novel and the film have proven to be crucial identificatory resources for Hungarian lesbians, who have gradually appeared from the closet since the official end of communism. Éva Szalánczki's plight has become perhaps the most important historical and discursive record of lesbian visibility, on which lesbian activists have drawn to construct their own very different kind of emergence into postcommunist representation.[5]

The first postcommunist novel written about lesbianism, *Kecskerúzs*, or *Goat Lipstick* (Magvető, 1997, Budapest), by a lesbian writer who uses the pseudonym Agáta Gordon, engages in conversation with its single predecessor to stake out a different kind of lesbian subjectivity "within" but also "outside" the law, one no longer constituted in isolation. There is a conscious effort in *Goat Lipstick* to create a literary tradition, a "minor literature" of sorts in the Deleuzian sense, which deterritorializes language, connects the individual to political immediacy, and produces a collective assemblage of enunciation, turning a most personal story political (Sándor 1999). But this kind of allegorization is deployed for the purposes of lesbian identification, resisting allegorical incorporation by the national body.

The continuities between the two novels, landmarks in the constitution of a lesbian community, are numerous and intentional, going far beyond the overt references in *Goat Lipstick* to passages in Galgóczi's novel. Both texts are caught in the ambivalence between capitulation to and a critique of nationalistic ideologies of gender and sexuality. But Galgóczi's tragic, isolated lesbian commits suicide—importantly, on the border of the nation, by border guards' guns. Gordon's protagonist, even though she sinks into paranoia and depression and ends up in the psychiatric institution where she writes her autobiographical text, nevertheless belongs to a secret collectivity and is able to inhabit a lesbian space built from a collection of found images and texts. Where Galgóczi's lesbians inevitably and tragically come up against absolute borders and binaries determined by the allegorizing logic of nationalism, Gordon's heroines hide among texts, quotations, and images that represent these borders as malleable. Even more important, Gordon's lesbians take pleasure in this textual hiding. "Hiding, the incorporation of a role and the incorporation of a self is almost luxurious in this novel, an enjoyed and excessive game" (Sándor 1999).

The difference between these two texts of Hungarian lesbian-feminist becoming can be captured with reference to Teresa de Lauretis's distinction between "films that represent 'lesbians' " and "films that represent the problem of representation" (1991, 224). While, to me, these categories are in continuity rather than in neat separation, it is much more true of *Goat Lipstick* than of *Another Love* that it proposes lesbianism as "*a question of representation*, of what can be seen." In Gordon's novel, lesbianism is "not merely a theme or a subtext of the film, nor simply a content to be represented or 'portrayed' "—as it certainly is in *Another Love* and the film *Another Way*—"but is the very problem of its form: how to represent a female, lesbian desire that is neither masculine, a usurpation of male heterosexual desire, nor a feminine narcissistic identification with the other woman" (de Lauretis 1990, 22).

*Goat Lipstick* is a paradigmatic text of postcommunist lesbian feminist emergence in that it both identifies with the earlier text and transforms it in the course of a collective, critical process of postcommunist reinterpretation. While *Another Love* was swallowed up almost completely by the heteronormative categories of the national and silenced after the end of communism, Gordon and her interpretive community take a critical, poststructuralist stand toward the same categories. Éva Szalánczki identifies as her role model the rebellious spirit of Sándor Petöfi, a revered Romantic male poet and patriotic revolutionary. Éva's search for what she calls lesbian "nature" was bound to fail within the patriotic parameters imposed by the search itself. Gordon, by contrast, foregrounds the way her heroine constructs lesbian subjectivity as a patchwork of allegories of reading (Balogh 2002). While Éva's story is retrospectively constructed in a realistic manner by a fascinated male police officer, the embodiment of state power, in Gordon's text the hiding protagonist's self-fashioning is communicated in a fragmented way through found poetry and punctuation-free, floating sentences without clear boundaries, evoking a "playfully dislocated, placeless subject" (Sándor 1999). Beáta Sándor characterizes this discursive, repetitive self-creation as playful, rendering borders and limits much less permanent than they are in Galgóczi's novel and Makk's film. Even being "in" and "out" are just subtle distinctions. "Small signs gain their meaning gradually and playfully, and through spatialized performances: they make a certain sense in one space and at a certain time and are without 'meaning' at another." Even the body of the lesbian is malleable, androgynous, metaphorically mixing with animals such as centaurs and goats. This self-creation corresponds to the poststructuralist notion of the subject as something precarious, formed in a process of repetitive contradiction, "irreducible to the humanist essence of subjectivity" that characterizes the male subject of modernism (Sándor 1999). Gordon, like Butler, leaves the sign "lesbian" permanently unclear.

The work of the Budapest Lesbian Film Collective, who represent the vanguard of feminist theorizing and activism in Hungary, further exhibits and crystallizes the ambivalence toward nationalism that characterizes Gordon's text. On the one hand, their films and activism maintain a critical distance from the homophobic institutions and practices of the nation-state and media discourses, which tend to portray lesbians as exotic animals reduced to their "queer" sexuality and eroticize "lesbian" sex in heterosexual porn.[6] There is also obvious enjoyment in hiding, in the intimate transgressions and subversions of the boundaries of what being bound by a nation-state and national language allows. On the other hand, there is a marked effort to construct lesbian representability that is by definition Hungarian or wishing to be established as part of a national cultural tradition. The latter is manifest in gestures small and large, from adopting the national "we" in the festival report with which

I begin this chapter through Gordon's effort to assert a retroactive historical continuity with her only predecessor, which feeds into collective work to create a decidedly Hungarian lesbian national mythology and way of communication.

Both attitudes are evident in the documentary made by the collective subsequent to *Goat Lipstick*'s publication, *Pilgrimage to the Land of Goat Lipstick* (2005). The video documentary follows a group of women, including Agáta Gordon herself, as they revisit the places and events of the novel. It goes back and forth between events of the day, including a bus ride from Budapest and a hike up to the cottage that saw the secret beginning of a lesbian community, and events of the night, as the group sits around the fire and Agáta and her former lover, the two main protagonists of the novel, take turns recollecting how lesbians from Budapest gradually and secretly inhabited the area. The storytelling is pleasurable and witty, interrupted by frequent and intimate laughs, conjuring up lesbian identities in a discursive process that refers not only to the actual events but also to their mythical and lyrical legitimation in Gordon's book, from which the film's intertitles quote to introduce new sections. Lesbian storytelling functions as a complex game of recognition, in which participants employ the mainstream national community's fear of naming lesbianism and turn it into a pleasurable hide and seek: the first couple "lived here in a way that no one knew about them and still no one does," as Gordon begins the tale.

At the same time, as the story around the campfire unfolds, the observer also becomes aware that an indispensable source of the intimacy and recognizability within this lesbian community is their shared attachment to a particular cultural and historical register of Hungarianness. Blind dates recognize each other by the literature they read, the music they listen to, and the Budapest museums and bookstores they frequent—the very emblems of culture from which Hungarian nationalism forges its immanence, eternity, and superiority. In other words, the critical distance from nation and nationalism, which often manifests itself in subversive transgressions and eroticized prohibitions, coexists with a desire to be seen, to be placed within, a specific national history and culture.

This ambivalence toward national culture can be better understood in terms of Homi Bhabha's account of the ambivalence of the nation as a narrative strategy, manifest in the divide between the performative and pedagogical functions of nationalism. He explains, "In the production of the nation as narration there is a split between the continuist, accumulative temporality of the pedagogical, and the repetitious,

recursive strategy of the performative. It is through this process of split-
ting that the conceptual ambivalence of modern society becomes the site
of *writing the nation*" (Bhabha 1994, 145). Rather than the homogeneous and horizontal view proposed by nationalist historiography, whose
reference point is an unchanging "people," the "people" is a complex
rhetorical strategy of social reference repetitively produced and confirmed within a set of discourses.

> We then have a contested conceptual territory where the nation's people must
> be thought in double-time; the people are the historical "objects" of a nationalist
> pedagogy, giving the discourse an authority that is based on the pre-given or
> constituted historical origin *in the past*; the people are also the "subjects" of a
> process of signification that must erase any prior or originary presence of the
> nation-people to demonstrate the prodigious, living principles of the people as
> contemporaneity: as a sign of the *present* through which national life is redeemed
> and iterated as a reproductive process. (Bhabha 1994, 145)

The paradox of the dual time of nationalism, the split between the
pedagogical mission that attempts repetitively to reinscribe and perform
what it represents as horizontal, homogeneous, and unchanging, "surmounting" the traces of such continual construction, has an explicit
gendered reference. Anne McClintock captures this reference in her own
description of the temporal contradiction of nationalism between a
frozen past and a dynamic future, which is resolved through the idea of
the hierarchical racial family of nations, on the one hand, and through
a gendered distribution of time within nationalism, on the other
(McClintock 1995). The paradox also recalls, once again, Butler's poststructuralist idea of the reiterative construction of gender. Furthermore,
as I discuss earlier, it is inherent in the very notion of Jameson's "national
allegory," as postcolonial critics such as Reda Bensmaia point out, precisely with reference to Bhabha's work (Bensmaia 1999).

*Pilgrimage*'s mythical, semireligious travel to and repetitive resettling
of the "land" discursively identified in the novel *Goat Lipstick* performs
and foregrounds the very process Bhabha describes, whereby the nation's
people are continually re-created in a process of "dissemination" rather
than originated as such at a specific point in time. The "people" who
are being created in the film are united precisely in a critical consciousness of heterosexual norms and assumptions, and in an intentional effort
to conjure up a retrospective tradition that begins with *Another Love*
and *Another Way* and continues with *Goat Lipstick* and *Pilgrimage*,
which retells the already fictionalized events to add another layer of
reiterative performance.

**Figure 4.3**
Still from *Puszta Cowboy* (Budapest Lesbian Film Collective, 2004).

*Puszta Cowboy* (see figure 4.3), a parodic short made by the Budapest Lesbian Film Collective and presented at the 2004 *Cineffable* in Paris, offers another way in which nationalism is revealed to be a patchwork of the "arbitrary signs and symbols that signify the affective life of the national culture," as Ernest Gellner defines it (Bhabha 1994, 142). While nationalism is in no way contingent or accidental, Gellner argues, it is made up of cultural shreds and patches that are often arbitrary historical inventions (Bhabha 1994, 142). *Puszta Cowboy* opens by citing one such precious cultural shred, the epic poem *Miklós Toldi* written by eminent Hungarian Romantic poet János Arany (legendary friend of Sándor Petőfi, Éva Szalánczki's role model) in 1846. The poem itself recasts the adventures of folk hero Miklós Toldi to create an inspiring allegorical narrative and enduring role model for the nation seen as in perpetual need of defense from more powerful enemies. In the poem, Toldi, a peasant boy of extraordinary strength and impeccable moral fortitude, rises from his humble surroundings on the Hungarian plains (the "puszta") to become one of the king's most loyal soldiers in the fight against foreign intruders. The poem has become a part of the national literary pantheon, recognizable and memorized by every Hungarian schoolchild. It also lent itself well to the communist state's folk mythology, which was instrumental in the nation-state's pedagogical mission to create a unified "people."

In *Puszta Cowboy*, a voice-over recites the memorable beginning stanza that describes the lonesome but powerful figure of Toldi standing tall in the hot, dry landscape. However, what we actually see is a transgendered Toldi on horseback, wearing a cowboy outfit, in a land-scape identified as the Wild West. The poem is immediately thrown outside the "continuist, accumulative temporality" of the pedagogical (Bhabha 1994, 145). After the initial gesture to *Toldi*, the film deviates from the poem and employs the generic markers of the Western to tell the story of the hero's quest for his lover, who had been kidnapped by her former lover. After an Indian leads Cowboy Toldi to his adver-sary's hideout, a shootout occurs, represented as alternating shots of the actual actors and shadow cartoon figures, which further reduces the Western to core allegorical elements of recognizability and simultane-ously renders Toldi's narrative a didactic allegorical tool. All the roles, which in actual Westerns act as codes that glue together the gendering, racializing, and nationalizing of the spectating subject in a seamless process, are played by lesbians, members of the Lesbian Film Collective (see figure 4.4).

What we end up with is a deliciously disorienting carnival with mul-tiple crossings: those of genres, national cultural traditions, cinematic conventions, as well as gendered and sexualized roles. By projecting the Western's desert scenery onto the backdrop of the Hungarian Puszta and the cowboy, the problematically sexualized embodiment of American manliness onto the mythical embodiment of Hungarian heroism, the film reverses the process whereby "the scraps, patches and rags of daily life [are] repeatedly turned into the signs of a coherent national culture, while the very act of the narrative performance interpellates a growing circle of national subjects" (Bhabha 1994, 145). The rags and patches of the

**Figure 4.4**
The duel in *Puszta Cowboy* (Budapest Lesbian Film Collective, 2004).

cultural fabric are revealed to be substitutable—by those of other nationalisms, as well as by those taken from global popular culture. The transgendered American cowboy/Hungarian folk hero thus becomes the double, the figure of the nation's repressed, who emerges from nationalism's effort to maintain the illusion of the nation's eternal present through "a consistent process of surmounting the ghostly time of repetition" (Bhabha 1994, 145).

The filmmakers thus foreground how nationalism as a narrative strategy repetitively re-creates its "people" in a continual performance of narrative coherence, to translate Bhabha's theory of nationalism into de Lauretis's gendered terms. At the same time, members of the filmmaking group and of the mother organization Labrisz spend much of their energy engaging in the kind of "pedagogical" mission that characterized the goals of the second feminist wave in the West. Their work for the recognition of domestic partnership or a fair antidiscrimination law that recognizes sexual minorities necessarily seeks visibility within the parameters of the nation-state and the European Union, employing the nation's own strategies of regulation and containment.

One of Labrisz's most controversial pedagogical projects in this regard is the program Queer Identities and Knowledge, supported by the European Union's Phare Democracy Project. The idea was to bring information about homosexuality and actual lesbian, gay, transgendered, and bisexual (LGTB) people into the very fortress of the nation's pedagogical effort, the institution of education. To this end, Labrisz sent out a letter to all high schools in Hungary, offering to organize and moderate conversations with groups of students around issues such as the hidden history of LGTB people in human societies, the reasons why such people remain invisible, the concepts of homophobia and discrimination, and ways in which students themselves can battle prejudice. A textbook edited by the Labrisz collective, *Not Taboo Any More* (2002), accompanies the educational initiative and discusses these questions in greater detail. A subsequent phase of the initiative is planned to introduce the program into teacher training.

*Pilgrimage* and *Puszta Cowboy* pose lesbianism as the very problem of representation, as an identity that is impossible to conceive of unless one is able and willing to rethink engrained notions about the absolute boundaries of subjectivity, gender, and nation. The Queer Identities and Knowledge project implies that lesbian, gay, bi, and trans differences can be captured, named, and accommodated in the pedagogical language of nationalism and the nation-state. It is fueled by a desire to be an organic, positive part of a high cultural, national heritage, to have a voice within the institutions of the state. In this regard, the program continues a project that began with the first film made by the collective, *Mihez kezdjen egy fiatal leszbikus a nagyvárosban?* ("*What Should a Young Lesbian Do in the City?*" [2000]), a film its makers consider "infotainment," the creation of lesbian representations that are likable and truthful, providing a safe mirror of identification for lesbians.

Unlike their first film, however, Queer Identities and Knowledge actively and directly reached out to the heterosexual mainstream. It turned out to underestimate the depth of homophobia: Labrisz's letter to schools received hateful rejection at worst and indifferent silence at best. They were able to hold conversations in only seven schools. Hate mail, parliamentary speeches, and media announcements by educators and politicians across the political spectrum emphasized the nation's commitment to the "normal" upbringing of a "normal" generation and expressed outrage at Labrisz's "veiled recruiting mission" to spread "deviance." As a parliamentary representative put it, this was similar to a pimp's promoting sex tourism. The news media unanimously questioned the "expertise" of the gays and lesbians involved with the project (most of whom are teachers, psychologists, social scientists, and college students) at addressing students. Mainstream psychological experts recommended on national television that high schoolers who feel "different" should turn to real, medical experts, who can cure them of their sickness (Seres 2001).

Labrisz members' faith in the potential success of such a program is another manifestation of their ambivalence toward nationalism, which amounts to a regional pattern for postcommunist feminist and lesbian groups: a radical awareness of the impossibility of representing lesbian difference within nationalist discourse, and a radical assumption of belonging and representability by virtue of sharing the language and culture that binds "the people" together in a more affective and powerful fashion than is the case in Western nations. A sympathetic analysis assesses the success of Labrisz's school program:

This is a rare sociological moment: it has managed to reach the widest social consensus, that based on homophobia. According to the shared knowledge of Hungarian society, homosexuality spreads by conversion and automatic model-following; high school students are especially likely to get it. And, given that it's a disease, it has to be cured by experts. Gay people are responsible for the dissolution of families, the high rate of divorce and alcoholism, for sexual harassment at the workplace, and for domestic violence against women and children. Gay people are to be blamed for the underproduction of Hungarians; and lesbians are especially suspicious since they are all feminists. (Seres 2001, translation mine)

Even in the face of such intense public rejection, the desire to carve out a history of presence within national culture is as crucial for Labrisz and the Film Collective as is the desire to connect with lesbians and feminist discourses beyond the borders. Their "transnational" orientation has inspired the collective to adopt feminist "third-wave" models of carnival and a playful, camp aesthetics of activism, both in the form of live events (e.g., in the annual Gay Pride parade and LGTB film festival, drag balls, and parties) and through the media (e.g., a strong Web presence and a lesbian radio show). They have also translated, disseminated, and adapted queer and poststructuralist feminist theories in the past decade.[7]

*Eklektika Dance Club*, a 2003 documentary made by the Film Collective, registers the creation and success of a queer dance club located in Budapest's Café Eklektika. While same-sex dancing initially offered the safety of role-playing and performance to gay and lesbian couples otherwise reluctant to come out in public, some of them have recently gone on to win international gay games competitions. Similar to *Pilgrimage*'s, the film's narration jumps back and forth in time, between scenes of painting and remodeling, as workers prepare the building for dancing lessons, and scenes of the first clumsy baby steps on the floor intercut with interviews with the dancers and glamorous vignettes from international gay games competitions. A true identity game unfolds along with the increasingly confident dance moves. As a participant comments, dancing liberates and sustains queer identities because one does not have to think of oneself in terms of categories such as "man" and "woman." Another adds, "Queer dancing is very much in line with the [poststructuralist] feminist approach in that if you reach a certain skill level, you can swap roles."

Staking out identities within and across national borders through a playful and performative aesthetic reaches its epitome in the group's most recent, forty-five-minute documentary about an international drag king workshop organized in Budapest. Narrator-codirector-participant "Dédé" introduces and comments on the events. Two German drag king workshop coordinators from Berlin were invited to transform a group of Hungarian and other European lesbians temporarily into heterosexual men—a fascinating experiment that is supposed to provide one with an embodied experience of the workings of gender. An important lesson

**Figure 4.5**
The makers of *Bandage, Socks and Facial Hair* (Maria Takacs, 2006). (Courtesy
of the Budapest Lesbian Film Collective)

transpires in the course of the day as the women learn how to appropriate space, talk, and eat like men, decking themselves out with facial hair,
men's clothing, and a sock in a strategic position to lend them more
authentic manpower (see figure 4.5). There are many different kinds of
"being men," and these ways of being men translate into certain national
stereotypes: a German woman dons a black turtleneck and black-rimmed
glasses to become a type of German intellectual. A woman from Bulgaria
becomes a long-haired Latin heartthrob in a flowing, flower-patterned
shirt. One Hungarian participant chooses to be a road robber, a mythical
folk hero from the national past. Dédé herself identifies her male persona
as an "intellectual."

What is striking about Dédé's performance of the "intellectual" in
particular is that her appearance changes very little in the transformation. The ease with which her body shifts from lesbian to a type of,
supposedly straight, man provides an important clue to the questions
of how and why Eastern European lesbian-feminists can sustain such a
marked ambivalence toward nationalism. The intellectual performed by
the "kinging" Hungarian lesbian brings together a particular register of
Hungarian culture and the most playful, theoretically informed register
of transnational queer culture. An essay in the recent *Drag King Anthology* assesses "kinging":

As dykes, our choice to king it up and create arenas for drag king culture is a political, liberatory move with deep resonances for shaking up outdated, oppressive gender systems and sexual codes, as well as our own potential for power. Queers and trannies do more than survive (and live) at the margins of society; through the exaggerations, perversions, and transmutations we create, we push human behavior to a futuristic edge. Drag kinging produces new erotics, new genders, and new forms and modes of power. (Bradford 2003)

Dédé is able to inhabit the "intellectual," a type that is at once a signifier and referent of national allegory as well as a recognizable emblem of masculinity across the Eastern European region, because, as I elaborate in chapter 5, the "intellectual" stands for an inherently androgynous type of masculinity, whose boundaries of performance are already rather fluid.

## The National Artist as a Queer Character

As a fitting instance of the confusions that characterize the shifting gender relations of postcommunist culture, the Hungarian, by definition male, critical establishment was paralyzed by Agáta Gordon's *Goat Lipstick*. It is a novel that not only represents lesbian relations thematically but also self-reflectively allegorizes the text's lesbianism as a narrative strategy and thereby exposes the gender prejudice of the supposedly neutral and absolute aesthetic criteria that establish the national canon. Trying to find a way to assess the novel within the categories of "national literature," one critic came up with a possible solution: the pseudonym "Agáta Gordon" may hide a male author (Györffy 1997). In this case, the novel can be dismissed as aesthetically reproachable because it elides erotically charged representations of sexual acts between women. "Paradoxically, the pornographic depiction of lesbian relations would guarantee the literary value of Gordon's novel within the boundaries of official literary criticism" (Balogh 2002, my translation).

Within the tenuous gender relations of cultural nationalism lies one likely answer to the question I raise at the beginning of this chapter. The ambivalence that characterizes the work of lesbian activist-artists in particular and emerging Eastern European feminist groups in general should be interpreted in relation to the ambivalence inherent in postcolonial Eastern European nationalisms. On the one hand, these nations submit themselves to a voluntary colonization, performing Europeanness according to the logic of "almost but not quite" in the sphere of imagination and culture, rather than in those of economy or politics. The performative aspect of these nationalisms is thus always more apparent, always likely to be taken up by subversion, than is the case with nations whose nationalisms are better established in the pedagogical languages of economic and political "progress." The affective relations that provide the glue of nationalism are grounded in the discursive, tenuous stuff of poetry and other arts, unlike the pride that many Americans may feel about their government's military and economic power or that English or Dutch people may feel about their countries' past glory and democratic institutions. The shifting, tenuous ground of nationalism is reflected upon and performed in a wide range of masculine performances, which even leave some room for identification and allow for continuity with masculine intellectual roles performed by lesbians. Lesbians, who are otherwise unrepresentable in terms of binary gender roles, inhabit the porous, liminal borders between masculinity and femininity opened up by artistic masculinities, which even incorporate male homosexuality and traditional femininity in postmodern Hungarian culture.

At the same time, precisely because the narrative boundaries of nationalism are permeable, the institutions of the nation-state—education, the media, the legislation, the legal system, health care, and so on—are compelled to reinforce the pedagogical mission of nationalism in excessively rigid ways. While lesbians are able to carve out small spaces of representability in national literature and culture along the borders of binary gender roles, they find themselves facing walls of exclusion when they demand nonprejudiced political representation in the areas of domestic partnership or marriage rights, adoption, legal age of consent, antidiscrimination laws mandated by the European Union, employment, and education.

Furthermore, because of the inherent "universality" of Hungarian and other Eastern European "poetic" nationalisms, based on imagining a shared European heritage, lesbian activist-artists who hail from other European nations are able to identify with selected patches and rags of national culture. At the same time, while Europe is conceived of as a shared home for Hungarian, German, or French lesbians within the EU, those from proper, core European countries are not bound by the infinitely more rigid and discriminative practices of Eastern European nation-states even if they choose to live there. This explains Kremmler's and Forestier's curious claim that they represented Hungary at a film festival in Paris.

For emerging lesbian communities in Eastern Europe, a postcolonial, transitional place where the nation has a tight allegorical grip on the aesthetic and political representation of sexuality, the transnational avenues of contact made possible by global media and informational technologies are a vital identity resource. Instances of play and performativity constitute transnational connections among lesbian representations even when, or especially when, they are buried under allegories that disavow such a performative potential. For lesbians in postcommunist cultures, it is politically crucial not to engage in an essentialist opposition to heterosexuality, which would support the nation-state's own essentializing and divisive strategies. Rather, their activism, which brings together both high and popular registers of culture, asserts a continuity between hetero- and homosexuality, exposing the psychoanalytic insight that homosexuality is heterosexuality's very precondition in that identity is always based on exclusion, and thus homosexuality plays a role in all identity formations (Fuss 1990, 110).

What follows from this discussion of postcommunist lesbian ambivalence toward the nation is that it is difficult and problematic to issue feminist judgments without falling into multiple traps of ethnocentrism. It is neither reliable to consider the work of Eastern European feminists only in their specific national contexts, nor in a regional or global brushstroke, typically from a liberal feminist point of view. Only the simultaneous presence of all these frameworks can yield enough specificity to unpeel layers of contradiction and make one understand how nationalism can prevent and enable lesbian identities at the same time.

Rosi Braidotti recently noted that feminism had been caught up in a culture of lament.[8] Nowhere is this more true than in Western accounts of the situation of Eastern European women, particularly of lesbians. While the pain, anger, and deprivation that such accounts emphasize is real, such depictions result in a partial picture. A more complex look at the historical, political, and theoretical environment from which the stories of Eastern European women come may reveal postcommunist lesbian feminist emergence to be an exciting and instructive development for feminism.

# 5

## From Poetic Pornography to Creative Consumption: Masculinity in Play

### Who Is the Eastern European Man?

The Budapest Lesbian Film Collective's video *Bandage, Socks and Facial Hair* (2006), which I discuss in chapter 4, documents what is very likely to have been the first drag king workshop in the postcommunist region. I screened the video to a group of academics and media professionals from various post-Soviet countries during a graduate seminar on post-Soviet media change.[1] The majority of the audience criticized the film because, as they argued, it took for granted the universality of what Kaja Silverman calls "assertively phallic," traditional masculinity (Silverman 1992). The film documents how the Berlin-based workshop leaders taught the participants, most of whom hailed from Eastern Europe, how "real men" walk, talk, eat, and sit. Of course, evoking the "assertively phallic" stereotype in an exaggerated fashion is part of the drag king performance, which "pinpoints and exploits the (often obscured) theatricality of masculinity" (Halberstam 1997, 104). As I show in chapter 4, the workshop participants successfully customized and localized the stereotype in their diverse, androgynous performances. However, the postscreening discussion revolved around the general observation that the confident, phallic man, who walks like a cowboy, spreads his limbs in a chair to take up the most possible space, and talks only when he has something important to say, has very little relevance when it comes to "typical" Eastern and Southern European masculinities.

In a similar vein, Dimitris Eleftheriotis (1995, 234–237) rightly notes that Euro-American theoretical paradigms are not very useful when discussing Eastern and Southern European masculinities. While there are identifiable types—the "intellectual" or the "violent Balkan man"—providing a taxonomy will not be adequate and will not qualify as the introduction of masculinity studies to the postcommunist region. As I show in this chapter, Eastern and Southern European masculinities are elusive, almost fictional, because of their shared register of hyperperformativity. I argue in the previous chapter that local nationalisms have historically tried to compensate for their permanent cultural, political, and geographic instability by sustaining especially strict and conservative regimes of gender. Nationalism has not only rendered gendered and sexualized minorities virtually invisible but has also placed the entire burden of representing the nation on men, a burden men could only fail to carry. Sociological data show, again and again, the abhorrent health statistics, life expectancy, record-high suicide rate, and alcoholism of Eastern European men. These statistical data are rarely analyzed beyond excessive pork and alcohol consumption. The self-destructive consequences of the impossible national expectations of manly performance would be very hard to understand within the traditional boundaries of the social sciences alone. At the same time, the mission to provide the patriarchal backbone for the nation has also lent at least some men tremendous privilege—those who are chosen, or appoint themselves, to carry the traditional Romantic banner of national culture. Until recently, national artists and intellectuals have had an unparalleled representational playing field, in which they could perform a range of femininities and masculinities, as well as ethnic and racialized personas.

Let me unfold this dense summary step by step. First, I trace the elusive, performative masculinity of the national artist to the Romantic origins of cultural nationalism in Eastern Europe. I pay particular attention to the way in which *poetry* has traditionally cleared and secured a space for the identity games of national intellectuals and artists. I explain how this space-clearing intensified in the communist period and has shifted into various mediated forms of crisis-management in the postcommunist era. The discussion lingers on these past two decades and on a set of representative films, which signal a crisis of masculinity and nationalism in locally specific ways: in the playful poetic sensibilities of Hungarian postmodern culture, in the ultraviolent performances of manhood in carnivalistic post-Yugoslav films and post-Soviet films from Russia, and in a set of aesthetically hybrid films from the Czech Republic, Romania and Hungary that focus on the conjunction between consumption and the gendered body in all its grotesque material functions.

## The Homoerotic Poetics of European Cultural Nationalism

"The Eastern European intellectual" or, by an almost coterminous name, "the artist," is a hybrid and culturally variable category, who is nevertheless a recognizable type across the region. Maciek Tomczyk, the rebellious protagonist of *Man of Iron* (Andrzej Wajda, 1981); Louka, the musician in the center of the Oscar-winning *Kolya* (Jan Sverák, 1996); or Hendrik Höfgen from an earlier Oscar winner for best foreign film, *Mephisto* (István Szabó, 1980), are all artist-intellectual brothers: They are short on muscles but abundant in verbal expression. They are self-conscious, narcissistic, masochistic, often tragic and self-destructive, prophetic, and, above all, extremely vulnerable. They correspond to director András Jeles's characterization of the artist as a man who "mesmerizes the audience. He is often a furious, conceited, hostile character, who is accompanied by a group of fine ladies following him everywhere with teary eyes" (Jeles 1999, 9).

The artist is a Romantic type, whose persona has its roots in European nationalisms. Joep Leerssen recently proposed that we should study nationalism in Europe as a complex set of interconnected cultural phenomena, a "truly international European pandemic" (Leerssen 2006, 566), whose various manifestations need to be studied in their mutual contacts, as part of a comparative cultural history. He argues that Romanticism, another European pandemic, which overlaps on many points with the emergence of nationalism, provides a good analogy in that it has been studied precisely in this integrated way: not as a trend sociologically generated by a political or economic infrastructure, but as one mobilized through the Europewide cultural communication and dissemination of ideas (566). Leerssen's revision implies that in the post-Wall era of increasing European integration, it is crucial to reevaluate how the historiography of European nationalisms has been tainted by Cold War ideology and to acknowledge the degree to and the ways in which European cultures have been interconnected since the inception of nationalisms.

At the same time, one needs to be careful not to overlook regional differences and their ideological implications, which have haunted European cultural nationalism since the beginning and intensified in the course of the twentieth century. Following John Hutchinson's seminal work on cultural nationalism (Hutchinson 1987; 1994), sociologist György Csepeli identifies an important difference between the nationalisms of Western and Eastern European states. He describes only the latter as "cultural" because, in the absence of the proper, enduring institutions of the nation-state that characterized Western European nationalisms, their Eastern counterparts are grounded in an imaginary and largely "cultural"—literary, artistic, symbolic—identification with the European nation (Csepeli 1991). In other words, Eastern nationalisms are inherently contingent, perpetually engaged in a voluntary but unacknowledged mimicry of proper Europe.

Even though Eastern European nations are predominantly white and have not been part of modern colonial empires, the particular and sustained importance of culture to compensate for a missing, more "authentic" ground, the need to reinvent the affective power of nationalism despite changing borders and vulnerability to more powerful nations, makes Eastern European nationalisms comparable to postcolonial nationalisms. Milan Kundera called this condition an "East Central European complex": a psychological condition that results from the absence of geographical and historical permanence within the region, whose borders and very name are permanently uncertain. Kundera claims that East Central Europe is politically in the East, geographically in the middle, and culturally in the West (quoted in Nowicki 1995, 21). György Bence calls East Central Europe a "political kitsch," while György Konrád considers it a "cultural concept," which emerged in the face of the repeated failure of states in the region to maintain national independence (Nowicki 1995, 21–22). Beverly James argues that utopianism, mysticism, idealism, and romanticism, evidenced in the strength of nationalism, a passion for poetry, and the popularity of heroism and martyrdom, has united the region for centuries and provided a fertile ground for communism (James 1999, 302).

Since Eastern European cultural nationalisms are so evidently based on what Homi Bhabha calls the discursive "scraps" and affective "rags" of nationalism (Bhabha 1994, 145), as I elaborate in chapter 4, they are also in constant danger of being exposed as such. The Romantic self-image of cultural nationalisms, the longing for perfect Europeanness, is both expressed and compensated for in an assumption of cultural and intellectual equality with or even superiority to Europe. Stanislaw Baranczak repeats a widespread Eastern European cliché when he calls East Central Europe "the kingdom of the intellect" (Nowicki 1995, 22). The allegorical embodiment, high priest, and prophet of this "kingdom" is the Eastern European artist. His extraordinary talent for poetic abstraction is supposed to bridge the gap between the particular (by definition national) and the universal (by definition European). Nationalist historians—Palacky, Iorga, Hrushevsky—were not so much scholars as "myth-making intellectuals," who "combined a 'romantic' search for meaning with a scientific zeal to establish this on authoritative foundations" (Hutchinson 1994, 123). The truest voice of nationalism and the paradigmatic figure of the national community is the poet. The Hungarian Sándor Petöfi and the Polish Adam Mickiewicz were Romantic national poets, in whose figures and work nation and poetry have mutually and perpetually reinforced each other in the affective appeal they issue to citizens. Poetry, the "purest" expression of national culture, and nation are inseparably united, making nations poetic, poetry inherently national, and the poet the emblem of cultural nationalisms.

Nationalism is "a special kind of contemporaneous community," which "language alone suggests—above all in the form of poetry and songs" (Anderson 1983, 145), a "deep, horizontal comradeship" that "spills into and out of libidinal economies in ways that are at once consistent and unpredictable" (Parker et al. 1992, 5). But the special importance accorded to poetry as the affective glue of nationalism also confers privilege on national artists, who become the chosen representatives of collective desire. Edward Said characterizes some of the great nationalist artists of decolonization and revolutionary nationalism—"Tagore, Senghor, Neuda, Vallejo, Césaire, Faiz, Dawish and . . . Yeats (Said 1990, 73) as "prophets and priests, among them poets and visionaries," who took the "insufficient yet absolutely crucial first step" toward decolonization by recovering the land, at least in imagination, from the colonizing outsider (76–77). He writes,

With the new territoriality there comes a whole set of further assertions, recoveries and identifications; all of them quite literally grounded on this poetically projected base. The search for authenticity, for a more congenial national origin than is provided by colonial history, for a new pantheon of heroes, myths, and religions, these too are enabled by the land. And along with these nationalistic adumbrations of the decolonized identity, there always goes an almost magically inspired, quasi-alchemical redevelopment of the native language." (79)

Czeslaw Milosz describes the symbiosis of nation and poetry in his *The Witness of Poetry* in a similar manner:

My corner of Europe, owing to the extraordinary and lethal events that have been occurring there, comparable only to violent earthquakes, affords a peculiar perspective. As a result, all of us who come from those parts appraise poetry slightly different than do the majority of my audience for we tend to view it as a witness and participant in one of mankind's major transformations. (Milosz 1983, 4)

The modern nation and the modernist love lyric have similar gender structures: both rely on women as symbolic resources in order to secure the circulation of "love" within a male, homosocial network. Rachel Blau DuPlessis establishes lyric, love, beauty, and woman as the four foundational elements of a conceptual cluster on which love poetry is traditionally built, and among which desire circulates according to the rules of a heterosexist economy (DuPlessis 1994, 72). Feminist theorists of nationalism have shown that nationalism also maintains a homosocial form of male bonding and legitimizes a fixed distribution of gendered labor. Anne McClintock observes that the temporal anomaly embedded in the foundational narrative of each nation—that between a backward, fixed, mythical past and a progressive, forward-thrusting future—is resolved through a naturalized gender divide: men represent the active, political, future-oriented element of the nation, while women serve as its inert source and essence, as reproductive vessels of population and tradition, gaining membership only through their family ties to men (McClintock 1995, 356–370). Nationalism satisfies an erotic need: it is experienced and represented as the love of a country, while the national imaginary is nurtured by figures of women: land and language are anchored in female tropes (Heng 1997, 30). This exclusion of women is by no means merely symbolic or cultural. As Nira Yuval-Davis explains, the divisive logic of nationalism is in accordance with an entire social philosophy at the center of the notion of citizenship, which was constructed in terms of the "Rights of Man," a social contract based on the "fraternity of men." Women's exclusion was "part and parcel of the construction of the entitlement of men to democratic participation, which conferred citizen status not upon individuals as such, but upon men in their capacity as members and representatives of a family" (Yuval-Davis 1998, 403).

## (Post)communist Poetic Pornography

The erosion of communism, which greatly accelerated after the collapse of the Iron Curtain, has also exposed the gendered and sexualized colonial dynamic that has haunted the image of the universal-national, poetic intellectual. This process began in the 1980s with the reinvigoration of poetic forms of expression (to counter the imposed aesthetic of socialist realism), an emphasis on individuality (in the face of forced collectivism), and the development of a peculiarly post-Romantic, modernist variety of postmodern culture. This postmodern culture produced ambivalent representations, which foregrounded the impending crisis of nationalism and the collapse of the naturalized boundaries of masculinity as conjoined processes. I briefly point to two trends that signaled this dual crisis in postmodern Hungarian culture, "the happiest barracks," where these tendencies were most pronounced due to the thawing of communism and the liberalization of the economy under the reign of János Kádár's "goulash communism": one trend is the appearance of male figures who walk and eroticize the no-man's-land between homo- and heterosexuality; the other one is feminized or female artist alter-egos.

Perhaps the best-known instances of male artist characters whose appearance and subjectivities "open in a variety of ways onto the domain of femininity" and foreground "castration, alterity and specularity," to import Kaja Silverman's description from a different context (Silverman 1992, 3), are the protagonists of István Szabó's "Central European trilogy" (Paul 1994), all played by Klaus Maria Brandauer. The first such persona is Hendrik Höfgen/Mephisto, whose homosexuality in the Klaus Mann novel that serves as the basis for the film *Mephisto*, is excised by the director. He is effeminate but engages in sexual relationships with women. Importantly, Höfgen is an actor, who already enjoys a wider range of legitimate gender performances within heterosexuality than ordinary men do. But his identity becomes increasingly compromised by his collaboration with Nazi leaders. After a series of increasingly desperate attempts at consolidating his slipping persona in front of mirrors and onstage, by the end of the film he is reduced to a castrated, powerless figure. The eponymous protagonist of *Colonel Redl* (1984) is a closet homosexual, living his life as a military officer in constant fear of being found out. When he finally is, he is forced to kill himself. Klaus Schneider, the protagonist of the third film in the trilogy, *Hanussen* (1988), is a soldier turned prophet, whose superhuman telepathic ability to connect with people and see Europe's grim future at the eve of the Second World War lends him a broader, polymorphous range of sexualities, which makes him irresistible to women and men alike.

The other relevant tendency within 1980s and 1990s postmodern culture in Hungary is a striking thematic concern in literature and film with femininity and the female body. Sándor Weöres's epic poem *Psyché*, written throughout the 1970s, provided the model for a set of literary and filmic texts in which the woman protagonist—beautiful, often racialized, ravenously sexual but at the same time submissive and nurturing, victimized, and idealized—embodies the male artist's attempt to both represent and anchor his slipping masculine identity in the "natural" female body. The symbolic emasculation that intellectuals had suffered as a result of a long history of inferiority to the real Europe, exacerbated by Soviet colonization and co-optation by the communist state, required compensatory representation in the realm of gender. Psyche, a fictional nineteenth-century, half-Gypsy woman and poet, "is the virtual creation of a life-style and a new possibility for life. The dream of late rococo, early biedermeier literature in an independent and free Hungary, where poets are not burdened by the need to express the crucial problems of society and the nation but are free to devote themselves to the common manifestations of love, joy, and sorrow: this is the dream of a Hungarian literature, European in character," as a Hungarian literary critic deciphers the allegory (Vajda 1988, 20).

Such an allegory is even more pronounced in the film version of *Psyché* (*Nárcisz és Psyché*, 1980), a central reference point of postmodernist, post-Romantic filmmaking in Hungary and regionwide, an "emblematic key opus of Hungarian and East Central European 'post' cultures," the model of a European narrative style (Peternák 1995, 4), and a "secret artist-autobiography" (Forgách 1996, 6). The director, Gábor Bódy, has been identified as the "archetype of the Romantic artist" (Forgách 1996, 4), whose eventual suicide has been called on to immortalize and justify other artists' heroic "search for self-expression" (5). *Nárcisz és Psyché* inspired a host of successors, most notably the novel *Seventeen Swans*, the autobiographical love story of a brilliant and beautiful young half-Gypsy woman poet, written by a certain Lili Csokonai. The male critical public reacted with anxiety to the fact that a woman would write about her own sexuality with almost pornographic openness, until it transpired that prominent postmodernist male writer Péter Esterházy was hiding behind the pseudonym. The novel was subsequently adapted for the erotica-filled film *Érzékek iskolája* (*School of Sensuality*, András Sólyom, 1996).

Such texts embody the curious phenomenon of what I call "poetic nationalism." Authors such as Bódy and Esterházy have explicitly rejected the political mission of the Eastern European artist to represent the nation, a dictate implied in "national poetry." However, they have retained the privilege to play afforded by the heritage of cultural nationalism. They redirected their national mission in terms of the liberation of the individual from the "super-politicized communication" of socialism and from the Lukácsian concept of "aesthetic reflection"—the pivotal notion of the centrally prescribed relationship between socialist art and cultural politics (Töttössy 1994, 882–883). Paradoxically, the reinstatement of the unified individual, the ideological nucleus of the Enlightenment and of modernist humanism, implies that such individuals stand outside of ideology altogether, on the very metaphysical terrain of the Romantic national artist-prophet and his masculine privileges.

Relinquishing the right to represent the nation and turning national poetry into playful, poetic nationalism was thus not an unequivocally progressive development. It was not a voluntary gesture, either. By the 1980s, in Hungary, Czechoslovakia, Poland, and Yugoslavia—the most liberal states among the Soviet satellites—it had become increasingly difficult to maintain the appearance of a clear-cut opposition between the oppressive system and an intellectual-led resistance. Most intellectuals celebrated in the West as "dissident" were directly supported and thus co-opted by the regimes. Censorship had eroded into a game on which both sides depended (Paul 1983, 209; Quart 1988, 192). It has recently been revealed that Szabó and Bódy themselves worked as spies for the secret police (Kovács 2005).

In the Hungary of the 1980s, while communist slogans about collectivism and equality continued to be rehearsed in public, capitalist forms of economy proliferated, allowing citizens relative prosperity within the "second economy" (Kolosi and Rose 1999; Kapitany and Kapitany 1995; Lengyel 1999; Hankiss 1990). Zygmunt Bauman refers to similar changes throughout Eastern Europe as the "postmodern stage" of communism—a period when needs became something to be celebrated and enjoyed, not simply to be satisfied (Bauman 1992, 169).

It is hardly surprising that late-communist films often relied on the game metaphor to reflect on the operation of the regime in double talk. Romanian director Mircea Daneliuc's films *Glissando* (1985) and *The Conjugal Bed* (1993) are perhaps the most explicit examples (see Pethö 2005). The repeated deployment of prostitution and pornography as metaphors of political corruption is an even more telling symptom of the celebration of needs in postmodern communism. It foreshadows the full-blown invasion of consumerism in the years following the fall of the Wall. When it comes to allegorical representations of eroticism, none of the later films could match the exuberance of Dusan Makavejev's surrealist erotic allegories. *W. R.: Mysteries of the Organism* (1971) resurrects the subversive ideas of German psychoanalyst Wilhelm Reich and sets up an analogy between the repression of sexuality and the mind control exercised by communism. Late-communist allegorical comedies such as *Egészséges erotika* (*Healthy Eroticism*, Péter Tímár, 1985) and *Falfúró*

(*The Wall-Driller*, György Szomjas, 1985) follow in Makavejev's footsteps by offering erotic heterosexual spectacle to depict the decaying, self-prostituting era of 1980s communism.

Pornography as an expression of poetic nationalism is also prominent in the work of Hungarian writer Péter Esterházy. He introduces his book *Kis magyar pornográfia* (*Little Hungarian Pornography*) (1995) this way:

> This is the author's most East European book, and his most helpless, too. It was written in 1982–83, in the overripe period of the Kádár era, under small, Hungarian pornographic circumstances where pornography should be understood as meaning lies, the lies of the body, the lies of the soul, our lies. Let us imagine, if we can, a country where everything is a lie, where the lack of democracy is called socialist democracy, economic chaos socialist economy, revolution anti-revolution, and so on. . . . Such a total, all-encompassing lie, when from history through green-pea soup, when from our father's eyebrows and our lover's lap everything is a lie, not to mention this theoretical yet very tangible presence of threat, all this makes for a highly poetic situation. (1995, v–vi)

While it is the collective "we" that is being corrupted by communist oppression, in the book only the prostitution of women's bodies is depicted as natural and deplorable. Men's political prostitution by other men is always metaphorical, tragic, temporary, and ultimately ennobling through the suffering imposed. It appears that the violence implied in "pornography" is attributed entirely to the nebulous communist regime, while its real victims within the national "we" are really only men, since, for women, prostitution is only natural. Evoking naturally erotic female bodies helps to set off the indignity suffered by male bodies as a result of their metaphorical prostitution.

Esterházy's 1994 novel, *Egy nö* ("*A Woman*," translated into English as *She Loves Me*, 1997), exacerbates the gendered division within the national "we" and retroactively establishes male dignity. The cover features a naked female arse extracted from an erotic Egon Schiele painting, combining marketing appeal with an allusion to the novel's European high modernist aspirations. It also identifies men as the proper national reading subjects, whom the narrator addresses in ninety-seven short, numbered segments, all titled "A Woman." Each of these segments wallows in breaking discursive taboos as they detail the narrator's various sexual encounters with women. Much like in the cover illustration, women's identities are pornographically and poetically reduced to bodies and body parts, "beautiful and ugly, kind and nasty, fat and bony, monogamous and promiscuous, seductive, negative, rebellious and voracious" (quoted from jacket, Esterházy 1995). However, two strategies elevate the book above mere pornography: the narrator's superior, often sarcastic tone and play with language—a distancing effect—and the haunting, selective reliance on national allegory as a deciphering strategy, demonstrated in this excerpt:

There is this woman. She loves me. (I have decided you love me, I said to her once, a very long time ago, although I mention this only in passing.) She has it in for the commies. As much as she loves me, that's how much she hates the commies. . . . For instance, during the first freely elected gentlemen's government, our relationship was nothing to write home about. Nothing irredeemable happened, it's just that . . . in short, we limited our discussion to the household chores and sending the children off to school, and she never broke into tears when she looked at me, she didn't flee, screaming, from me in her underwear, jumping over tables and chairs, she didn't open the bathroom door on me when I was inside.

Not so after the elections! Ah! So you're back, are you!, and those cute little starry eyes of hers flashed like the very devil. They lay sprawling over this country for forty years. And these assholes went and voted for them! I keep mum. I'd rather not say that these assholes are us, the country. *I* didn't vote for them, and don't you go on saying it, even as a joke, and if you voted for them in secret, I'm going to kill you. What a sweetheart. I don't even try to calm her down, I wouldn't dream of it: memories of Tuscany. Why, they can't even speak the language properly, she screeches. Inside me, everything is stretched tight as a bow, that's how close I feel to her. They robbed us blind, and now they're playing Mr Clean! They crippled this nation, and now they're shooting their mouths off. I turn white, my hands tremble. I hear the beating of my heart. Trade union lobbyists!, and she squeezes my balls, but with so much feeling, passion and oomph, it would suffice to rebuild the nation. (Esterházy 1997, 157–158)

I have singled out Esterházy precisely because he is one of the most progressive Eastern European public intellectuals and role models, comparable in status within literature to Slavoj Žižek in critical theory. Esterházy has an international reputation and reach. Most of his writings have been translated into other languages and some have been turned into films. He is often expressly critical of of ethnocentrism and nationalism. Yet the gendered political privilege of his status as a national intellectual remains invisible and unrepresentable to himself. On the one hand, he dismisses the allegorical politics of talking for the national "we" in sarcastic terms. On the other hand, he asserts his "natural" place in the all-male family of Hungarian artists, as in a collection of his newspaper columns, *Az elefántcsonttoronyból (From the Ivory Tower, 1991)*: "I am an indebted and grateful son and product of Hungarian literature, and, at the same time, I am someone who is indifferent to some of the important traditions of this literature; for instance, the fact that it makes the collective its central value. I am not attracted by the heroism that follows from this. Then I would rather be a woman writer than a real man" (Esterházy 1991, 77, my translation). My intention is to point out the paradox embedded in this impossible separation: a rather stunning blindness to the gendered politics of representation and a simultaneous blindness to the particular construction of cultural nationalism that affords men this very privilege of representation. It is unproblematic for him to isolate political representation in the sphere of public, state politics from metaphorical, poetic representation in the untouchable sphere of art, where, as he blatantly puts it elsewhere, "those who can speak must speak for those who cannot," (1991, 18) and where he "will allow politics as little weight in [his] writing as, for instance, the weight of a light female shoulder" (72). The imagery of the fixed and natural female body repeatedly serves to naturalize the artist's limitless metaphorical performances.

As a result of decades of public communication during which "information [had been] the most valuable article of commerce" (Arpad 1995, 22), cynicism and fantasy became indispensable resources for survival. Artists' escape from oppositional politics into "pure poetry" and postmodern play afforded a relatively safe place allegedly beyond ideology, where they were able to speak for the nation without taking political responsibility for doing so. The safety of this place was ensured to a great extent by its masculinity. The universal, modernist individual that these playful poetic discourses rescued from the emasculating public spheres of economy and politics was unquestionably a man. The female, feminized, queer, ambiguously sexualized, and racialized protagonists of such texts serve two opposing purposes: they symbolically compensate for the Romantic national playing field that intellectuals had irrecoverably lost, and they allegorically represent the declining class of male intellectuals and their individual artistic autobiographies.

## Masculinities in Crisis

I have reflected on the gendered performance of nationalism in Eastern Europe in the last, eroding phase of state socialism in order to highlight the continuity that "before" and "after" studies of the "Transition" often obscure. Setting up the almost-forgotten or nostalgically remembered "before" and the triumphant or convulsive "after" as sharp divisions has unfortunately hindered the processing of lessons that studies of nationalism and the global media could draw from the dissolution of one of the grandest historical experiments. Such lessons would critique the blind acceptance of national homogeneity, the stubborn refusal to pay attention to identities other than national, the failure to rethink the intellectual's mission, and the walls between culture and political economy in studies of Eastern Europe.

The release of post-Wall cultural, political, and economic flows finally affords us the perspective to see the 1980s as a time of gendered confusion, formerly obliterated by Cold War frameworks of selection and interpretation. I want to emphasize the fact that such neglected representations of gender play in late-communist, post-Romantic, modernist film and literature anticipated an impending, full-blown crisis of masculinity and nationalism. If we take to heart Leerssen's remapping of cultural nationalism as a European phenomenon and bridge the artificial divide between studies of Eastern European nationalism in the social sciences and studies of culture in Slavic studies, we will see, in Miroslav Hroch's words, that cultural preoccupations "do not passively 'reflect' or 'follow' social developments or political movements but that they tend to anticipate them"; they "stand at the beginning of the alphabet" (Leerssen 2006, 562). This view is also consistent with Fredric Jameson's argument that films' overt messages are inevitably obscured by their filmmaker's co-opted situations. Jameson shows how an emerging class consciousness of late capitalism thus becomes "figurable" in the "raw material" of Hollywood entertainment films before any other means of representation make it apparent in the culture (Jameson 1985, 719). The political, like sex, helps the entertainment industry "reinvest its tired paradigms, without any danger to itself or to the system" (720). In a similar vein, new kinds of allegorical identity politics became figurable in the poetic, (post)modernist, pornographic film and literature of late socialism. These new meanings anticipate the subsequent, more explicit questioning of hegemonic masculinities and nationalisms. Of course texts are what they do for a community at a particular place and time (Suleiman 1997, 53). With Jameson, I assume that audiences are sensitive to such formal contradictions, even if they are not yet articulated in public discourses.

The postcommunist ideological opening has finally provided the paradigms to name some of these inherent contradictions. Postcommunist events in Eastern Europe have made it evident how profoundly masculine identities in the region are dependent on and embedded in nationalisms. To observers it is often incomprehensible that there is no such thing as "man" (or "woman") without always already and primarily being a Czech, Serbian, Russian, or Hungarian. This insistence on performing perfect national manhood, and grounding it in a fixed and naturalized gender divide is so important because clear-cut ethnic, cultural, and linguistic divisions and state borders have been impossible to maintain in the region. The collapse of borders after 1989 has necessitated the compensatory reinforcement of rigid gendered borders within and among nations.

There is now a substantial amount of critical feminist literature on the post-1989 backlash against women, the postsocialist hostility against feminism, the efforts to reestablish an all-male public sphere, and the introduction of new kinds of discriminatory policies against minorities—all in proportion to the loss of power that men have experienced as leaders and actors in the new EU-rocentric democracies. This has led to the most violent results in the wars of Yugoslav succession and the most repressive policies in the ban against abortion in Poland. "We will nationalize those bellies!" as a Polish senator proposed shortly after the collapse of communism (Watson 1993, 75). Scholars have analyzed the situation in terms of the "rise of masculinism" (Watson 1993), "anti-feminist backlash" (Goven 1993; Occhipinti 1996; Mihancsik 1999; Eisenstein 1993; Dolby 1995), or, rather, "backlash before feminism" (Graff 2003), and the emergence of "male democracies" (Eisenstein 1993, 312–314). Post-Wall democracies introduced a number of measures across the region to regulate women in order to conjure "real men" back into being, or at least account for their "disappearance" (Graff 2005; Galambos 1999; Hirsch 1999; Kovács 1998; Schubert 1999; Salecl 1994).

## The Nostalgic Return of the Artist

Immediately following 1989, nationalism in the region became overtly appropriated by right-wing parties in an aggressive and simplistic fashion. This rendered the role of the playful, Romantic intellectual, hanging on to the memories of dissent assigned to him in the grand performance of the communist Big Brother show, finally obsolete. However, the sensitive, androgynous artist, inexplicably irresistible to women, did not disappear altogether. His figure became nostalgically resurrected as a reminder of a different, peaceful, cultural kind of nationalism, a fossil much like a piece of the Berlin Wall, and, as such, something produced primarily for Western consumption on the nostalgia market. Louka, the misanthropic musician in *Kolya* (Jan Sverák, 1996) or Hradno, the music teacher in *The Elementary School* (Jan Sverák, 1991) are such dinosaurs. The international market rewarded *Kolya* with an Academy Award and continued to produce its own nostalgic-mythical Eastern artists: the mysterious, amnesiac Polish piano player genius, played by *Good Bye Lenin!*'s *Ostalgie*-affected Alex, actor Daniel Brühl, who winds up in England in *Ladies in Lavender*, or Roman Polanski's pianist (*The Pianist*, 2002), played by a dreamy Adrien Brody, whose music is able to withstand Nazism and save his own life, which is evidently more worthy of saving than that of others. The most blatant statement about the Romantic power of musical play, channeled through the supreme talent of the Artist, is István Szabó's postcommunist film *Meeting Venus* (1991).

The film was inspired by Szabó's own adventure as an opera director: he had staged Wagner's *Tannhäuser* at Paris's Opera Europa a few years before making the film (Zsugán 1985, 12). The film's protagonist, Hungarian conductor Zoltán Szántó—whose name is strikingly similar to the director's—is an idealized embodiment of the Eastern European intellectual, who has shed the allegorical burden of being a national artist by 1991, and is finally able to fulfill his Romantic destiny as the universal representative of European (high) culture. Accordingly, the film was produced by the British David Puttnam; Klaus Maria Brandauer, who plays the protagonist in Szabó's earlier trilogy, is replaced in the lead role by French actor Niels Arestrup, and the setting shifts from Eastern Europe to Paris, Europe's cultural capital. Most members of the international cast led by Szántó bear names typical of their nationalities, some of which are translations of one another: Taylor, the American singer's name, and Schneider, the name of the German singer, for instance, are translations of the Hungarian "Szabó." This playfulness signals the fact that the era of grim national historical drama is over. We are dealing with a comic allegory of the new Europe, appropriately set on the stage of the Opera Europa.

Szántó's Faustian dilemma is familiar from *Mephisto*—a choice between political commitment versus artistic freedom or, in *Tannhäuser*'s analogous onstage story, duty versus love. While in *Mephisto* the continuity between stage and life could be argued to convey an ironic sense that reality is always produced in performance, the allegorical dimensions of *Meeting Venus* seem unconvincing—the likely reason for the critical failure of the film. The film begins with Szántó's literal transition to the West: he is shown going through immigration at de Gaulle Airport. As we watch him being singled out and examined at customs, his point of view is firmly established as hegemonic through his voice-over, reading a letter addressed to his wife, supposedly reflecting on the incident in retrospect: "Is it my face that irritates them? Or just the stale smell of Eastern Europe? They make me feel like a man entering the drawing room with dog shit on his shoes." The Eastern European artist, presented as the "black man of Europe," arrives in the land of youthful dreams, as he identifies Paris, with a rather melodramatic baggage of shame and guilt. However, this Eastern Europeanness, visibly written on his body as much as on his passport, miraculously disappears in the course of his work on the opera. Once in the realm of music, the past, along with his debilitating historical memories, simply dissipates. When the former East German singer, Schneider, asks him for a favor later on, appealing to their shared Eastern-bloc memories, Szántó reflects in voice-over: "I had no idea what the man was talking about."

In the narrative logic of the film, it is the appeal to the absolute and natural authority of Music, and specifically Wagner's music, that allows Szántó's European intellect to become perfectly released from his Eastern European body. It is also Wagner's music that affords him the ethical authority to tame his rambunctious musicians: "First I have respect for Wagner, and then to myself," he declares. "You're playing like children! It's an insult to Wagner!" he bursts out during a rehearsal. Szántó is seen, precisely, to grow above everyone else. His mature, dedicated artist's world sharply contrasts with the comically depicted confusions of what seems to be a child care center, where everyone is selfish, sulking, or hysterical.

The appeal to the allegedly apolitical sphere of music and the universal mastery of Wagner—notwithstanding the Eurocentric legacy of such an appeal—serves to represent the conductor's role as that of a humble mediator between the universal and the particular. Szabó comments on this mediatory role in an interview: "Everyone has a creative part in his soul. The creative process is everyone's problem, whether you're an opera singer, a filmmaker or a baker" (Paul 1994, 197). The film, however, sends a very clear message that an opera singer and filmmaker stand a much better chance of representing the universal than a baker. In a fashion that almost parodically fulfills feminist and postcolonial critiques of Eurocentrism, Szántó's transformation from the abject not-so-white man of Europe into a fully legitimate and by definition white European intellectual is conditioned on distinguishing himself from homosexuals in the cast and on conquering a host of women. Unlike in *Mephisto*, where it is Höfgen's black postcolonial lover Juliette who "naturalizes" him as a straight white man, the chief device of remasculinization this time is the very embodiment of Westernness—none other than Glenn Close, playing the Swedish diva Karin Anderson. Besides his cultural connection with European music, implied in the Hungarian artist's cultural nationalism, it is Szántó's relationship with this archetypal woman of the West that turns him into someone who is always already European.

Miss Anderson becomes Szántó's only ally against the rest of the Opera Europa. She is seduced by the erotic charge of Szántó's unconditional identification with the music (see figure 5.1). This is a nostalgic, wish-fulfilling reconstruction of the artist's charisma, similar to that surrounding the music teacher in Jan Sverák's *Obecná Skola (The Elementary School*, 1991), made the same year, at a time when this charisma was swiftly becoming a thing of the past. Szántó's heterosexual virility is confirmed in the repeated attempts of female singers to seduce him (something that seriously undermines the film's credibility) and in his positive distinction from gay men: Hans-Dietrich, the set decorator; his American partner, the singer Steve, who bounces from one nervous breakdown into another; and Gábor, an emigrant Hungarian administrator who works for the opera. Gábor is depicted as a duplicitous, overweight bald man and a closet homosexual, whose crudeness represents the "wrong" kind of Eastern European masculinity.

In one of the letters to his wife in which Szántó comments on his adventures in voice-over, he sums up the reasons for the opera's troubles this way: "Bureaucrats pretend to be artists, and artists, bureaucrats. Impossible! . . . Apparently, due to democracy, nobody really seems to care about the *Tannhäuser*. Except, perhaps, Miss Anderson." In contrast with the resistance to the magnificent demon of communism conjured up in the constant comparisons that haunt Szántó's tenure at the Opera Europa, the everyday identity politics of Western democracies appears to be irritating, pitiful, and senseless. The two managers of the opera repeatedly remind him that he is not in "Stalinist" times anymore, that "democracy is a hard game," and that the West does not operate by "dictatorship." The film's joke is on them, however:

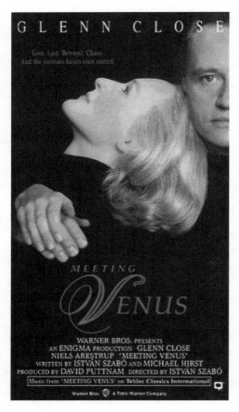

**Figure 5.1**
The winning combination for a new European culture: Glenn Close as Swedish
diva Karin Anderson, and Niels Arestrup as Hungarian conductor Zoltán Szántó
in *Meeting Venus* (István Szabó, 1991).

they rely on stereotypical Cold War concepts of Eastern Europe, and
their own style of management is highly subjective, favoritist, and
sometimes even dictatorial. Through the allegorical microcosm of the
Opera Europa, democracy appears to Szántó/Szabó as a set of competing
mini-dictatorships, essentially an anarchic situation, which precludes
collaboration. The musicians' union tries to control rehearsal schedules
as a means of negotiating with the management. The orchestra sabotages
rehearsals in protest against the Opera Europa's sponsorship of unfavor-
able transnational companies. Even the curtain is subject to conflicting
political interests. Szántó's response is, "I can't stand this democracy
of yours."

I would like to foreground the relationship of the particular and the universal that is articulated here in representations of geographically specific masculinities. If, as Slavoj Žižek claims, democracy and "politics proper" are synonymous (Žižek 1998, 989), then Szántó/Szabó's dilemma is really about how to conduct politics in a postcommunist, post-Wall Europe, about the necessity and possibility of a universal ethics that does not sacrifice the political representation of the particular. The film stages a paradigmatic encounter between the postcommunist Eastern European intellectual and the "real" Europe. In globalizing Europe, the space for politics proper is increasingly threatened by the "onslaught of the multitude of particular identities of a postmodern, all-embracing social body" (Žižek 1998, 996). The film's representation of this encounter betrays Žižek's hope that the initial, mutual post–Cold War disappointment of Eastern and Western Europe would result in a productive new paradigm of politics proper (1004). But Žižek's evaluation leaves out of consideration the continuing alliance between Eurocentric universalism and dominant masculinities.

Some degree of ethical universalism is clearly necessary to achieve effective political representation. Politics proper requires that the singular should appear to stand in for the universal against the particular power interests of a ruling group (989). Far from being mutually exclusive, subjectivity and universalism are two sides of the same coin (1003). But it is doubtful whether, as Žižek implies, the universal subjective stance can really occur to any individual, even if only "in principle" (1003). Or whether, in Szabó's words, everybody can be "an artist in his soul." Yet in the film, this inherently masculine and Eurocentric subjectivity succeeds in creating solidarity across various group allegiances thanks to Wagner's music, which, through the conductor's divine mediation, evokes multinational Beauty and Love in the end. During the first performance, the curtain fails to rise because the technician in charge is on strike. Under Szántó's guidance, however, the singers perform the entire opera in front of a closed curtain. The suggestion is that the power of the music and Szántó's supreme talent do not need to be enhanced by cheap spectacle. The audience is mesmerized by the opera without visual excess. Even Szántó's betrayed and hurt wife, watching the performance on television at home, is shown to be moved and forgiving.

By the end of the film, the Hungarian artist who arrived in Paris with his Eastern European burden becomes a transcendent European subject, unbound by national, ethnic, and sexual identities, embodying Miss

Anderson's *ars poetica*, "freedom is inside." This state of universality, however, has nothing to do with political representation. Democracy and politics are simply rendered insignificant. This version of the "universal," instead of pointing to a way out of the postmodern "postpolitics" of democracy as a game, which Žižek derides, simply trivializes the importance of particular identities and group interests. By taming and uniting the Opera Europa in Wagner's Romantic spirit, Szántó shows actual, "corrupted" Europe what "absolute" European values are—at least in the interpretation of the last Eastern European artist.

### Carnivalistic Balkan War Games

In an entire cycle of postcommunist films, made in places where the transition has been accompanied by border disputes, violent confrontations, displacement, and war, the double crisis of masculinity and nationalism has been represented as much less serene although no less nostalgic. Unlike Szabó's haughty intellectual, who distances himself from political power struggles, angry, violent young men take justice into their own hands in a host of postcommunist films. They have been let down by their governments and mobilized by the revisionist and fascist promises of right-wing nationalist parties. They have also been left behind by a fast-moving, globalizing world where class distinctions are increasingly sharp and where some will make it to Europe and others will not. In their frustration, they go on a rampage against everyone who does not embody their ideal of the pure ethnonational subject. It is instructive to compare *Meeting Venus*'s mobile artist, looking down on and conducting Europe from the stage in order to bring an enduring Eastern European fantasy to visual fulfillment, with the angry, violent men who are not only stuck in their Balkan and post-Soviet homes, at the bottom of the social hierarchy of the New Europe, but quite often literally operate in a criminal underground.

Aleksei Balabanov's *Brothers* are gangsters, as are the characters of Pyotr Lutsik's *Okraina* (1998). *Luna Park* (Pavel Lungin, 1992) follows the emergence of Andrei, leader of a skinhead gang, from a bunkerlike gathering space used to beat up homosexuals, Jews, and other aliens. In one of the convergences that reveal the intimate, mutual dependence between nostalgic masculine investment in artistic play and a wish to show the corporeal masculine violence of the transition, Andrei, the neo-Nazi, is gradually transformed by his bonding with his long-lost father, a Jewish musician. His father's irresistible bohemian personality, no less than his music, tames Andrei so that at the end of the film he breaks from his gang and rides away on a train with his father.

The wars of post-Yugoslavian succession also inspired a series of films that revolve around disgruntled, disillusioned, cynical, and violent men. These protagonists behave much like Szántó's childish performers, but with incomparably more violent consequences. Films such as *Before the Rain* (Milcho Manchevski, 1992), *Underground* (Emir Kusturica, 1995), *Powder Keg* (Goran Paskaljevic, 1998), *Ulysses's Gaze* (Theodoros Angelopoulos, 1995), *No Man's Land* (Danis Tanovic, 2001), *Pretty Village, Pretty Flame* (Srdjan Dragojevic, 1996), and *Wounds* (Srdjan Dragojevic, 1998) have received considerable attention (see Marciniak 2006, 129–148; Longinovic 2005; Žižek 1996; Iordanova 2001; Levi 2007; Ravetto-Biagioli 1998). They have been Oscar nominees and winners, and recipients of festival successes and critical acclaim. They have been interpreted as documentation, as reflection on and symptoms of the Balkan Wars into which the former Yugoslavia erupted in the 1990s. I restrict my analysis here to the tendency of these films to represent men of the Balkans as the violent, immoral, animalistic, criminal others of rational, cool, and democratic Europe, which Szántó's transcendent musician eagerly performs in a classic instance of colonial mimicry. I look at these violent and corporeal masculinities in relation to what the films represent as an insane, explosive, carnivalistic game, continuously dancing in the gray zone between reproducing and subverting, exoticizing and rejecting European stereotypes of the Balkans as a global powder keg.

Unlike the sensitive artist characters of films from somewhat less volatile postcommunist places, the protagonists of these films tend to be manly men, whose powerful, dangerous, and attractive physicality has contributed to the stereotype of the wild Balkan man (Bjelic 2005). Even when he is an intellectual, he is physically powerful, as is Macedonian journalist Aleksandar Kirov, the hero of *Before the Rain*, played by Rade Serbedzija, whose other credits include *Mission: Impossible II* (John Woo, 2000), *The Saint* (Phillip Noyce, 1997), and *Snatch* (Guy Ritchie, 2000). These protagonists operate on a terrain that is perpetually in danger of explosion, as the title *Bure Baruta* (translated as *"Powder Keg,"* as well as *"Cabaret Balkan"*), suggests. The most explosive moment for Szántó occurs when he loses his temper over the singers' bickering and bursts into an angry, improvised song, a list of the ethnonational stereotypes the cast members are not able to transcend. Karin Anderson joins in the song, making this moment of abstracted passion, mediated through music, a confirmation of their love for each other and a turning point in the narrative. Films about men caught up in post-Yugoslav and post-Soviet wars have no use for such intellectual distancing and certainly no need for classical music. They are passionate folk heroes come to life, descendants of the mythical national leaders created by Romantic national writers and poets (Iordanova 2001, 116). But unlike leaders of the past, they come without any moral mission or qualms, any commitment to anything but their own criminal interests. The equally mystical and nostalgic ethnic belonging in which they have been misled to believe blows up in their faces or is understood to be a farce from the start.

Kusturica's *Underground* has become the most often referenced and controversial piece of this cycle. Divided into three parts, "War," "Cold War," and "War," this "mythopoetic" film (Ravetto-Biagioli 1998; Levi 2007) presents an episodic, fragmented, surreal vision of the history of Yugoslavia from World War II to the post-Yugoslav wars, centered on a love triangle: Two friends, Marko and Blacky, vie for the favors of the pretty and opportunistic Natalia. After the war, Marko emerges as a hero of anti-Nazi resistance and leaves Blacky in an underground cellar along with many other people, deceiving them into believing that the war is still on. For several decades, Marko and Natalia, now married, use those trapped underground for slave labor to manufacture weapons, which they then sell on the international black market. The slaves, including Blacky, escape only when the walls of the cellar break down in the drunken aftermath of an underground wedding and the prisoners find themselves in the middle of an East-West tunnel system used for trafficking. Marko, Blacky, and Natalia meet again in the 1990s, when another war rages in the former Yugoslavia. Blacky is in charge of paramilitary groups, who eventually kill Marko and Natalia. In the film's epilogue and most mythopoetic moment, all the protagonists of the film, dead and alive, reemerge for an exuberant celebration on the bank of the Danube. The piece of land they occupy gradually separates from the mainland and floats down the river like a magical island—a defining metaphor of Yugoslavia, according to Kusturica (Iordanova 2001, 114), and an optimistic ending to a dark film permeated by cynical black humor.

Marko is a celebrated poet and politician, a corrupted version of Szántó's intellectual, one who is also a racketeer involved in various sneaky schemes. But it is the figure of the film's director that ignited an international controversy, which implicitly revolved around the role of the (Eastern) European Romantic artist as a man. Intellectuals from the

Balkans and from Western Europe, including Slavoj Žižek and Peter Handke, took actives roles in the debate that ensued about Kusturica's moral responsibility. An ethnic Bosnian from Sarajevo, Kusturica made a film in Belgrade in times of Serbian aggression against Bosnia. Because *Underground* was allegedly cosponsored by Milosevic's government, it was placed under close international scrutiny. Even though Kusturica explicitly refused to take sides, it appeared that parts of his film could be interpreted as pro-Croatian and pro-Serbian (Iordanova 2001, 111–159). Dina Iordanova argues that the storm around Kusturica, which made the director somewhat melodramatically announce that he would retire from filmmaking under the weight of attacks, revived the Romantic concept of a special moral code for the artist, "to whom traditional norms cannot apply, but who rather lives in a state of perpetual self-assertion, playfully casting aside firm commitments and violating rules in the name of sustaining a frivolous, creative personality" (130).

Szabó and Kusturica converge in this unspoken appeal to the special rights of the artist. Although they represent it differently, they have both inherited the legacy of Romantic nationalism and sustained an essentialist relationship to the geopolitical ground from which the creative genius grows, and which also provides the foundation for the particular, essentialist masculinity of their protagonists. In the work of both directors, women tend to be secondary devices, objects of exchange between the men, or even impediments to men's goals, prone to treason and betrayal (Longinovic 2005, 46). On several occasions, Kusturica publicly compared the post-Yugoslav state of affairs to a natural disaster that originates in ancient and incurable enmities, rooted in the "seismic" Balkan ground, beyond everyone's control (Iordanova 2001, 125–126). This is a regionally specific variation on the Central European argument that Hungarians, Poles, and Russians are naturally poetic, which underscores Szabó's nostalgic conception of his post-Wall European-Hungarian artist.

*Underground*, along with other post-Yugoslav war films, triumphed in the festival circuit and has been distributed worldwide. At the same time, these "Balkan" films have a different, less reverent relationship to high culture than Szabó's *Meeting Venus* and its conductor protagonist do. As Dusan Bjelic argues, films such as *Wounds*, *Cabaret Balkan*, and *No Man's Land* employ the Hollywood idiom and stereotypical news media representations of the barbaric quagmire of the Balkans—no different from current representations of Iraq and the rest of the Middle East—to perform them back to Western audiences (Bjelic 2005). This "performative destabilization," particularly the exploitation of the image of the "wild Balkan man," draws on the use of ultraviolence and humor in films such as *The Player* (Robert Altman, 1992), *Pulp Fiction* (Quentin Tarantino, 1994), and *Natural Born Killers* (Oliver Stone, 2004). Much like Mickey and Mallory Knox in *Natural Born Killers*, Pinki (Dusan Pekic) and Kraut (Milan Maric), the main characters of *Wounds*, are "TV vampires," whose main inspiration in life is the crime reality show *Puls Asfalta* (*Pulse of the Asphalt*), which features and glorifies real-life Serbian criminals "brought to you by Democracy Light," according to its cynical headline (Bjelic 2005, 113). Like other films in the genre, director Dragojevic attacks state-controlled Serbian television and its nationalistic media culture centered on violent, popular spectacle (113). One of the most incredible peaks of ethnic violence, wrapped in nationalistic media spectacle, was the "wedding of the century" between turbo folk singer Ceca and Serbian warlord Arkan, which took place in Belgrade in the winter of 1995 and was estimated to have cost $250,000 (Iordanova 1998). The culture of militarization and violence in postcommunist Serbia actively cultivated political propaganda through television, which equated violence with patriotism, rewarded war criminals with honors for heroes, and promoted popular culture with its kitsch macho-pornographic content as the model to emulate for youth (Kronja 2006).

Kriss Ravetto-Biagioli and Pavle Levi call the disruptive, subversive aesthetic of post-Yugoslav films "mythopoetic" (Levi 2006, 90; Ravetto-Biagioli 1998). Ravetto-Biagioli adopts Pasolini's use of the term, for whom mythopoesis is a "disruptive exposé of (1) the generalization of myth and cultural truths; (2) the dissemination of this generalized 'unreality' via television and popular media; and (3) the dislocation of generalized cultural truths from any sense of immediacy or intimacy" (Ravetto-Biagioli 1998, 43). In the films' treatment, these "truths" involve what Bogdan Denitch calls "the nationalism of poets, novelists, historical mythmakers, overimaginative ethnographers, and irresponsible populist demagogues" (Denitch 1996, 17). They also involve Europe's unacknowledged investment in maintaining the image of the uncivilized Balkan other, a mechanism eloquently described by Baudrillard (1993) and Žižek (1994, 210–217). Myth in films like *Underground* and *Ulysses's Gaze* works "as a genre of subversion, one that expresses multiple histories, truths and uncertainties, one that abstracts linear and spatial narratives and uses epic as a device for diffusing ethnocentrism. More than supporting what Mikhail Bakhtin calls a 'creative understanding' or a 'dialogical mode of representation,' this subversive use of myth, poetry and fragmentation constitutes a radical refusal of paradigms of transcendence" (Ravetto-Biagioli 1998, 49).

Kusturica, in particular, provides a carnivalistic vision of Yugoslav history, which recalls popular and folk-mythic modes of representation (Ravetto-Biagioli 1998, 50). The explosive, no-barriers, hybrid aesthetic of *Underground*, its bizarre humor, and its recurring absurdity evoke a series of antecedents that include Rabelais, Hieronymus Bosch, Terry Gilliam, and Federico Fellini (Iordanova 2001, 112). Pavle Levi associates Kusturica's eclectic style with the 1980s Bosnian popular subcultural movement New Primitivism (Levi 2007, 62). In rock culture, as much as in poetry, painting, theater, and film, the New Primitives focused their attention on the little people, small-time crooks, and petty thieves on the margins of society. They favored expressions that appropriated the popular culture of entertainment, sports (soccer games), street jargon, and local fashion (63). New Primitives "performatively transformed" Hajrudin Krvavac's popular 1971 war film *Walter Defends Sarajevo*, a Yugoslav Western and a centerpiece of the Partisan war film genre, whose purpose was to disseminate socialist propaganda (63–66). As Levi explains, one of the most influential and sophisticated manifestations of neoprimitivism was *The Top List of the Surrealists*, a radio program subsequently turned into a television show. With exposure to an all-Yugoslav audience, consolidated in the heart of state television, *The Top List of the Surrealists* confronted the alarming tendencies that began to penetrate and fragment Yugoslavia by the mid-1980s: ethnonationalism, religious intolerance, and the rise of vulgar xenophobic and racist myths, which followed a predictable Manichaean pattern of exclusion (68).

The affinity between the rebellious critical spirit of the New Primitives and Kusturica's propensity to excess is evident. If Szabó's artist characters try to transcend the limitations of their bodies and sublimate desires in the rarefied sphere of Beauty, where only the select few get to play, Kusturica's play is "difficult to contain, often destructive, even murderous; but it is also liberating—expressive of an unbound spirit and unconditional freedom" (Levi 2007, 85). His vision of the Yugoslav nation can be characterized as magical realist, configuring the nation as "enchanted" (86), engaging in libidinal exuberance, perpetual festivities, intoxication, and eroticization, offering heightened scopic gratification (90–91)—unlike Szántó's repressed conductor, who communicates the Beauty of music through the abstracted faculty of sound, without self-serving spectacle.

The exuberance of the absurd also links post-Yugoslav films with those of the Yugoslav Black Wave of the late 1960s and early 1970s, identified with filmmakers such as Zivojin Pavlovic, Aleksandar Petrovic, and Dusan Makavejev, whose *W. R.: Mysteries of the Organism* (1970) created an international stir (Longinovic 2005, 36). The films of the Black Wave (*crni talas*) were blacklisted for their social criticism. Similar to post-Yugoslav films, they mixed styles, including cinema verité, nouvelle vague, newsreel footage, fascist propaganda, Hollywood action, war, and gangster films, to address subjects such as machismo, urban poverty, and ethnic minorities (Ravetto-Biagioli 2003, 459).

Unlike Szántó, the Central European artist who is eager to transcend the "dog shit on his shoes" and reminds the cartoonish, bickering figures that populate the Euro-bureaucracy of Opera Europa of the European cultural values eternalized by masters such as Wagner, filmmakers from the post-Yugoslavian Balkans have no choice but to engage in and with the powerful discourses of Balkanization that have orientalized and fixed the region in its image of backwardness and tribalism (see Todorova 1997). Their only choice is to put "truth," along with fixed identities, into crisis by means of the carnivalesque, grotesque, absurd, and black comedy. As Kriss Ravetto-Biagioli argues,

The treatment of truth one finds in these films functions more along the lines of a Nietzschean ass festival than a Bakhtinian celebration of multiplicity. The logic of the ass festival is more than merely oppositional and counter-hegemonic. It laughs in the face of what Nietzsche calls the tarantulas—spirits of gravity who preach equality but are secretly vengeful. The laughter of the ass is designed to lure cloistered dogmatists "out of their den of lies" and expose their demands for justice as appeals for "revenge against all those who are not like us." The excessive carnivalesque theatricality of the ass festival treats societal preoccupations as purely performative. However, in a self-critical move, it also hyperbolizes the role of the ass/artist in such a spectacle. (Ravetto-Biagioli 2003, 457)

One of the most evocative instances of this self-mocking carnivalesque mode is the character of the master of ceremonies, who announces the film *Bure Baruta* ("*Powder Keg*" or "*Cabaret Balkan*") in the film's prologue. He promises, "Tonight I'm going to fuck with you, children!" (see figure 5.2). This self-mocking stance would not occur to Szabó's dignified artist, whose stage is elevated over popular tastes and forms of culture. According to Tomislav Longinovic, the master of ceremonies' direct address of the voyeuristic and, it is assumed, Western audience is an explicit poetic reference to "playing" the Western eye. "The intentional identification with the Western (mis)perception of local identities

**Figure 5.2**
Goran Paskaljevic's *Bure Baruta* ("*The Powder Keg*" or "*Cabaret Balkan*," 1999).

is used as a basis for a performance of cruel uncertainty, where lies and truths are no longer distinguishable" (43). The master of ceremonies foreshadows the theater of cruelty that is to come.

The position of being watched by the West through the camera eye requires the common masculine subject to perform some exceptional act beyond good and evil. It is an automatic invitation to desublimate civilizational prohibitions, opening up the abyss of fraternal hatred. The loss of subjectivity under the new temporal demands brings men to the edge as they engage in the torturer/victim game of mutual annihilation (43).

Bjelic calls this a "musical chair power game," perpetuated by sexism and racism. As in *Pulp Fiction*, where Marsellus Wallace is entrapped and sodomized by a white racist but then, in his turn, gets a hold of a loaded shotgun to get "medieval" on the "hillbilly boy's ass," the global power grid in which the city of Belgrade is a mad powder keg is a tyranny without a tyrant (Bjelic 2005, 116). Pinki and Kraut in *Wounds*; Milan and Halil in *Pretty Village, Pretty Flame*; or Ciki and Nino in *No Man's Land* have no other way of leaving the mad system but by shooting each other. This game exposes the homoeroticism at the heart of nationalism. Branka Arsic claims that Serbian nationalism is due entirely to the suppressed homosexuality of Serb men (Arsic 2003)—a motif that occurs in virtually all post-Yugoslav films.

The carnivalistic theater of cruelty that such films perform turns national historical figures and ethnic types into comic book characters (Levi 2007, 96). In his analysis of *Underground*, Tomislav Longinovic notes that the artificiality of the film's plot is enhanced by intertitles and an exaggerated acting style that evokes silent films and "transforms the Yugoslav subject into a cross between animal and cartoon" (42). This is already evident in the film's beginning sequence, which shows the bombing of the Belgrade zoo by the Nazis. "The noble strivings of heroic freedom fighters are replaced by the comically exaggerated outbursts of the characters aware of their own farcical status inside the grand narratives of politics and history" (42). Unlike Szántó's artist, however, who can see the peoples of Europe only through this stereotyping lens, the caricatures in the Balkan films I reference here "provide a way of *unthinking* any romanticization of violence, from national myths of victimization that call for retribution, to heroic (humanitarian) duties of protecting the planet from would-be tyrants and 'barbaric peoples'" (Ravetto-Biagioli 2003, 464).

### Virtual Balkan War Games

As it is demonstrated by the news each day, war is a strategic, homoerotic power game, an extreme sport that is fought to the death according to established rules. Post-Yugoslav films also foreground this darkly ludic dimension of war: it is performed for the pleasure of consumers around the world, in a deadly reality-show-infotainment sandwich. The bloodier and more tragic the post-Yugoslav war became, the harder it became to negotiate its immediate commodity status, its absorption in the playful practices of global media consumption. Even the numerous art exhibitions that confronted the "return" of the Balkans and Balkanization in Western public discourses[2] have been argued to backfire by depoliticizing the war, rendering "the Balkans" a marketing and branding tool in the service of a superficial multiculturalism (Avgita 2007).

Those who want to avoid both the rock of fragmenting, violent ethnonationalism and the hard place of a paralyzing, demonizing artificial unity implied in the recent rediscovery of the "Balkans" by global media have no choice but to acknowledge and confront both processes. Members of Personal Cinema, a group of media artists, programmers, and curators formed in 2001, for instance, acknowledge that Balkanization is a global media process and want to wrest the pacifist, progressive idea of "democracy" and "ethics" from the anti-intellectual tendencies of the global war on terror. One of their many projects is the multiplayer online game the *Making of Balkan Wars: The Game*, which takes on "the abuse of the Balkans as framed in the media, Hollywood and video games" and wants to "reveal what the media mean from the inside and to play a 'dirty game'" (Spyropoulos 2007, 172). This multiuser, 3-D, first-person perspective game is a virtual space that hosts forty videos, documentaries, sounds, images, and texts contributed by more than fifty artists from sixteen countries. Each exhibit ponders the notion of the Balkans, the media, identities, and the war.

*The Making of the Balkan Wars: The Game* is an example of the way older and more recent practices and technologies of play merge in post-communist Europe. Its makers set out to critique the narrow definition of highbrow art preserved by exhibitions about the war such as "Blood and Honey" and "In the Gorges of the Balkans." The game format offers an interactive interface freely available on the Internet. It incorporates geopolitical war games and epic video games but does not tempt the player to destroy and kill. After choosing an avatar that represents a "Balkan" character, one explores various spaces that characterize the Balkans. The process is supposed to create a virtual "identity factory"— also the name of one of the game spaces. It showcases and thus denaturalizes the production of Balkan and Eastern European mythologies, deconstructing the complex labels "Balkans" and "Balkanization" the way Maria Todorova and other scholars have done,[3] turning it into a phenomenon that describes a global state of fragmentation and crisis (Spyropoulos 2007, 172). In game spaces identified as "The Mall," or "The 'National' Prison of Balkana," the avatar is able to observe and participate in a distilled version of the tragic game in which the Balkan wars and subsequent labels of Balkanization have been constituted. Artists who have contributed their work use humor and parody in their often irreverent photos and other illustrations, character sketches, scripts, music, storyboards, dioramas, videos, and essays. In the course of spatial exploration, the player's contribution to "balkanization" and "de-balkanization" is measured by the game, taking into account how much time the player spends in front of specific exhibits and interacting with other players. The goal is to keep the two in balance. The spaces provide various interpretations of the social, historical, and cultural elements of the Balkans (see figure 5.3).

**Figure 5.3**
Still from the *Making of Balkan Wars: The Game* (Personal Cinema Collective, 2002).

The question so often asked in the wake of the war, "What is the Balkans?," is reformulated here as part of the larger question, "Can we separate what we know as the essence of 'the Balkans' from how we know it?" (174). The game foregrounds democracy as a process of democratization rather than a fixed state of "truth" to achieve. Democracy is reconstituted in Hannah Arendt's sense as an agonic game (see Tully 1999).

*The Making of Balkan Wars: The Game,* along with an accompanying documentary, also available online on the Personal Cinema home page, are intended to undermine the sensational spectacle of war and reclaim the stereotypes of the Balkans presented by the global news media. It is dedicated to critiquing the real historical war game in a form that acknowledges the media commodification of the Balkans. The members of Personal Cinema see their work as "tactical media." Geert Lovink, David García, and Krzysztof Wodiczko define tactical media as a means for the small and the weak to move fast across the physical or media and virtual landscapes, and become the hunter instead of the hunted (Spyropoulos 2007, 175). The Personal Cinema group considers the game to be in continuity with the theater in that the interface does not masquerade as "innocent," as in corporate games. Rather, it is displayed as a temporary museum whose goal is not the least "to question the meaning of an interface or platform that hosts arts" (175). However, the tendentious goal and the "artistic" roots of the game also limit its "fun" potential and thus its reach. The makers seem fully aware of the irony that, while they intended the game to be a critique of large Balkan exhibitions, at the end of the day, the game works like a virtual exhibition. In fact, one is most likely to encounter the game in the context of these same exhibitions across Europe (Personal Cinema Project 2005).

The group is characteristically reluctant to give up on the tradition and potential of art as a political practice, even though, with Peter Lunefeld, they contest the notion of a singular oppositional avant-garde (Spyropoulos 2007, 177). But they are equally reluctant to embrace and mystify new media technologies as inherently more progressive or democratic by virtue of their realism, speed, and interactivity. In fact, unlike technophiles, they "prefer to be boring" and continue to invest in narrative at the expense of technical know-how (177). This duality of caution toward new forms and technologies of play—reminiscent of Lev Manovich's caution about "totalitarian interactivity"— and critical reliance on older technologies and notions of play (such as narrative and poetry) is typical of postsocialist attitudes, crystallized in the wake of the global news focus on the Balkans. Personal Cinema draws on Huizinga's *Homo Ludens* to articulate the centrality of this dual meaning of play to their political practices and vision for the new Europe:

Spectacle, metaphors, any kind of imaginary constructions or myths, and even the creation of language is a form of play. Of course, we can fall into the trap of reading play as a form of abstraction that defines the whole world, like Capital does for Marx and Deleuze, or Simulation and the Real for Baudrillard, or Information and the Capital for McKenzie Wark, Love and Hate for the Pope, and so on. . . . In exactly the same way, play is related to games like Grand Theft Auto. The point here is that play cannot define the whole world but, on the other hand, it is more than just a search for fun. . . . Play is directly related to the construction of and obedience to rules and consequently to ideology, doctrines and, most important of all, ethics. . . . Play does not reveal what happened in the Balkans. But it makes us reread what an imaginary construction like the Balkans means. (Spyropoulos 2007, 179–180)

On a larger scale, Personal Cinema calls for the emergence of representation and distribution systems that respond to the local, the individual, even the unprofitable, producing and distributing multimedia works such as film, video, documentary, video games, CD-ROMs, software, and so forth through noncommercial, independent channels. The aim is a critical engagement of the public, offering alternatives to the increasing global homogeneity of media, particularly in support of minority groups

(Personal Cinema 2005). Andy Deck and Ilias Marmaras's 2000 manifesto reads,

Lacking coordination and investment, independent artists and filmmakers settle into the reactive procedural contexts that are industrially produced. Not surprisingly these contexts require skills that are very similar to those demanded by the advertising and entertainment industries, which exert the most influence over the further evolution of media technology. Personal Cinema II explores roles that can be elaborated by artists and filmmakers that are not conducive to the death of art and cinema. . . .

Technological innovations have established new rules for engagement with a public that has become accustomed to increasingly frenetic and effortless media. The amply demonstrated utility of the new media for the purposes of marketing now motivates creative practices that short-circuit, parody, deflate, and digress from the imperatives of consumption. . . .

While relevant distribution systems are clearly in a state of flux, historical parallels with the emergence of film and radio would lead us to believe that this fluid condition will not last. What would it mean for digital media and distribution systems to assume a stable configuration? Would such a configuration be something other than an apotheosis of marketing? Would it more resemble extreme sports, violent video games, or the archive of artifacts that are conventionally known as cinema? (http://www.personalcinema.org/warport)

Perhaps the most explicit and promising fusion between the two senses and practices of play evoked here is Personal Cinema's *Secondary Transludic Borders* project. Its conception reminds one of the controversial art collective Neue Slowenische Kunst (NSK), or New Slovenian Art, founded in 1984. NSK's inspirations are rooted in European avant-garde movements such as Surrealism and Dada. They have taken an active, parodic, and political stand against nation-states, borders, and totalitarianism through a variety of art practices. In 1991, they declared their own (virtual) transnational state. They have issued passports and founded embassies in actual cities. *Secondary Transludic Borders*, as the name indicates, approaches actual and virtual borders with the decidedly playful means of tactical media. The goal is to identify and transcend the corporeal, geopolitical, and social borders that global capitalism enacts in order to naturalize its power structures.

Participating artists are particularly critical of the emerging class that controls the "vectors," that is, the media that enable movement in space. Secondary Transludic Borders established its presence in one of the privileged global vectors of communication, Second Life, in order to complicate borders that demarcate identities in "first life." Participants wish to exploit the virtual online environment's potential for identity games, which is in marked opposition to the collective fixation on static identities in the highly nationalistic first-life environment of the Balkans. They are particularly invested in unfixing the first-life borders of gender, sexuality, bodies, nations and communities, land and property, work and commerce, and languages. The interactive performances and venues for this project took place in an actual location, the biennial art fair ArtBrussels (April 2007), as well as in the project's virtual center in Second Life.

## Consuming Games of Masculinity: *Little Otik* and *Hukkle*

The films I discuss in this final section betray a similar transitional sensibility and a corresponding openness to hybrid aesthetics, a willingness to throw identities in play and borders into construction. My primary interest remains in the ways in which the films suggest that processes of media globalization and Europeanization have upset boundaries of gender and nation. While the films' ludic aesthetic shares a regional affinity for the carnivalesque and the absurd with post-Yugoslav films, in the Balkan region the experience of the war sustained a distinct thematic center. The filmic identity games I examine in this last section, in turn, converge in their preoccupation with *consumption*. Consumption recurs as a theme in the characters' continual eating and processing of food, each other, and media; as an allegorical concern with global and European capitalism's, particularly the media's, appropriation of local memories, space, and art; and as a political and ethical practice in which the filmmakers themselves also engage. The gendered practice of mediated consumption is crystallized in two particularly rich feature films, *Hukkle* (György Pálfi, 2002) and *Little Otik* (Jan Svankmajer, 2000), in which I anchor my discussion.

Both films should be seen as part of a global cycle of films that meditate on the conditions of late capitalism through the allegory of obsessive eating and cannibalism. Crystal Bartolovich, in an essay provocatively titled "Consumerism, or the Cultural Logic of Late Capitalism," notes this pattern in relation to films such as *The Cook, the Thief, His Wife and Her Lover* (Greenaway, 1989), *Eat the Rich* (1987), *Consuming Passions* (1988), or *Parents* (1988). The theme reaches back to Pasolini's last film *Saló, or the 120 Days of Sodom* (1975) and Ferreri's *The Big Feast* (1973), and also incorporates Cronenberg's "body horror" cinema (*Naked Lunch* [1991], *Videodrome* [1983]) or Michael Haneke's *The*

*Seventh Continent* (1989). Bartolovich traces the concern with consumption and cannibalism to a global "crisis in appetite." She refers to Antonio Gramsci's claim that crisis occurs "when the old ways are dying and the new cannot yet be born," which results in "morbid symptoms" (quoted in Bartolovich 1998, 234).

I read *Hukkle* and *Little Otik* as manifestations of such a global crisis in appetite, readable in ways that are also specific to the historical moment of postcommunist European transitions. They evoke other cannibalistic and consumption-oriented reflections on global crisis, such as Makavejev's outrageous pornography of vulgar-Marxism in *W. R.: Mysteries of the Organism* (1971), or the Brazilian political-aesthetic tradition of carnivalesque, grotesque, and cannibalism. Applying an even wider historical lens, the two films could be identified as neobaroque, borrowing Angela Ndalianis's parallel between baroque aesthetics excess and contemporary ludic, global media entertainment (Ndalianis 2005). Jan Svankmajer's films have also been described variously as gothic, mannerist, and alchemist (see Cherry 2002; Wells 2002). *Hukkle* has been called a village ethnography as well as a nature film, has been compared to *Microcosmos: Le peuple de l'herbe* (Claude Nuridsany and Marie Pérennou, 1996) and has invited a Deleuzean framework. Both filmmakers' work may be characterized as "surrealist documentary," not in the sense of "film as record" but in that of "film as recognition": they both reveal the underlying value systems and relations beneath rationalized, civilized cultures, confirming Svankmajer's view that the surreal exists *in* reality, not *beside* it (Wells 2002). By virtue of uncovering the hidden, grotesque, terrifying underbelly of post-Enlightenment modernity, both films qualify as "docu-horror," "politically charged horror," or what Paul Wells calls "agit-scare" (Wells 2002), where horror resides in the recognition that global culture is driven by obsessive and compulsive needs.

The filmmakers' responses to a sense of global crisis and postcommunist transition are motivated by the shared legacy of European art cinema trying to find a space within cultures in radical transition between national cinema and consumer-oriented transnational media. They exhibit a European ambivalence toward Hollywood entertainment cinema and inherit the dissident role of the artist who is a man. They also share a regional, antisentimental attraction to black humor and the grotesque tradition of Ionescu, Kafka, and Gogol. At the same time, they continue distinct national traditions: *Little Otik*'s aesthetic and philosophy are deeply rooted in Svankmajer's association with the

Czechoslovak Surrealist Group and in an even older legacy of politically motivated Czech puppetry (Holloway 1983; Richardson 2006). *Hukkle*'s younger director, Pálfi, draws on the Hungarian allegorical, poetic-pornographic engagement with the body, discussed earlier in this chapter. Both filmmakers are also indebted to local folk traditions. *Little Otik* adapts a Czech fairy tale about a Pinocchio-like tree root, which comes to life as a result of paternal woodwork and maternal desire, but quickly turns out to be a monster who devours everybody in sight. The particular resurrection of the folktale pattern of cannibalism to critique modern consumption also situates the film within a global production of children's media, alongside popular animated films such as *Spirited Away* (Hayao Miyazaki, 2001) and *Monster House* (Gil Kenan, 2006) (see Baltazar 2007). In turn, Pálfi adopts the ironic gaze of the ethnographer inherited from the tradition of Hungarian village ethnography of the early 1900s (Imre 2004). The filmmakers' engagement with Hollywood genres—most evidently the horror and the thriller—is informed by such complex local-national-regional inspirations. In the following, I attempt to draw a conceptual map of the joint crisis of masculinity and nation over this cluster of multilevel frameworks, which converge in postsocialist identity play.

## Cannibalism and Gendered Conspiracy

Both films have been firmly contained in the critical appreciation of their respective auteurs, thanks to a cult following of Euro-American cineastes. *Little Otik* has been rightly seen as both an organic part of Czech surrealist animator Jan Svankmajer's long career and a potential new beginning in his oeuvre, given the fact that animation takes a backseat to a fairly traditional live-action plot in this modern-day horror fairy tale. Pálfi's first feature has been deemed a promising and unique new direction in European art cinema. As I argue, these films' preoccupation with food, consumption, cannibalism, and the grotesque body, and their similar mixing of styles, techniques, and genres, including animation and live action, point to a shared sense of the postcommunist "crisis" that has befallen Eastern European national cultures and their representative artist masculinities.

*Little Otik* transports the story of the eponymous folktale character, a humanoid tree root that comes to life to satisfy an infertile couple's desire for a child, into a dilapidated postsocialist urban tenement. The word *otesánek*, the name of the character and the film's title in Czech,

**Figure 5.4**
Nurturing the monster of consumption in *Otesánek* ("*Little Otik*," Jan Svankmajer, 2000).

joins the word for "to hew" with the diminutive suffix -*ánek*. Figuratively, it also refers to a person who devours everything. After Mr. Horák jokingly presents the root to his wife, Horáková, her passion for a child drives her to fake pregnancy and to "give birth" to Otik, the root-baby, whose craving for food matches the dimensions of his mother's pathological motherly desire (see figure 5.4). The more he eats, the faster he grows, quickly devouring the cat, the social worker, and eventually his own parents. The only person who is on to the pattern is the preteen daughter of the Horáks' neighbors, the precocious Alžbětka. As is often the case in Svankmajer's tales, the child is more mature than all the adults. While Horáková's regression to her fantasy of doll play has released a horror narrative, Alžbětka is able to control not only the resident pedophile's vibes toward her—communicated in the film through Alžbětka's subjective vision of an animated hand reaching out of the old man's bulging zipper—but also to predict Otik's, the monster's, moves after discovering the "script" in her book of fairy tales. Her periodic reading of the tale, represented in two-dimensional animation, prefigures the real-life events happening next door. In the end, Alžbětka is able to contain the monster in a locked chest in the cellar and bring the tale to its predicted conclusion.

**Figure 5.5**
The old man whose hiccups provide the digestive rhythm for *Hukkle* (György Pálfi, 2002).

*Hukkle*'s plot is so hidden under allegorical narrative layers and aesthetic distractions that it defies description. The title, an onomatopoeic word, refers to the hiccups that provide a steady digestive rhythm throughout the film, moving the plot along and structuring its various elements. The old man who performs the hiccuping is an inhabitant of the Hungarian village where the film takes place (see figure 5.5). But this toothless, grinning, silent man is no more of a character than the rest of the village dwellers (of the actual village of Ozora, where the film was shot). The camera observes the villagers as they perform various daily tasks with the same uninhibited and bemused curiosity with which it observes the local fauna and flora: a dying cat, as it turns into a disintegrating carcass and a pile of sun-dried bones in an accelerated sequence; a mole's underground journey to the surface, filmed from the animal's point of view, culminating in its merciless murder by a hoe-wielding old woman, who throws the dead mole to her dog to eat; an underwater sequence that follows a frog as it is swallowed by a catfish, which, in turn, gets caught on a fishing hook and is consumed by a human, whose digesting body is penetrated by the X-ray vision of the camera; and a gigantic pig repeatedly strolling down the street, looking for mates. Even though a rich variety of noises substitutes for human dialogue, the apparent village ethnography hides a murder plot: The men of the village, who periodically gather at their makeshift outdoor bowling alley, become fewer and fewer in number. One by one, they are being poisoned by a mysterious white liquid cooked up from the blossom of the white lily, which is gathered, processed, exchanged, and fed to the husbands by their silent wives.

Acts of consumption and digestion structure and punctuate both films. In *Hukkle*, all living creatures are caught up in an accelerated cycle of incessant consumption and decay. Similar to many of Svankmajer's earlier, animated films, food and eating are at the center of *Little Otik*, as well. At the very beginning of the film, as the Horáks arrive home from the hospital after learning the devastating news that they cannot have children, Mr. Horák has surrealist visions of babies sold like fish at the market and then emerging from watermelons. Discussions in the neighbors' apartment invariably take place around the dinner table, punctuated by close-ups of food and on the drooling, hungry face of Alžbětka's barking, insensitive father. He is mesmerized by acts of consumption in television commercials, which mingle with his own hallucinations. Of course, baby Otik himself is the very embodiment of monstrous, cannibalistic consumption.

Michael Nottingham suggests that the fixation on food and consumption in Svankmajer's films is a manifestation of what he calls the "folk-festive" mode, whose ideological and aesthetic underpinnings are to be found in the grotesque, in black humor, and in the filmmaker's unique surrealism. Mikhail Bakhtin's account of the carnivalesque in *Rabelais and His World* is particularly relevant to analyzing this ludic aesthetic cluster (Nottingham 2004). Bakhtin focuses on the jubilant preindustrial world view that crystallizes in Rabelais's writing: it is characterized by the unrestrained, spontaneous energy of the masses, which finds expression in irreverent humor, folk rituals, and a preoccupation with food, the mouth, defecation, sex, and various other grotesque operations of the body (Nottingham 2004, 3). Robert Stam, in his analysis of Brazilian carnivalesque culture, refers to Bakhtin's distinction between closed/deaf and open/hearing cultures. A transition from the former to the latter, a process of "decentering," occurs when a national culture loses its self-sufficient, sealed-off character and becomes conscious of itself as only one among many (Stam 1989, 122).

Stam's account of Latin American art is equally useful for approaching Eastern European manifestations of the grotesque and carnivalesque. It provides a more specific grounding for Gramsci's definition of *crisis* in transitional postcommunist cultures' recent tendency toward decentralizing, centrifugal aesthetic forces: "Latin American art is necessarily parodic, caught in specular games of doubling and redoubling, an art for which . . . 'naiveté is forbidden'" (Stam 1989, 122). However, in Brazilian modernist art, carnival and cannibalism were employed as subversive political and aesthetic strategies, most notably in the anthropophagy movement of the 1920s. Oswald de Andrade's *Cannibalist Manifesto*, as well as the movement's *Cannibalist Review*, set out to devour and incorporate techniques of superdeveloped countries precisely to oppose neocolonial domination (Stam 1989, 122). Cannibalism as a metaphor entered the language of the avant-garde in Europe but never led to a cultural movement or ideology as it did in Brazil in the 1920s under Andrade's leadership, in the 1950s' recycling of popular culture, or in the Tropicalist movement of the 1960s (126). Whereas Latin American cultures are carnivalesque in a literal sense— as an expression of polyphonic cultures, where carnival is woven into the very fabric of national identity—carnival remains a textual phenomenon in Europe for the most part (128). While such a subversive, politicized use of cannibalism and the carnivalesque has also emerged during moments of crisis in Eastern and Southern Europe—most recently in the Balkan films I discuss earlier in this chapter, or in *The District* (Áron Gauder, 2004), discussed in chapter 3—Eastern European national cultures' uncritical Eurocentrism constitutes a further limitation of such politics. In Brazil, centuries of cultural mixing and hybridity, the simultaneous and visible presence of waves of colonization, have resulted in what Stam characterizes as a "carnival culture." In Eastern Europe, however, carnivalesque subversions have remained tied to national cinemas and artists, protected from excessive contamination by popular forms.

In Latin America, carnival has remained a collective ritual, which gives voice to symbolic resistance to internal hegemonies of class, race, and gender, and allows minorities to take over for a moment the symbolic center of national life (Stam 1989, 129). This happens briefly in the recent Hungarian animated film *The District*, when the multicultural underclass forces of the ludic ghetto chase away the government representatives. Carnival here connotes a "profoundly democratic and egalitarian impulse," a collective catharsis, a social and interactive form of *jouissance*, where the marginalized play out imaginary roles (129). But even in *The District*, the film's somewhat condescending, parodic thrust holds up a derisive, condescending mirror to the two main underclass characters, the Roma bar owner and the white-trash pimp. They do not deserve our sympathy because they are nothing but criminals about to resubmerge in their world of booze and prostitution.

Svankmajer's repeated engagement with the themes of consumption and cannibalism, however, is comparable to the Tropicalism of the late 1960s. Tropicalism drew inspiration from the Brazilian modernism of the 1920s but fused aesthetic internationalism with political nationalism. It aggressively mingled folkloric and industrial, native and foreign, resulting in what Bakhtin would have called "textual polyphony." Joaquim Pedro de Andrade's 1969 adaptation of Mário de Andrade's 1928 novel *Macunaíma* uses cannibalism as a critique of repressive military rule and of the predatory capitalism model of the Brazilian economic miracle. The nation devours its own people in an allegory that mixes high and mass-mediated traditions (Stam 1989, 150). In a similar vein, food's function as a source of abundance and renewal and a symbol of collectivity is inverted in Svankmajer's animated films. Otik himself is a version of Macunaíma, a Rabelaisian protagonist with a grotesque body. Such heroes, whose prototype is Rabelais's Gargamelle, glorify the body in its obscenity, as it is overcome by "tragicomic seizures like sneezes and orgasms" (Stam 1989, 158)—or hiccups, as in the case of the old man in *Hukkle*. In *Hukkle*, the old man's grotesque hiccuping dominates the soundscape, rendering human speech inconsequential, noiselike—divesting it of any expressive, rational, or artistic function.

The grotesque body, again familiar from Bakhtin's account of the medieval carnivalesque, is on display in both films. Otik, a root, is literally a substratum, comparable to Bakhtin's material bodily lower stratum (Nottingham 2004, 21). *Hukkle*'s camera descends under the surface several times to root around in the soil and water, to try to find decaying bodies of men and animals. For Rabelais, the festive laughter of the carnivalesque dispelled the boundaries of sacred and profane, official and unofficial, the "joyous superabundance" of humanity (Nottingham 2004, 7). Bakhtin's idea of Rabelais's grotesque body would also describe Otik: "As a shifting series of vortexes of energy, the site of unanchored polysemy and radical differentiality, the grotesque body is given to excess, and thus to the gigantism and hyperbole of its artistic forms—its outsized noses and swollen buttocks, and the masks that emphasize metamorphosis and the 'violation of natural boundaries' " (Stam 1989, 159).

But Otik's grotesque body is more monstrous than subversive: it is the embodiment of evil and hostile forces of consumption, the latest in a series of menacing representations of food and eating in Svankmajer's work. In Svankmajer's early Kafkaesque short, *The Flat* (1968), a tenant is trapped in an apartment where objects prevent him from eating.

His spoon has holes, his fork bends, and his hard-boiled egg resists all his attempts to break it. Larger forces enlist objects in a conspiracy against the helpless individual—clearly reflecting on the existential conditions of the artist under socialism in the aftermath of the crushed 1968 anti-Soviet revolution. The theme most memorably returns in the three-part short *Dimensions of Dialogue* (1982). In the third part, two clay men's heads play a bizarre, surrealist game of "rock, paper, scissors." They alternate sticking out their tongues, which hold new objects each time. When the objects do not match, the "dialogue" breaks down and becomes increasingly destructive. In the live action-animation feature *Conspirators of Pleasure* (1996), nonspeaking characters play even stranger, sexualized games. Two neighbors destroy each other in the course of a game that involves elaborate costumes and the ritual consumption of a chicken. Other characters, whose perverse pleasures are intertwined, include a popular TV reporter, who gets sexual stimulation from caressing fish; her disconnected husband, whose life revolves entirely around constructing a massage machine made of a variety of brushes; the reporter's secret admirer, who builds a multihanded structure around his television set that rubs his various body parts pleasurably when his idol appears on TV; and a mail carrier, whose secret passion is rolling up bread into a million tiny balls and sucking them up through tubes to plug all her cavities.

In Svankmajer's monumental animated film *Faust* (1994), Faust finds an egg in the middle of a loaf of bread, which releases forces of darkness when cracked. The postcommunist triptych *Food* (1992) presents perhaps the most damning reversal of the positive connotations of eating. In the first part, "Breakfast," a person sits at a table across from another person, who turns out to be a vending machine of sorts. When the diner follows the instructions and consumes the food and drink dispensed, he turns into the machine himself. The last shot reveals a long line of people waiting outside to take their turn in becoming consumption machines. In the second part, "Lunch," two diners, ignored by waiters in a restaurant, engage in an eating competition, in the course of which they devour everything in sight, including each other. "Dinner" takes the theme of cannibalism to the furthest extreme: the subjective camera follows the gaze of unseen diners as they observe their food. A shot of the first one's wooden right hand leads to the discovery of his left hand on his plate, ready to be eaten. Subsequent meals serve up other body parts, including feet, breasts, and a penis. Svankmajer's surrealist adaptation of Lewis Carroll's novel, *Alice* (1988), also features acts of cannibalism, including the White Rabbit's shocking meal of the sawdust that spills out of his own wounded body.

Consumption, food, and sexuality are pleasures that have gotten out of control—a far cry from the collective joy of the medieval carnivalesque. Nottingham writes, "In Rabelais's world, the mouth is the means of expressive exchange that facilitates community, as well as the point of negotiation with the earth through nourishment, and the spirit-world through the breath. The folk-festive conception of food is as an emblem of popular empowerment, not ancillary but central to the potential for inverting social hierarchies" (Nottingham 2004, 13). Instead of the collective regeneration that follows the carnivalesque subversion of hierarchies, in Svankmajer's absurd universe we are left with empty play with the forms of the folk-festive. His films "reflect a surrealist approach that marries bleak existentialism with the absurd, replacing Bakhtin's emphasis on joviality and the carnivalesque with the black humor much lauded by Breton" (5). The promise of collective utopia is replaced by the reality of a dystopian totalitarian state, followed in the postcommunist period by a dystopian global consumer society—from Big Brother to *Big Brother*. Svankmajer has commented, "This civilization eats everything. It eats nature, whole cultures, but also love, liberty and poetry and it changes these into the odious excrement of the society of consumption and mass culture."[4] Food becomes a symbol of commodification, coupled with violence, individual isolation, and death.

This reversal of the Bakhtinian carnivalesque similarly illuminates *Hukkle*'s concerns with consumption. Food here is poison, which leads to death instead of regeneration. While all of Svankmajer's films have an almost universal allegorical dimension that cannot be reduced to a representation of the communist regime, the horror of *Little Otik*'s reworking of the folktale is precisely in the difficulty of pinning down the meaning, the origin of the horror. In a similar vein, *Hukkle* depicts an indifferent universe, in which people and other living beings are caught up in a near-natural process of senseless consumption. Conversely, since the film makes repeated efforts to call attention to the artificial, mechanical construction of its amplified soundscape, it hints at the possibility that "nature" exists primarily or exclusively as a set of manipulated images and noises, as a subject invariably transformed by audiovisual technology and served up for human consumption.

In *Hukkle*, food is consumed along with media—a theme also articulated through the figure of Alžbětka's father in *Little Otik*, while human communication is as impossible as it is in *Conspirators of*

*Pleasure* or *Dimensions of a Dialogue*: the shepherdess wears head-phones to transport herself from her dreary life into another world of sounds, and the investigating policeman's mother watches a telenovela on TV. The only actual human dialogue we hear in the movie comes from a global television show. There is nothing apparently tragic about this all-consuming universal digestive rhythm. No character in the film shows any remorse, sorrow, or other emotion. After the grandchild visit-ing from the city dies by accidentally licking Grandpa's poisoned food, the dead child's parents and grandparents follow the little coffin to the cemetery with the same vacant expression with which they had earlier consumed their dinners or with which the policeman's mother watches the soap opera.

Conspiracy is a common trope in Eastern and Central European films, which carry on a Kafkaesque cultural heritage of experiencing modernity as an imprisoning universe with inscrutable rules. Unlike in *The Trial*, *Colonel Redl*, and many other Eastern and Central European texts, however, in *Hukkle* there is no hero, and the conspiracy is an almost justifiable alliance of hardworking women who otherwise do not appear threatening at all. The kind of feminizing conspiracy that the film repre-sents through an alliance of women has more to do with that in *Video-drome*, *The Truman Show*, or *The Matrix*, where human subjects do not know that they are used, rendered passive, and being force-fed an elec-tronic diet that divests them of communicative agency and freezes them in spiritual death. But even in the latter two films, there is hope for redemption, for an escape back to reality. *Hukkle* conveys anxiety about conspiracy in the much larger sense that, as Fredric Jameson argues in *The Geopolitical Aesthetic*, constitutes the logic of the emerging system of postmodernism (Jameson 1992, 9–31).

The film represents a transition from the Manichaean, typological allegory, itself drawing on the Central European experience of existential anxiety captured by Kafka, to an allegory of the national that can no longer think of itself as authentic, truthful, and isolated from global postmodernism. The oscillation between the national and the global as primary conceptual and emotional frameworks of identity is repre-sented in *Hukkle* as emasculating. The film's allegorical structure makes figurable a certain gendered class consciousness specific to Eastern Europe—that of intellectuals who are forced to redefine their earlier taken-for-granted role, who have hopelessly slipped behind the economic elite in the social hierarchy, arriving at the position that Western Euro-pean and American intellectuals occupy.

**Figure 5.6**
Female conspiracy in *Hukkle* (György Pálfi, 2002).

Women in *Hukkle* are not simply powerful; they are murderers (see figure 5.6). They act like automatons, as if programmed by a remote control. If the irresistible mechanism of global consumption that has come to replace a more familiar and tangible form of political oppression is the ultimate evil in the film, consumption is also linked with evil femininity. Women are the addressees of most advertisements, the allegorical agents of a new order, turned active criminals by the power channeled through them by global commercial media. Alžbětka's father in *Little Otik* is a cautionary image of what happens to men who yield to the seductive, feminizing power of commercials: they will become clueless, ridiculous, devoid of authority.

Feminists such as Ann Douglas and Tania Modleski have persuasively contested the hierarchical conceptual opposition between passive, feminine consumption and active, masculine production, and have detected a masculine bias in the association between mass culture and femininity.[5] Such an association, while relatively new in Eastern and Central

European representations, is also motivated by a gendered class anxiety about the loss of European high art's prestige. Pálfi's eclectic, genre-mixing aesthetic strategy seems to resist the elitist hegemony of ideal meaning. However, what is passive and corruptive about global mass culture is isolated in the film as part of a female regime, rendered in feminine images. Pálfi's strategy is similar to Baudrillard's, who, Modleski argues, describes the feminized masses as a "gigantic black hole" outside of language, meaning, representation, and politics, while he celebrates the revolutionary potential of mass culture. Similar to "woman" in psychoanalysis, Modleski writes, the masses can no longer be spoken for in the collapse of sociality, the end of both the public and the domestic sphere, which characterizes Baudrillard's model of simulation (Modleski 1991, 31–32).

The metaphysical aspect of female monstrosity is not to be ignored here. The film's flirting with Hollywood genres encourages associations between the poison-brewing female conspiracy and the figure of the witch, a recurring representation of the monstrous feminine in horror films. *Hukkle* only hints at where the source of power is in the new order of media globalization, if there is such a center. Toward the end of the film, the hiccups suddenly stop and the earth begins shaking. The apocalyptic moment is brought on by an American fighter plane which, according to the script, is coming from the nearby American army base of Taszár. While the film does not claim that the women are agents of a specifically American kind of media imperialism, the local intellectual climate of anti-Americanism would make the link unmistakable.

Whose anxieties underpin the apocalyptic vision of a feminine conspiracy against fragile men in a world where consumption, vaguely associated with the United States, replaces communication? What does the policeman realize after the plane charges under the village bridge in a striking computer-generated special-effects phenomenon? In the last scene of the film, the policeman sits at a wedding table exasperated, as the camera pans around to reveal a young, indifferent bride and an oblivious, older groom, and we hear a chorus of village women sing a song about being orphaned—the only other instance besides the TV scene where human language is uttered in the film.

The theme of conspiracy, which also recurs in Svankmajer's work, is most evident in his *Conspirators of Pleasure* (1996). A truly transitional piece, conceived in the 1970s and completed in the 1990s, it links communist and postcommunist identity games organically under the theme of conspiracy. All the characters are fundamentally alienated from one another and are connected only through their conspiratorial dedication to their secret individual pleasures. Their innocent games have tragic consequences. The film shows that Svankmajer saw no great difference between the social conditions during and after communism (Richardson 2006).

*Hukkle* and *Little Otik* are both thriller-horrors that subtly link monstrous consumption with women. *Hukkle* was inspired by a series of real-life murders committed in 1929 by a large group of women who used arsenic systematically to murder their husbands and fathers-in-law in the actual Hungarian town of Nagyrév. The mass murders were hushed up at the time but brought enduring shame to inhabitants of the town, and their legacy is alive even today. It is quite likely that a feminist historical investigation would find evidence of early gendered "civil disobedience" in the murders. It is also telling that only a foreign filmmaker dared to engage the historical legacy head-on: Dutch director Astrid Bussink's documentary *The Angelmakers* (2005) revisits Nagyrév and investigates the murders retrospectively. If one is not familiar with the actual events, it is possible to miss the significance of the gendered conspiracy in Pálfi's film altogether. Most reviews have avoided tackling the issue as well, underscoring the fact that this is the least consciously processed register of the film. The author of a Hungarian review notices the fact that women systematically kill men as "female spiders devour males." But, in interpreting this pattern in relation to a larger social context, he dissolves the gender difference he had just identified within the old national "we," which he automatically extends to "humans" caught up in the struggle for survival (Sólyom 2004).

What is obvious is that women of the village feed, nurture, hunt, gather, and kill. Men, by contrast, play, fish, sit, and sleep, and are fed by women or are taken by women to see the doctor. Women are strong and determined while men are feeble—with the arguable exception of the policeman, who is one of the few male survivors. While the film does not issue an ethical commentary on the murders, the way it presents the women's daily, mind-numbing tasks of plucking chicken, cooking and heating up meals, feeding men, and watching men eat reminds one of Chantal Akerman's *Jeanne Dielman* (1976) and induces similar sympathy for the housewife whose days are spent in mindless service.

In *Little Otik*, it is a woman's desire for a child and a precocious girl's curiosity about sexuality that create and feed the monster that eats people (see figure 5.7). In a similar vein, in *Hukkle* the monster grows out of an infertile terrain, whose reproductive incapacity is allegorical

**Figure 5.7**
Alžbětka in *Otesánek* (*"Little Otik,"* Jan Svankmajer, 2000).

but most causally tied to women's and men's sexual inadequacy in a hostile environment obsessed with consuming. It is not far-fetched to see this motif as linked with the crisis of masculinity engendered by the postcommunist erosion of patriarchal-nationalistic structures, which unleashed a conservative backlash against women who defy naturalized gender hierarchies and take on public responsibilities at the expense of motherhood and domestic duties. In media depictions across the region, women's recent, limited empowerment, also supported by the European Union's policies of gender equality, has routinely been represented as a voracious appetite with sexual overtones, a hunger for commodities, power, and men. At the same time, as I argue earlier, men's anxiety over recognizing that consumption is "feminizing" the nation has been represented as the disappearance of "real men."[6]

Feminists have had much to say about the gendered implication of the grotesque body in horror films. Wayne Booth argues that Bakhtin, much like Rabelais, addresses himself to men and assumes a male audience, leaving women out of the conversation altogether (Booth 1982). Mary Russo also reveals Bakhtin's failure to incorporate the social relations of gender in his theory (Russo 1986). Robert Stam, however, claims that Bakhtin's analysis may be compatible with feminism. He considers Bakhtin's view of the body not phallocentric but "marginocentric" (Stam 1989, 163). While Bakhtin rarely addresses sexuality directly, he asserts that in modern society food, drink, and copulation lose their link to the social whole and become a petty private matter, the stuff of "romantic love" and fertility (Stam 1989, 160). This view is compatible with Svankmajer's representation of the grotesque monster, a universal, allegorical representation of merciless consumption.

## Transnational Body Cinema

Stam argues that Bakhtin subverts the usual hierarchy of the senses by rendering smell and taste equally important as sight, the sense usually trusted to confer epistemological authority (Stam 1989, 159). Svankmajer's surrealist practice similarly mingles sensory experiences. His use of collage encourages an associative rather than rational understanding, deliberately bypassing dialogue (Richardson 2006, 123). The result is often what Breton called poetic metaphor (Nottingham 2004, 2): the union of two realities that are usually considered widely separate. As it has been repeatedly pointed out, Svankmajer's animated films and even individual images have a tactile quality. They are sensually, not simply visually, present, calling to life everyday objects in a fashion that invariably threatens the individual and visualizes the absence of the collective (Nottingham 2004, 6 and 125). His constant mixing of animate and inanimate objects in a grotesque fashion simultaneously evokes horror and comedy, recalling Freud's notion of the uncanny. Svankmajer has called himself a necrophile because he is fascinated by communicating with dead things, objects that are witnesses to a forgotten, or potentially repressed, history, which he then re-animates in his narratives (Wells 2002).

This necrophilic relation to repressed history also animates Pálfi's subsequent feature, *Taxidermia* (2006), a monstrous historical allegory of socialism. Perhaps the most shockingly tactile of the rare collection of grotesque bodies in the film is that of the taxidermist, who eventually sews his own body into a stuffed, live puppet. Svankmajer's credo as an animator, for whom living beings are often incapable of human communication but inorganic objects come to life, resonates with *Taxidermia*: "For me, objects are more alive than people, more permanent and more expressive—the memories they possess far exceed the memories of man. Objects conceal within themselves the events they've witnessed. I don't actually animate objects. I coerce their inner life out of them—and for that animation is a great aid which I consider to be a sort of magical rite or ritual."[7]

The shift from the abstraction of language to the expressivity of Bakhtin's "lower bodily stratum" has been a recurrent focus of European art cinemas, especially during times of crisis. Balkan film and art provide many recent examples. In a similar vein, Jurij Murasov argues, drawing on Bakhtin's work and Antonin Artaud's theater of cruelty, that post-Soviet art has a tendency toward body-oriented performances "that may be interpreted as a form of media discourse on the conflict between the ear and the eye, between verbality and visuality" (Murasov [n.d.]). Vlad Strukov discusses the animated work of postcommunist Russian art collectives in similar terms, including the work of Andrei Bakhurin, whose flash animation characters "occupy a liminal space between humans, dolls, monsters ('freaks') and insects," and whose surreal narratives "occasionally lack any cohesion or linear development" (Strukov 2005). Along with other recent Romanian films, Paul Arthur situates Christian Puiu's *The Death of Mr. Lazarescu* at the center of the "meta-genre" of "corporeal cinema." Corporeal cinema consists of grim allegories that are preoccupied with "Eastern Europe's recent historical convulsions," including Béla Tarr's, Alexander Sokurov's, and Emir Kusturica's films as well as films from other cultures, similarly preoccupied with a play with realism, such as Jafar Panahi's *Crimson Gold* (2003), Pablo Trapero's *Crane World* (1999), and Catherine Breillat's *Fat Girl* (2001) (Arthur 2006).

Along similar lines, Laura U. Marks argues that hybrid cinema, in which autobiography mediates a mixture of documentary, fiction, and experimental genres, characterizes the film production of cultures in transition and people in identity flux (Marks 1994, 245). Such films are produced in contentious relation to dominant languages and are properly termed a minority form. Svankmajer's and Pálfi's concern with eliciting the repressed memories of silent people by interrogating the historical layers preserved by objects has the same archaeological quality that Marks, following Deleuze's notion of the archaeology of the image, attributes to hybrid cinema. Such a cinema confounds official history, private recollection, and simple fiction. Marks adds, "if Deleuze's understanding of perception is traced back to its borrowing from Bergson, these disjunctions within the sense information offered by a film can evoke other sorts of memory that slip from dominant discourse, namely memories encoded in senses other than auditory and visual" (245). Marks agrees with Deleuze that the visual and the verbal are different orders, irreducible to each other, creating, in the cinema, a necessarily disjunctive record of "truth." However, she claims—in an argument further elaborated upon in her book *The Skin of the Film*—that there are other, even less easily coded orders, which also leave their traces on audiovisual media.

Experimental diasporic cinema digs between strata, using a mixture of filmic languages to tell the unofficial stories of exile, emigrant, or culturally mixed people. Where multicultural categorizing keeps difference in its place, hybridity is unpredictable and generative. When someone's experience does not fit into the categories provided, it brings back the histories that are repressed—just as a fossilized fragment visibly recalls the forgotten struggles of past generations. Hybrids reveal the process of exclusion by which nations and identities are formed. (251)

With Deleuze, Marks argues that films made by minorities tend to evoke memories that are at odds with and are often consciously opposed to the official image repertoires. These recollection images act like "radio-active" fossils in that they embody traces of events whose representation has been buried but can be reactivated (253). Svankmajer's work relies precisely on such a relationship to objects as fossils, which can be reactivated only through tactile memories. These memories take one back to childhood, the time of the first preverbal sense, touch. Pálfi's rejection of verbal language and the stylistic and generic hybridity of his work also rest in such a minority relationship to the collective national past and the global/European future. People in his village are not seen using the national language to communicate. There is a rich sound track, but it is entirely made up of amplified, often artificially created noises—doors slamming, animals moving, a garbage truck making its rounds on dirt roads, even the growing of plants. The film foregrounds the technical manipulation of image and sound—most shockingly in the special effects sequence at the end of the film, in which an American fighter plane swoops under the local bridge causing a minor earthquake in the village. The documentary effort, then, is rendered unreal, or hyperreal, by underscoring the use of state-of-the-art surveillance and simulation technology.

The film's official Web site (www.hukkle.hu) further extends its address to the technologically savvy and playful by inserting credits, a shooting diary, and information about the director and the cast within clever interactive visual games positioned against shadow-puppet-like stock images of a generic village: a stork, a house, a bench, and a pond. One can move around the circular site horizontally, arriving at the same spots again and again with no apparent escape, emulating the cruel, imprisoning rhythm of life in the filmic village. As one navigates the site, a hand-shaped icon keeps appearing to reveal information, which then emerges from the stork's beak, from a half-empty bottle, or from under the roof of a house. The village is a puppetry set—a place that allows for the allegorical manipulation of formulaic, simple images and lives. In addition to a visual ethnography, an allegorical village film, a nature show, and what a critic calls the current international mini-genre of subtitle-free, deliberately "quiet projects" (Young [n.d.]), there is also a thriller element in *Hukkle*. Thus, the film also functions as a Hollywood genre film fused into a European art film, somewhat like a documentary in David Lynch's style. The viewers are motivated by narrative suspense to figure out why the murders occur and how the film will end. Even if there is no single key to the puzzle, there is a certain allegorical coherence to this "film style game" or "artistic experiment," as the director introduces it on the Web site.

The film successfully taps into and replicates the experience of a transition from an order embedded in the relative safety and isolation of the national community to a frightening but also liberating global order. In this new world, community can be reproduced only virtually, from a variety of camera angles, manipulated by digital technology and sophisticated editing; and the national language is muffled under a combination of noises that obliterate the difference between organic and artificial. The village is a frozen image of the past, a memory of the idealized national community that, the film's ironic distance and painstakingly constructed realism imply, may never have existed in the first place. Watching the old man sit on a bench in front of his house all day, men playing leisurely bowl games in the street, or a shepherdess tending to the herd are reminders of a world about to disappear or already nostalgically staged for the tourist's camera. The village as allegorical tableaux mobilizes local reflexes of an older, typological kind of reading familiar from the Cold War, prompting the audience to decode an abstract film language that masks a politically unutterable message. But this expectation gets sidetracked and undermined by the expectation of reading a Hollywood genre film: who is committing the murders and why?

Eastern European viewers and fans of Eastern European cinemas worldwide will recognize the national artist's effort to create something "authentic and autonomous," qualities that, critics repeatedly lament, are hard to come by in the derivative land of postsocialist cinemas. A Hungarian critic, in his evaluation of the less-than-stellar film crop of the late 1990s, declares that in order to create free and autonomous artistic fiction, one needs "absolute hearing." In *Hukkle*, the modernist-

Romantic masculine urge to flaunt the genius's superhuman hearing is tamed by a degree of humility before the new, all-devouring black hole of postmodern technocapitalism. The film's unconventional soundscape is characterized by this ambiguity between hubris and humility. Do the sound effects create progressive heteroglossia in the Bakhtinian sense of socially generated contradictions, which constitute the subject as the site of competing discourses and voices (see Shohat and Stam 1994, 215)? Is the purpose of privileging sound to suppress the modernist gaze associated with the claim to authenticity? Or does the emphasis on the technological manipulation of noises and images create a "pseudo-polyphonic discourse" in the manner of television commercials? Does bypassing human language mean renouncing the truth-seeking effort of historical films as it does, for instance, in *Latcho Drom* (1993), Tony Gatlif's film about Romany history told entirely in musical vignettes, which I discuss in chapter 3? Does Pálfi's listening subject assume historical "response-ability" instead of the grudging historical responsibility of the national artist called on to reify an abstract truth? Does Iain Chambers's description of the postmodernist, listening subject describe the viewer addressed by Pálfi's film?

In the dispersal of a single History, whose omniscient word legislates the world, I begin to hear composite voices crossing and disturbing the path and patterns of the once seemingly ineluctable onrush of "progress." In the movement from concentrated sight to dispersed sound, from the "neutral" gaze to the interference of hearing, from the discriminating eye to the incidental ear, I abandon a fixed (ad)vantage for a mobile and exposed politics of listening—for a "truth" that is always becoming. (Chambers 1996, 51)

The politics of listening remains ridden with ambiguity in the film. The act of listening is foregrounded, but the "speaking" human subjects remain silenced, objectified. Many of the noises are generated by the playful filmmaker himself. Whereas most films of the 1980s were enwrapped in explicitly male intellectual experiences of compromising with oppressive powers, in the world of *Hukkle*, the artist hides behind the allegorical, hiccuping character of an old villager. But the structural contradiction of the allegorical form foregrounds the ambiguity of his mission; analogical distance from the character also implies the recognition of similarity to the character. The artist, no longer sponsored by the state and justified in his role as the Romantic voice of the nation, is feminized by a culture that forces him to promote and sell himself with audiovisual tricks and clever websites.

Rey Chow's reading of *King of the Children* (Chen Kaige, 1987), based on a novel of the same title by the Chinese writer Ah Cheng (1984), sheds analogical light on the gendered plight of the national artist. In the film, a young man, Lao Gang, comes to an isolated, rural school to be a schoolteacher—much like Pálfi's invisible urban observer, the director's alter ego, gains access to the life of Ozora. Both films are concerned with the struggle of the intellectual class for self-definition among hostile circumstances. In both cases, this class redefinition is short-circuited by what Chow calls the narcissism of the male intellectual. Chow redefines the psychoanalytic description of narcissism, which Freud primarily applied to female patients, as "an effect of cultural marginalization or degradation" (Chow 1993, 109). She argues that Lao Gang bypasses the sexuality represented by actual women in favor of "men's play," the male child, and a bond with nature. Like many other characters in 1980s Chinese film and literature, he is self-absorbed, passive, and thus "feminine," characteristics that Chow reads as symptoms of the symbolic impotence of Chinese male intellectuals, who are reluctant to perform their national duty of symbolic cultural procreation in post–Cultural Revolution Chinese culture (111). Chow's analysis applies to post-Soviet East Central European intellectuals by analogy. The intellectual's loss of power is more complete and self-conscious in *Hukkle* than in *King of the Children* or in earlier East Central European films, however (see Imre 2001).

The community that both *Hukkle* and *Little Otik* address are film buffs and film students, the audiences of international film festivals. While it would be too bold to claim that the films provide new models for postsocialist filmmaking, they both bring a new kind of energy to the world cinema scene because they break out of imprisoning categories such as "national" and "regional" while they continue filmmaking and philosophical trends rooted in local tradition. Their particular hybridity allows for the coexistence of the familiar fear of totalitarianism and a more postmodern, shapeless fear of the global conspiracy of consumerism. They cross the two main routes that postsocialist filmmaking has followed in the past fifteen years: they do not continue to lock film production into high modernist art, nor do they simply or cynically satisfy audience desires for entertainment. Much like Kusturica and other post-Yugoslav filmmakers, or the artists of the Personal Cinema collective, they use stylistic play and black humor to sustain art as the site for the collective processing of crisis and transition. Crystal Bartolovich argues that Greenaway's *The Cook, the Thief, His Wife and Her Lover* remains limited in its potential for political intervention because it criticizes only the thief—the crude, loud, and distinctly lower-class consumer—as the embodiment of cannibalism, the cultural logic of late capitalism. The criticism is issued from the point of view of the cook, the wife, and the lover, who are all sophisticated and refined characters, restrained in their consumption, worthy of "Greenaway's high table"—unlike most of the film's viewers (Bartolovich 1998, 237). Such a charge can be leveled at Eastern European films such as *Hukkle, Little Otik,* or *Underground* only to a certain extent, since their directors—unlike the Szabó of *Meeting Venus*—seem quite conscious of the fact that their place is the equivalent of the "low table" in the post–Cold War European geography of power. In their depictions, the Eastern European artist as a man is very much implicated in the logic of cannibalism and is rapidly losing his Romantic-national privileges as a result.

Perhaps the most appropriate representation of the ambivalent, in-between Eastern European artist at this historical moment is Dracula. He is the product of a sprinkling of local historical memory enhanced by a large amount of Western exoticization. Dracula has recently been embraced as "native" and repackaged for foreign consumption in Romania and elsewhere (see Iordanova 2007). At night, he comes to life and becomes the king of horror; a shape-shifter; an undead human animal; an ambiguously sexualized, effeminate superman, who sustains his grotesque body entirely by consuming others. At dawn, he disappears and his daytime alter ego comes to life. His name might be Borat: a global hybrid, just like Dracula, but wrapped in stereotypes instead of legend, lacking even vampiric agency. But this is the beginning of another tale . . .[8]

# Conclusion

I argue for a politics rooted in claims about fundamental changes in the nature of class, race, and gender in an emerging system of world order analogous in its novelty and scope to that created by industrial capitalism; we are living through a movement from an organic, industrial society to a polymorphous, information system—from all work to all play, a deadly game.
Donna Haraway, "A Manifesto for Cyborgs" (2003, 20)

The *global* is everywhere these days. Politicians, corporate executives, school principals, university professors, and newsmakers constantly refer to globalization as something inevitable to celebrate, prepare for, or worry about. In everyday lives, the "global" evokes a mix of these emotions, a general sense of an accelerated shift toward fulfilling the modern dream, an unavoidable but almost metaphysically vague future of new technological and scientific frontiers and increasing mobility, but also of dwindling resources, permanent war and economic crisis, and ecological catastrophe. The sense of destiny about a global future has solidified since the end of the Cold War and the fall of communism in Europe, when the last obstacles to the neoliberal consumer-capitalist route were allegedly cleared out of the way. Since then, despite the multidirectionality of its cultural and economic flows, globalization has been sealed with a stamp that features the Statue of Liberty and the Disney logo.

The Wall came down in 1989, but the Cold War division between the "Old" and the "New" Europe has not disappeared. New walls have been erected around Fortress Europe in defense against immigrants, refugees, aliens, and fortune-seekers from the east and south. But such tensions have been downgraded from a global to a regional concern, the private affair of the European Union, which has been assimilating the lands beyond the Iron Curtain within its growing empire over the past decade. While Russia has continued to be a global player, much of its former empire has been easing closer to a united Europe. Other areas, such as the Middle East and China, have been identified in the past decades as the hot buttons of global economy and security, legitimated as such by U.S. economic and political interests and the U.S.-led war on terror.

This book is certainly not the result of a nostalgic yearning for the Cold War, when the area studies attention, supported by state department research money, was lavished on the Soviet empire. On the contrary, it is an argument against naturalizing a vision of globalization determined by neoimperial power interests. The area studies paradigm issued selected questions and found the selective answers it was paid to find. Globalization is not and should not be construed as a zero-sum game, a turf war among the peripheries for the attention of power centers. Rather, it is a dispersed and inscrutable set of political and economic games that are no longer played exclusively among nation-states. The "game" model usefully complements existing metaphors of globalization, such as "flow," "scape," and "network." The play/game metaphor underscores the increasing recognition that media flows are not simply one aspect of globalization but part and parcel of all transnational economic, political, and cultural exchanges. Media globalization implies that the power games of transnational corporations are inseparable from consumers' collective and individual identity games.

Political science alone is inadequate to map the complexities of such multilayered games, whose rules are permanently subject to shifts. It needs to be complemented by media and communication studies, an inherently interdisciplinary set of inquiries informed by cultural studies and the social sciences. As I emphasize in these chapters, the need for an interdisciplinary understanding of media globalization is particularly true for the post-Wall transformations in Eastern Europe. The play and game model allows one to analyze the changing aesthetic of postcommunist television, film, and new media practices as they are intertwined with the ideological and economic interests that motivate the power games behind simplistic evocations of globalization. Now that the Balkan wars have ended, the news cameras have turned away from the postcommunist region. However, the subsequent erasure of the forty-year experience of communism, and the failure to process the unprecedented historical experience of the transition from late communism to late capitalism in its complexity, is depriving our understanding of media globalization of valuable lessons. Rendering these events irrelevant or too obscure for navigating the unstoppable flow of capitalist globalization has effected a short-circuiting of historical memory, detrimental at a time when U.S.—and, by extension, global—media is inundated with political propaganda under the guise of innocent entertainment and spectacle, and when serious questions loom about the mediated power games in which the next generations will engage.

Unlike employing other models of globalization, which tend to emphasize its novel and distinctive qualities, seeing the postsocialist transformations in terms of shifting play practices that continually crystallize into new games also allows us to notice otherwise hidden continuities. Late-communist media entertainment in particular is rife with opportunities for studies of contradictory play practices, which fall neither under established notions of modernist high art nor under consumerist entertainment and undermine any strict opposition between communism and capitalism, production and consumption, state and market control, isolation and mobility, or work and play. Considering the fact that such ambiguities have characterized this in-between region—along with other peripheral areas around the world—for most of its recorded history, it is not at all clear that they will simply disappear once Eastern and Southern Europe "catch up" and become an indistinguishable part of a globalizing media world, in which local differences are preserved only for tourist attraction. Postcommunist changes continue earlier trends as much as they reflect radically new influences. While such influences are important, the feared mass conversion of the population to the church of American popular culture is yet to happen. Instead, as I argue, one observes a mix of enthusiasm and disappointment, resistance and acceptance. The specific histories of the aesthetic, economic, and political hybrids I discuss in the book—postcommunist reality programming, children's animation, post-Yugoslav carnivalesque films, ludic lesbian media activism, Roma hip-hop, or the Eurovision contest—hold out the possibility that the unique combination of communist and postcommunist media trends might yield alternatives to the all-encompassing logic of consumption and entertainment.

Adapting Donna Haraway's account describing contemporary cyborg identities, we are indeed part of a deadly global game, not the least because it is all play. Isolation, withdrawal, high-cultural contempt, resistance, and culture jamming have proven futile in resisting its converging temptations. We need to go beyond mere juxtapositions and comparisons, which often replay the same games rather than changing the rules. Ultimately, studies of media globalization should result in global, strategic media literacy efforts that connect researchers, media producers, and consumer citizens in a recognition of shared complicity with and interests against converging media conglomerates and confront these actors with their own ethnocentrism toward one another. My goal has been to show that the insight to be gained from the complex interdisciplinary analysis of the global peripheries is particularly important to a strategic mapping of transnational media trends. The New Europe is just one such peripheral resource of theoretical inspiration and historical precedent.

# Notes

## Introduction

1. "Play clearly represents an order in which the to-and-fro motion of play follows of itself. It is part of play that the movement is not only without goal or purpose but also without effort. It happens, as it were, by itself" (Gadamer 1996, 105).

2. It is impossible to do justice to the proliferation of the play metaphor in modernist thought. Psychoanalysis has been one of the most fertile fields for theoretical play, to which I give relatively little attention in this book. Sigmund Freud, Jacques Lacan, Louis Althusser, more recently Slavoj Žižek and Judith Butler, and countless other theorists adopt an ontological model that sees human life as an ongoing attempt to strive for the unattainable Real and simultaneously avoid the inevitably traumatic encounter with it. Symbolization, or the use of language, is a form of incessant "Fort-Da," a process of meaning making that originates in early childhood and keeps life from appearing meaningless.

3. In ethnographic field work, the "ludic turn" draws on earlier work by Huizinga (1955) and Geertz's (1974) opposition between work and play, investigations of the role of play in learning (e.g., Lave and Wenger 1991), studies of the significance of role-play and mimesis considered as embodied ways of knowing (e.g., Taussig 1993), and studies of the cultural, political, and ethical dimensions of engaging with informants through play (e.g., Lury 1998).

4. See, for instance, Frasca (2003) and de Mul (2005). See also the European collaborative research program Playful Identities: http://www.playful-identities .nl/flash/index.html.

5. For instance, Julian Sefton-Green asks if modernity is characterized by mass media culture, in what ways does digital culture break with or extend this paradigm? He urges us not to get so distracted by the hyperbole surrounding digital culture as to miss its continuities with more traditional forms of screen-based entertainment (1998, 5).

6. For instance, the deceptively named, Hungarian-language, invite-only site International Who Is Who, or "iwiw," has 2.6 million users registered with

their own personal details, in the country of 10 million. Rather than creating a cosmopedic space, digital technology, provided by Magyar Telekom, the former communist state telecommunications company-turned-subsidiary of Deutsche Telekom, seems to have reconstituted the national intimacy of an enormous family, which characterized the affective private sphere of late communism, while dispensing with the latter's oppositional culture-poaching function. Even though the multilingual interface was touted as a great innovation, which accompanied the change of the name from "wiw" to "iwiw," the site recently reverted to a Hungarian-only interface.

## Chapter One

1. "Homework," episode 149, season 7. First aired on CBS, September 30, 2002.

2. For a good summary, see Mizuko Ito (2008) "Mobilizing the Imagination in Everyday Play: The Case of Japanese Media Mixes." In *International Handbook of Children's Media and Culture*. Sonia Livingstone and Kirsten Drotner, eds.

3. In a recent roundtable discussion, five high-ranking Hungarian educational experts, all men, all with backgrounds in scientific or technological fields, enthusiastically discussed the smooth interaction between the state and the ICT "profession" in implementing new, technology-focused educational programs, parts of the tellingly named National Strategy of Informatics. One of the participants declared, "The country will only move forward if the citizen becomes a serious consumer of informatics, which will create a market. So the goal should be the mass proliferation of internet culture. For this, we need market-friendly policies that make the purchase of PC's and the use of the internet accessible for the citizen; and that make it possible for cable companies to provide internet services based on a flat fee. I see these as two of the most important directions we need to follow. The third one . . . is the continued production of educated people and independent intellectual capacities, which has always characterized Hungary" ("Kerekasztal beszélgetés" 1997).

4. http://europa.eu.int/europago/index.htm.

## Chapter Two

1. http://www.szoborpark.hu.

2. See, for instance, Sabrina Petra Ramet, ed. 1994. *Rocking the State: Rock Music and Politics in Eastern Europe and Russia*. Boulder, CO: Westview Press.

## Chapter Three

1. See, for instance: "A hazáról méltatlan, igaztalan hírt kelteni nem a hazaszeretet tárgykörébe tartozik: A zámolyi romák a jobboldali sajtóban," http://

www.mozgovilag.hu/2000/12/dec3.htm. IREX Policy Paper: "The Roma in Central and Eastern Europe," http://www.irex.org/publications/policy-papers/index.htm. "Slovakia's Unloved Ones," *The Economist*, March 4, 2000, vol. 354, no. 8160: 51. "ERRC Press Release: United Nations CERD Finds Slovak Anti-Romani Municipal Ordinances Violate International Law," http://www.errc.org/cikk.php?cikk=230. Johnson, Eric, "Beating Death of Romany Mars Slovakia's Image," http://www.romapage.hu/eng/hiren021.htm.

2. Timothy Cresswell discusses the historically engrained, racist association of mobility and homelessness with shiftlessness, unreliability, absence, and general disrepute—an assumption that implicitly valorizes sedentary, settled territorial nationalism as authentic. Timothy Cresswell and Ginette Verstraete, eds. 2002. "Introduction: Theorizing Place," in *Mobilizing Place, Placing Mobility: The Politics of Representation in a Globalized World*. Thamyris/Intersecting no. 9: 11–32.

3. See *Cinema Journal*'s special "In Focus" section on "The New Cold War" (fall 2004), 43.4, eds. Louise Spence and Dennis Broe; Neil Postman, *Amusing Ourselves to Death: Public Discourse in the Age of Show Business*, New York: Penguin, 1986.

4. The relationship of postsocialist states with "the West" deserves a closer inspection for its contradictions. These contradictions surface most clearly when one interrogates the situation of Romany minorities. Nation-states across the postsocialist region have split the notion of "the West" into morally charged opposites to serve their own political ends. Idealized "European" values and culture represent the "good" West, to which political parties solemnly swear to lead their charges back after the forced detour of communism. By contrast, aspects of globalization that undermine the process of enlisting loyalties in service of the "shared" national project prescribed by the state are relegated to the "bad" West. These aspects are often summed up simply under "globalization," and are often associated with commercialization and the way in which American "media imperialism" has targeted and invaded fresh Eastern European markets, bringing along a politics of identity seen as "imported" from a land kept under the terror of political correctness and affirmative action. The deeply engrained, institutionalized hierarchy of Eurocentric high culture and global popular culture helps to naturalize the good-bad West distinction, often swaying even progressive critics of state policies.

This hierarchy is also racialized: while nationalism and racism always go hand in hand, Eastern European nationalisms' eager emulation of the structures of European nationalism, in the absence of the latter's haunting imperial legacy, kept whiteness and white supremacy entirely submerged in nationalism until very recently. In other words, nationalism in Eastern Europe functions as a form of racism. Eurocentric modernist high culture, seen as the true legacy of Eastern European nations, is "naturally" white, that is, transparent. By contrast, the multicultural world of advertisements, Hollywood films, imported reality television shows, hip-hop music, global fashion, and video games are disturbingly colorful, threatening to reduce the whiteness of Eurocentric national cultures to the paleness of cultural death.

5. See György Csepeli, "Competing Patterns of National Identity in Postcommunist Hungary," *Media, Culture, and Society* 13 (1991): 325–339; Aleksandar Kiossev, "Megjegyzések az önkolonizáló kultúrákról," *Magyar Lettre Internationale* 37, summer 2000: 7–10; Róbert Braun, "Communities in Transition: Problems of Constitutionalism and Narrative Identity in Europe," http://www.replika.c3.hu/english/02/04braun.htm.

6. See "Fekete, sárga barátokat keres a cigányirtó fiú," *RomNet*, February 21, 2005. http://www.romapage.hu/hirek/hircentrum/article/74539; Nóra Papp, "Ciganyirto jatek az interneten," *RomNet*, February 15, 2005. http://www.romapage.hu/hirek/hircentrum-forummal/article/74511/1464/page/10; "Rasszista jatek az interneten," *Népszabadság Online*, February 16, 2005, http://nol.hu/cikk/352099.

7. See "Tiltakozás a TV2 *Bazi nagy roma lagzi* címü müsora miatt," *RomaPage*; http://www/romapage.hu/hirek/index.php?kozep=rsk777.htm. Miklós Györffy, "A vesztesek mint vásári érdekesség a médiában," *Radio Kossuth*. http://www/radio.hu/index.php/read/27044; Éva Farkas, "Magyar Bálint elítéli az Irigy Hónaljmirigy roma-paródiáját," *Magyar Radio Online*, http://www.radio.hu/index.php/read/26300; "Megsértette-e a TV2 a romákat?" *Magyar Radio Online*. http://www.radio.hu/index.php/read/26587.

8. For a historical analysis of the conflict of high culture and mass culture, and on the democratizing potential of the latter, see Strinati Dominic, *An Introduction to Theories of Popular Culture*. London: Routledge, 1995. See especially pp. 21–50.

9. "From Bad to Horrific in a Gypsy Ghetto," *BusinessWeek*, June 19, 2000: 24–E4; Nicola Solimano and Tiziana Mori, "A Roma Ghetto in Florence," *UNESCO Courier*, June 2000: 40.

10. *Paraszt*, the Hungarian term I have translated as "white trash," literally means "peasant," and refers to someone rude and uncivilized, regardless of job or location.

11. Kinyírsz, mer' csak szidni bírsz,
Hogy nem vagyok pretty, mint a Britney Spears,
de a bálványod nekem túl silány,
én egy MC-lány vagyok, egy MC lány.

Neked a tip-top csaj,
nekem a hip-hop zaj kell.
A termeted, mint egy King Kong, aszti!
Az agyad viszont egy ping-pong laszti,
baszki, aszkéta nem leszek miattad,
mint rakétának, az utam kiadtad,
de ki bánja, mikor a bálványa,
az ideálja nekem túl silány . . .

12. The term "discursive ghetto" is Hamid Naficy's. See Hamid Naficy, "Phobic Places and Liminal Panics: Independent Transnational Film Genre," Rob Wilson and Wimal Dissanayake, eds., *Global/Local*. Durham: Duke University Press, 1996: 120.

13. I am grateful to Christine Taylor, whose unpublished paper on Dutch multiculturalism and Ali B has provided the core of the information presented here.

14. From Ali B's official Web site: http://www.alib.nl.

15. German, Belgian, and Italian managers in the industry, in particular, take advantage of the new communication opportunities provided by the Internet or satellite TV as much as star candidates from Eastern Europe. This is the way the Russian Tatu duo or the Romanian Cheeky Girls have made it in Europe—the latter ironically resurrecting the Dracula myth and emphasizing the lesbian connotations of the vampire image, offering all this in a combination of Hungarian folk, rap, rock, and Gypsy techno. "Cigánytechno, balkánrock," *Népszabadság*, July 3, 2003, http://www.romapage.hu/kulthirnews2.php?id=223.

16. Anett Szalai, "Roma csillagok." A review of an international musical festival, held in Budapest in August 2000, notes that most of the Hungarian participants were Roma. It also predicts that, similar to many of their predecessors, some of these Romany musicians will end up with contracts with well-known Western bands. Klezmatics, "Filmszakadásig," *Magyar Narancs* 12.30, 2000: 27.

17. On Syndrom Snopp, see http://www.paranolmalz.cz. On contemporary Eastern European Gypsy music, see Zuzana Jurková, ed., *Romani Music at the Turn of the Millennium, Proceedings of the Ethnomusicological Conference*, Saga: Praga, 2003.

18. See http://www.gipsy.cz.

19. http://groups.yahoo.com/group/balkanhr/message/2029.

20. "SuperStar (Czech Idol) Is Romany Vlastimil Horvath," *Ceska Tisková Kancelár*, June 14, 2005; "Are Czechs Racists and Why They Resent Romanies?" *Ceska Tisková Kancelár*, June 13, 2005, http://www.ctk.cz.

21. "Három megasztáros kapja a Polgárjogi Dijat az idén," *Népszabadság Online*, May 5, 2005, http://www.nol.hu/cikk/361303; "Megasztár-Szupersztár: a meglepetés is hasonló," *Népszabadság Online*, June 13, 2005, http://www.nol.hu/cikk/365971; "Ki nyer a Megasztáron?" *Népszabadság Online*, May 14, 2005, http://www.nol.hu/cikk/362307; Márton Nehez-Posony, "A cigánysztár," *Népszabadság Online*, May 6, 2005, http://www.nol.hu/cikk/361401.

22. I take the term "new ethnicities" from Stuart Hall's essay of the same title in Nathaniel Gates, ed., *Cultural and Literary Concepts of "Race,"* London: Garland, 373–382.

## Chapter Four

1. See Martha Nussbaum's well-known attack on what she saw as the elitist, theoretical model of feminism she identifies with Judith Butler's work, which sees "struggles" of Indian and other Third World women for survival and emancipation as cut off from the mundane. Her article, "The Professor of

Parody," was originally published in the February 22, 1999 issue of *The New Republic.* http://www.tnr.com/archive/0299/022299/nussbaum022299.html. Gayatri Spivak (1999), among others, pointed to the hierarchy and condescension implied in Nussbaum's argument and mentioned poor Indian women's communities employing the very performative model of resistance to patriarchal structures theorized by Butler.

2. British colonialism criminalized and suppressed same-sex desire in a way that had not been the case in the Mughal era before. With the ideological aid of colonial theological Puritanism, the British influenced the suppression and erasure of same-sex desires not only through their cultural, economic, and legal systems but also through the anticolonial nationalistic movements they necessitated (see Syed 2002).

3. Paola Bacchetta discusses the activities of "Campaign for Lesbian Rights," a coalition among lesbian and feminist groups as well as leftist individuals and groups throughout India, which came about as a result of the Hindu Right's attacks on *Fire* in December 1998. Paola Bacchetta, "New Campaign for Lesbian Rights in India," *Off Our Backs* 29.4 (1999): 6. See also Bridget Kulla, "Why Has 'Water' Evaporated? The Controversy over Indian Filmmaker Deepa Mehta," *Off Our Backs* 32.3/4 (2002): 51–52.

4. David Paul writes, "At first glance the issues of lesbianism and censorship may strike one as unlikely twins, but a brilliant idea links them in this story. For Éva, sexual and political nonconformity are of one piece. Since she cannot accept the Party line on matters of sexual preference ... she can equally well reject the Party line on journalistic scandals" (1989, 192). Kevin Moss similarly accepts the filmmaker's explicit allegorical intentions without examining the discursive violence committed against the lesbian character: "In *Another Way*, then, Makk takes advantage of the similarities between political and sexual dissidence and constructs his film around the intersections of the two. Éva is both politically and sexually dissident, and the film shows how similar the devices used to conceal and reveal such dissidence are" (Moss 1995, 246).

5. For this information, I am grateful to members of the Lesbian Film Collective Katrin Kremmler, Magdi Timár, and Eszter Muszter, with whom I conversed at the Lesbian Film Festival in Budapest, July 4, 2004.

6. This was confirmed in my interviews with members of the group. This inherently essentialist exoticization of lesbian sex is precisely the reason why visual and other texts by lesbians avoid representing lesbian sex at all—much like Galgóczi and Makk did.

7. This, again, is very similar to the activities of Polish feminists, who have a hip-hop group and demonstrate against the ban on abortion and other neoconservative measures by church and state with campy street demonstrations and music. See Agnieszka Graff's article, "Lost Between the Waves? The Paradoxes of Feminist Chronology and Activism in Contemporary Poland." *Journal of International Women's Studies* 4(2), 2003: 100–116.

8. Keynote address, 6th European Gender Studies Conference, Lodz, Poland, September 2006.

## Chapter Five

1. The screening took place during the summer graduate course "Media Globalization and Post-Communist European Identities," which I codirected at the Central European University in July 2007.

2. For instance, "Inventing a People: Contemporary Art in the Balkans," curated by André Rouillé, touring exhibition, 1999; "In Search of Balkania," curated by Roger Conover, Eda Cufer, Peter Wibel, and Neu Gallerie, Graz, Austria, 2002; "European Contemporary Art: The Art of the Balkan Countries," curated by Miltiades Papanikolaou anjd Irina Subotic, State Museum of Contemporary Art, Thessaloniki, 2002; "Blood and Honey: The Future of the Balkans," curated by Harald Szeemann, Sammlung Essl Kunst der Gegenwart, Vienna, 2003; "In the Gorges of the Balkans: A Report," curated by René Block, Kunsthalle Fridericianum in Kassel, 2003, etc. For a more complete list, see Louisa Avgita and Juliet Steyn, "Introduction" to *Third Text*, vol. 21, no. 2, March 2007: 113–116; special issue on "Specifically Balkan Art."

3. Maria Todorova, *Imagining the Balkans*. Oxford and New York: Oxford University Press, 1997; Vesna Goldworthy, "Invention and in(Ter)Vention," in *Balkan as Metaphor: Between Globalization and Fragmentation*, Dusan Bjelic and Obrad Savic, eds. Cambridge: The MIT Press, 2002.

4. Quoted in the commentary on Svankmajer's film *Dimensions of a Dialogue*, at the Tate Gallery's 2002 Svankmajer exhibition, 2002.

5. Tania Modleski, "Femininity as Mas(s)querade," in her *Feminism without Women: Culture and Criticism in a "Postfeminist" Age*, New York: Routledge, 1991: 23–34; Ann Douglas, *The Feminization of American Culture*, New York: Knopf, 1977. See also Ien Ang and Joke Hermes, "Gender and/in Media Consumption," in *Mass/Media and Society*, James Curran and Michael Gurevitch, eds., London: Edward Arnold, 1991: 307–328.

6. See, for instance, Galambos K. Attila, "Nöi vonalak," *Filmvilág* 42.7 (1999), 22–23; Zsófia Mihancsik, "A láthatatlan nem: Magyar nök filmen," *Filmvilág* 47.7 (1999): 16–21; Brenda Cranney et al., eds. *Woman in Central and Eastern Europe: Canadian Woman Studies/Les Cahiers de la femme* 16.1 (1991); Zillah Eisenstein, "Eastern European Male Democracies: A Problem of Unequal Equality," *Gender Politics and Post-Communism*, Nanette Funk and Magda Mueller, eds., New York: Routledge (1993): 303–330; Ellen E. Berry, ed., *Postcommunism and the Body Politic*, New York: New York University Press (1995); Joanna Goven, "Gender Politics in Hungary: Autonomy and Antifeminism," in Funk and Mueller, *Gender Politics and Post-Communism: Reflections from Eastern Europe*, London: Routledge, 1993: 224–240.

7. Svankmajer was quoted in "The Magic Art of Jan Svankmajer," BBC2, 1992, produced by Colin Rose. See also Roger Cardinal, "Thinking Through Things:

The Presence of Objects in the Early Films of Jan Svankmajer" in *Dark Alchemy: The Films of Jan Svankmajer*, Peter Hames, ed., Westport, Connecticut: Praeger (1995): 78–95; and Michael Richardson, "Jan Svankmajer and the Life of Objects," chapter 8 in his *Surrealism and Cinema*. Oxford: Berg (2006).

8. On the intimate relationship between Dracula and Borat, see Nárcisz Fejes, "Borat's Cultural Learnings from Dracula." Unpublished manuscript, courtesy of the author.

# Works Cited

Almon, Joan. 2003. "The Vital Role of Play in Early Childhood Education." In *All Work and No Play*, edited by Sharna Olfman, pp. 17–42. Westport, CT: Praeger.

Anderson, Benedict. 1983. *Imagined Communities: Reflection on the Origin and Spread of Nationalism*. London: Verso.

Andrejevic, Mark. "The Pacification of Interactivity," *M/C Reviews*, October 25, 2001, http://www.media-culture.org.au/reviews/features/interactive/mandrejevic .html.

Appadurai, Arjun. 1994. "Disjuncture and Difference in the Global Cultural Economy." In *Colonial Discourse and Postcolonial Theory*, edited by Patrick Williams and Laura Chrisman, pp. 324–339. New York: Columbia University Press.

Appadurai, Arjun. 1996. *Modernity At Large: Cultural Dimensions of Globalization*. Minneapolis: University of Minnesota Press.

Appiah, Anthony. 1991. "Is the Post- in Postmodernism the Post- in Postcolonial?" *Critical Inquiry* 17 (winter): 336–57.

Arendt, Hannah. 1958. *The Human Condition*. Chicago: University of Chicago Press.

Arendt, Hannah. 1977. "What Is Freedom?" In *Between Past and Future*, pp. 143–172. Harmondsworth: Penguin.

Armstrong, Thomas. 2003. "Attention Deficit Hyperactivity Disorder in Children: One Consequence of the Rise of Technologies and the Demise of Play?" In *All Work and No Play*, edited by Sharna Olfman, pp. 161–175. Westport, CT: Praeger.

Arnold, Matthew. 2006. *Culture and Anarchy*. Oxford: Oxford University Press.

Arpad, Joseph T. 1995. "The Question of Hungarian Popular Culture." *Journal of Popular Culture* 29: 9–31.

Arsic, Branka. 2003. "Queer Serbs." In *Balkan as Metaphor: Between Globalization and Fragmentation*, edited by Dusan I. Bjelic and Obrad Savic, pp. 253–277. Cambridge, MA: The MIT Press.

Arthur, Paul. 2006. "A Meditation on *The Death of Mr. Lazarescu* and Corporeal Cinema." *Film Comment*, vol. 42, no. 3, (May–June): 44–49.

Avgita, Louise. 2007. "The Balkans Does Not Exist." *Third Text* 21, no. 2: 215–221.

Bachetta, Paola. 1999. "New Campaign for Lesbian Rights in India," *Off Our Backs* 29.4: 6.

Bakhtin, Mikhail. 1984. *Rabelais and His World*. Bloomington: Indiana University Press.

Balogh, Andrea P. 2002. "A leszbikus lét utópiái és realitásai Gordon Agáta *Kecskerúzs* címü regényében" ("Utopias and Realities of Lesbian Existence in Agata Gordon's novel, *Goat Lipstick*"). Unpublished manuscript.

Baltazar, Jodi. 2007. "A Devouring Way of Life: Consumption as Cannibalism in Children's Animated Film." Unpublished paper.

Barany, Zoltan. 1998. "Ethnic Mobilization and the State: The Roma in Eastern Europe." *Ethnic and Racial Studies*, no. 21 (2): 308–327.

Barber-Kersovan, Alenka. 2001. "Popular Music in Ex-Yugoslavia between Global Participation and Provincial Seclusion." In *Global Repertoires: Popular Music within and beyond the Transnational Music Industry*, edited by Andreas Gabesmair and Alfred Smudits, pp. 73–87. Sydney: Ashgate.

Barthes, Roland. 1977. "From Work to Text." *Image, Music, Text*. Trans. Stephen Heath. New York: Hill and Wang.

Bartolovich, Crystal. 1998. "Consumerism, or the Cultural Logic of Late Capitalism." In *Cannibalism and the Colonial World*, edited by Francis Barker, Peter Hulme, and Margaret Iversen, pp. 204–237. Cambridge University Press.

Batinic, Jelena. 2001. "Feminism, Nationalism, and War: The 'Yugoslav' Case in Feminist Texts." *Journal of International Women's Studies* 3 no. 1 (fall). http://www.bridgew.edu/SoAS/jiws/fall01/batinic.pdf.

Baudrillard, Jean. 1983. *Simulations*. Paris: Semiotexte.

Baudrillard, Jean. 1993. *Perfect Crime*, trans. Chris Turner. London: Verso.

Bauman, Zygmunt. 1992. *Intimations of Postmodernity*. London: Routledge.

Beck, John C., and Mitchell Wade. 2004. *Got Game: How the Gamer Generation Is Reshaping Business Forever*. Cambridge: Harvard Business School Press.

Benjamin, Walter. 2005. "Toys and Play: Marginal Notes on a Monumental Work." In *Selected Writings 1927–1934*, vol. 2, edited by Michael W. Jennings, Howard Eiland, and Gary Smith. Cambridge: Harvard University Press.

Bensmaia, Reda. 1999. "Postcolonial Nations: Political or Poetic Allegories?" *Research in African Literatures* 30, no. 3: 151–163.

Bessenyei, István. 1997. "Világháló és leépítés" ("World Wide Web and Deconstruction"). *Educatio* no. 4. http://www.neumann-haz.hu/tei/education/educatio/hu.prt.

Bhabha, Homi K. 1994. "DissemiNation: Time, Narrative and the Margins of the Modern Nation." In *The Location of Culture*, by Bhabha, pp. 39–170. New York: Routledge.

Bjelic, Dusan. 2005. "Global Aesthetics and the Serbian Cinema of the 1990s." In *East European Cinemas*, edited by Anikó Imre, pp. 103–120. London: Routledge.

Booth, Wayne. 1982. "Freedom of Interpretation: Bakhtin and the Challenge of Feminist Criticism." *Critical Inquiry* 9.1.

Böröcz, József. 1992. "Travel-Capitalism: The Structure of Europe and the Advent of the Tourist." *Comparative Studies in Society and History* vol. 34, no. 4 (October): 708–741.

Böröcz, József. 2001. "Birodalom, kolonialitás és az EU keleti bövítése," *Replika* 45–46 (November): 23–44. http://www.replika.c3.hu/4546/02borocz .htm.

Boyd, Todd. 2004. *The New H.N.I.C. (Head Niggas in Charge): The Death of Civil Rights and the Reign of Hip Hop*. New York: New York University Press.

Boyd-Barrett, Oliver. 1998. "Media Imperialism Reformulated." In *Electronic Empires: Global Media and Local Resistance*, edited by Daya Kishan Thussu, pp. 157–176. London: Arnold.

Boym, Svetlana. 2001. *The Future of Nostalgia*. New York: Basic Books.

Bradford, K. 2003. "Grease Cowboy Fever or the Making of Johnny T." In *The Drag King Anthology*, edited by Donna Jean Troka, Kathleen LeBesco, and Jean Bobby Noble, pp. 15–30. Binghampton, NY: Harrington Park Press.

Brinker-Gabler, Gisela, and Sidonie Smith, eds. 1997. *Writing New Identities: Gender, Nation, and Immigration in Contemporary Europe*. Minneapolis: University of Minnesota Press.

Buda, Zsuzsa. 1997. "A tanár mint harmadfajú Maxwell-Démon" ("The Teacher as Maxwell Demon of the Third Kind"), *Educatio* no. 4. http://www.neumann -haz.hu/tei/education/educatio/hu.prt.

Burton, Barbara, Nouray Ibryamova, Dyan Ellen Mazurana, Ranjana Khanna, and S. Lily Mendoza. "Cartographies of Scholarship: The Ends of Nation-States, International Studies, and the Cold War." In *Encompassing Gender: Integrating International Studies and Women's Studies*, edited by Mary Lay, Janice Monk, and Deborah Rosenfelt, pp. 21–45. New York: The Feminist Press, 2001.

Butler, Judith. 1993. *Bodies That Matter: On the Discursive Limits of "Sex."* London and New York: Routledge.

Cahn, Claude. 2002. "Fortress Europe." *Roma Rights Quarterly*, no. 2.

Caillois, Roger. 1961. *Man, Play and Games*. Chicago: University of Illinois Press, 2001.

Castells, Manuel. 1996. *The Rise of the Network Society*. London: Blackwell.

Chambers, Iain. 1996. "Signs of Silence, Lines of Listening." In *The Post-Colonial Question*, edited by Iain Chambers and Lidia Curti. London and New York: Routledge.

Cherry, Brigid. 2002. "Dark Wonders and the Gothic Sensibility: Jan Svankmajer's *Neco z Alenky* (*Alice*, 1987) in *Kinoeye* vol. 2, no. 1 (January). http://www.kinoeye.org/02/01/cherry01.php.

Chow, Rey. 1993. "Male Narcissism and National Culture: Subjectivity in Chen Kaige's *King of the Children*." In *Male Trouble*, edited by Constance Penley and Sharon Willis, pp. 87–117. Minneapolis: University of Minnesota Press.

Chow, Rey. 2001. "Gender and Representation." In *Feminist Consequences: Theory for the New Century*, edited by Elizabeth Bronfen and Misha Kavka, pp. 38–57. New York: Columbia University Press.

Clifford, James. 2002. *The Predicament of Culture. Twentieth-Century Ethnography, Literature and Art*. Cambridge: Harvard University Press.

Connor, Steven. 2005. "Playstations. Or, Playing in Earnest." *Static* 1, no. 1. http://static.londonconsortium.com/issue01/connor_playstations.pdf.

Couldry, Nick. 2004. "The Productive 'Consumer' and the 'Dispersed Citizen.'" *International Journal of Cultural Studies* 7 no. 1: 21–32.

Csepeli, György. 1991. "Competing Patterns of National Identity in Postcommunist Hungary." *Media, Culture and Society* no. 13: 325–339.

Cvetkovitch, Ann. 2001. "Fierce Pussies and Lesbian Avengers: Dyke Activism Meets Celebrity Culture." In *Feminist Consequences: Theory for the New Century*, edited by Elizabeth Bronfen and Misha Kavka, pp. 283–320. New York: Columbia University Press.

Czeizer, Zoltán. 1997. "Játék és tanulás az interneten" ("Play and Learning on the Internet"). *Educatio* no. 4. http://www.neumann-haz.hu/tei/education/educatio/1997tel/studies/1czeizer_hu.prt.

Dayan, Daniel. 2001. "The Peculiar Publics of Television." *Media, Culture and Society* 23, no. 6 (November): 743–67.

Debord, Guy. 1995. *The Society of the Spectacle*. New York: Zone Books.

de Lauretis, Teresa. 1987. *Technologies of Gender: Essays on Theory, Film, and Fiction*. Bloomington: Indiana University Press.

de Lauretis, Teresa. 1990. "Guerrilla in the Midst: Women's Cinema in the 1980s." *Screen* 31, no. 1: 12–25.

de Lauretis, Teresa. 1991. "Film and the Visible." In *How Do I Look? Queer Film and Video*, edited by Bad Object-Choices, pp. 223–263. Seattle: Bay Press.

Denitch, Bogdan. 1996. *Ethnic Nationalism: The Tragic Death of Yugoslavia*. Minneapolis: Minnesota University Press.

Dolby, Laura M. 1995. "Pornography in Hungary: Ambiguity of the Female Image in a Time of Change." *Journal of Popular Culture* 29: 119–127.

Domokos, Zsuzsa. 2004. "Vizuális illúzió" ("Visual Illusion"). *Támpont*, no. 1: 1.

Downey, John. 1998. "Full of Eastern Promise? Central and Eastern European Media After 1989." In *Electronic Empires: Global Media and Local Resistance*, edited by Daya Kishan Thussu, pp. 47–62. London: Arnold.

DuPlessis, Rachel Blau. 1994. "'Corpses of Poesy': Some Modern Poets and Some Gender Ideologies of Lyric." In *Feminist Measures: Soundings in Theory and Poetry*, edited by Lynn Keller and Cristanne Miller, pp. 69–95. Ann Arbor: Michigan University Press.

Dyson, Anne Haas. 1997. *Writing Superheroes. Contemporary Childhood, Popular Culture and Classroom Literacy*. New York: Teachers College Press.

Eisenstein, Zillah. 1993. "Eastern European Male Democracies: A Problem of Unequal Equality." In *Gender Politics and Post-Communism*, edited by Nanette Funk and Magda Mueller, pp. 303–330. New York: Routledge.

Eleftheriotis, Dimitris. 1995. "Questioning Totalities: Constructions of Masculinity in the Popular Greek Cinema of the 1960s." *Screen* 36 no. 3 (autumn): 233–242.

Ellis, John. 1982. *Visible Fictions*. London: Routledge.

Erasmus of Rotterdam. 1509. *In Praise of Folly*. Neeland Media LLC: Kindle Edition (digital), 2004.

Esterházy, Péter. 1988. *Tizenhét hattyúk*. Budapest: Magvetö.

Esterházy, Péter. 1991. *Az elefántcsonttoronyból*. Budapest: Magvetö.

Esterházy, Péter. 1997. *She Loves Me*, trans. Judith Sollosy. Evanston: Northwestern University Press.

Esterházy, Péter. 1995. *A Little Hungarian Pornography*, trans. Judith Sollosy. New York: Quartet Books.

Farkas, Éva. 2003. "Magyar Bálint elítéli az Irigy Hónaljmirigy roma-paródiáját," *Magyar Radio Online*. http://www.radio.hu/index.php/read/26300.

Fáy, Miklós. 1999. "Mit ér a vér, miszter fehér?" ("What's Your Blood Worth, Mr. White?") *Filmvilág* 42, no. 1: 24.

Feest, Christian. 2002. "Germany's Indians in a European Perspective." In *Germans and Indians: Fantasies, Encounters, Projections*, edited by Colin Calloway, Gerd Gemunden, and Susanne Zantop, pp. 25–43. Lincoln: University of Nebraska Press.

Forgách, András. 1996. "A késöromantika elöérzete" ("Premonitions of Late Romanticism"). *Filmvilág* 39, no. 2: pp. 4–7.

Franklin, Adrian. 2003. "The Tourist Syndrome: An Interview with Zygmunt Bauman." *Tourist Studies* 3: 205–217.

Franklin, Adrian. 2004. "Tourism as an Ordering: Towards a New Ontology of Tourism." *Tourist Studies* 4: 277–301.

Frasca, Gonzalo. 2003. "Simulation versus Narrative: Introduction to Ludology." In *The Video Game Theory Reader*, edited by Mark J. P. Wolf and Bernard Perron, pp. 221–236. New York: Routledge.

Foucault, Michel. 1997. "The Ethics of Concern for Self as a Practice of Freedom." In *Michel Foucault: Ethics, Subjectivity and Truth*, edited by Paul Rabinow, pp. 281–302. New York: The New Press.

Fuss, Diana. 1990. *Essentially Speaking: Feminism, Nature and Difference.* London: Routledge.

Gadamer, Hans-Georg. 1996. *Truth and Method*, 2nd ed., trans. Joel Weinsheimer and Donald G. Marshall. London: Sheed and Ward.

Galambos, Attila K. 1999. "Nöi vonalak" ("Feminine Lines"). *Filmvilág* 42.7: 22–23.

Garite, Matt. 2003. "The Ideology of Interactivity (or, Video Games and the Taylorization of Leisure"). Paper presented at the DIGRA "Level Up" conference. http://www.digra.org/dl/display_html?chid=http://www.digra.org/dl/db/05150.15436.

Gee, James Paul. 2003. *What Video Games Have to Teach Us About Learning and Literacy.* New York: Palgrave.

Geertz, Clifford. 1974. *Myth, Symbol and Culture.* New York: W. W. Norton and Company.

Gemünden, Gerd. 2002. "Between Karl May and Karl Marx: the DEFA Indianerfilme." In *Germans and Indians: Fantasies, Encounters, Projections*, edited by Colin Calloway, Gerd Gemunden, and Susanne Zantop, pp. 243–256. Lincoln: University of Nebraska Press.

Gilroy, Paul. 1998. "Race Ends Here." *Ethnic and Racial Studies* 21.5 (September): 838–847.

Giroux, Henry A. 1994. *Disturbing Pleasures: Learning Popular Culture.* London: Routledge.

Goven, Joanna. 1993. "Gender Politics in Hungary: Autonomy and Antifeminism." In *Gender Politics and Post-Communism: Reflections from Eastern Europe*, edited by Nanette Funk and Magda Mueller, pp. 224–240. New York: Routledge.

Graff, Agnieszka. 2003. "Lost Between the Waves? The Paradoxes of Feminist Chronology and Activism in Contemporary Poland." *Journal of International Women's Studies*, vol. 4, no. 2 (April). http://www.bridgew.edu/SoAS/jiws/April03/Graff.pdf.

Graff, Agnieszka. 2005. "The Return of the Real Man: Gender and E.U. Accession in Three Polish Weeklies." http://www.iub.edu/~reeiweb/events/2005/graffpaper.pdf.

Grewal, Inderpal, and Caren Kaplan. 1994. "Introduction: Transnational Feminist Practices and Questions of Postmodernity." In *Scattered Hegemonies: Postmodernity and Transnational Feminist Practices*, edited by Grewal and Kaplan, pp. 1–36. Minneapolis: University of Minnesota Press.

Groos, Karl. 1898. *The Play of Animals: A Study of Animal Life and Instinct*, trans. Elizabeth L. Baldwin. London: Chapman and Hall.

Groos, Karl. 1901. *The Play of Man*, trans. Elizabeth L. Baldwin. London: William Heinemann.

Györffy, Miklós. 1997. "A New Family Saga." *The New Hungarian Quarterly* 38, no. 147. http://www.hungarianquarterly.com/no147/p104.htm.

Györffy, Miklós. 2003. "A vesztesek mint vásári érdekesség a médiában," *Radio Kossuth*. http://www/radio.hu/index.php/read/27044.

György, Péter. 1997a. "The Global Dreamworld."

György, Péter. 1997b. "Iskola a határon" ("School on the Border"). *Educatio* no. 4. http://www.neumann-haz.hu/tei/education/educatio/1997tel/studies/hu .prt.

Györgyi, Annamária. 2001. "Feminizmus gyerekcipöben" ("Feminism in Baby Shoes"). *Heti Válasz* (*Weekly Response*) November 18. http://lektur.transindex .ro/?cikk=526.

Habermas, Jürgen. 1995. *Moral Consciousness and Communicative Action*, trans. C. Lenhard and S. W. Nicholsen. Cambridge, MA: The MIT Press.

Halberstam, Judith. 1997. "Mackdaddy, Superfly, Rapper. Gender, Race and Masculinity in the Drag King Scene." *Social Text 52/53*, vol. 15 no. 3–4 (fall/ winter): 104–131.

Hall, Stuart. 1990. "Cultural Identity and Diaspora." In *Identity, Community, Difference*, edited by Jonathan Rutherford, pp. 222–237. London: Lawrence and Wishart.

Hames, Peter. 1995. *Dark Alchemy: The Films of Jan Svankmajer*, edited by Peter Hames. Westport, Connecticut: Praeger.

Hames, Peter. 2002. "Way Our West: Oldrich Lipsky's *Limonadovy Joe aneb konska opera*" *Kinoeye* vol. 2 no. 15 (7 October).

Hankiss, Elemér. 1990. *East European Alternatives*. Oxford: Clarendon Press,

Haraway, Donna. 2003. "A Manifesto for Cyborgs: Science, Technology and Socialist Feminism in the 1980s." In *The Haraway Reader*, edited by Donna Haraway, pp. 7–45. London: Routledge.

Hartley, John. 2004. "Democratainment." In *The Television Studies Reader*, edited by Robert C. Allen and Annette Hill, pp. 524–533. London: Routledge.

Hendershot, Cyndy. 1995. "Postmodern Allegory and David Lynch's *Wild at Heart*." *Critical Arts 9*, no. 1: 5–20.

Heng, Geraldine. 1997. "A Great Way to Fly: Nationalism, the State, and the Varieties of Third-World Feminism." In *Feminist Genealogies, Colonial Legacies, Democratic Futures*, edited by M. Jacqui Alexander and Chandra T. Mohanty, pp. 30–45. New York: Routledge.

Hirsch, Tibor. 1999. "Pörén, buján, pajkosan: erotika és öncenzúra az ezredfor-dulón" ("Naked, Lewd, Playful: Eroticism and Self-Censorship at the Millen-nium"). *Filmvilág* 47.7: 24–27.

Holloway, Ronald. 1983. "The Short Film in Eastern Europe: The Art and Politics of Cartoons and Puppets." In *Politics, Art and Commitment in the East European Cinema*, edited by David W. Paul, pp. 225–251. New York: St. Martin's Press.

Horvath, John. 2000. "Alone in the Crowd: The Politics of Cybernetic Isolation." In *Culture and Technology in the New Europe*, edited by Laura Engel, pp. 77–103. Stamford, CT: Ablex Publishing.

Huizinga, Johan. 1955. *Homo Ludens: The Study of the Play Element in Culture.* Boston: Beacon Press.

Hutchinson, John. 1987. *The Dynamics of Cultural Nationalism.* London: Routledge.

Hutchinson, John. 1994. "Cultural Nationalism and Moral Regeneration." In *Nationalism*, edited by John Hutchinson and Anthony D. Smith, pp. 122–131. Oxford: Oxford University Press.

Huxley, Aldous. 1932. *Brave New World.* New York: Harper and Brothers.

Huyssen, Andreas. 2000. "Present Pasts: Media, Politics, Amnesia." *Public Culture* 12, no. 1: 21–38.

Imre, Anikó. 2001. "Central European Culture Today and the Problematics of Gender and Poetry." In *Comparative Cultural Studies and Central European Culture Today*, edited by Steven Tötösy, pp. 71–90. West Lafayette: Purdue University Press.

Imre, Anikó. 2004. "The Politics of Hiccups: National Cinema without National Language." *CineAction* 64: 8–17.

Imre, Anikó, ed. 2005. *East European Cinemas.* London: Routledge.

Imre, Anikó. 2006. "Play in the Ghetto: Global Entertainment and the European 'Roma Problem.'" *Third Text* 83 20, no. 6: 659–670.

Iordanova, Dina. 1998. "Balkan Weddings Revisited: Multiple Messages of Filmed Nuptials." Working paper.

Iordanova, Dina. 1999. "Eastern Europe's Cinema Industries Since 1989: Financing Structure and Studios." http://www.wacc.org.uk/de/content/pdf/1231.

Iordanova, Dina. 2000. "Mediated Concerns: The New Europe in Hypertext." In *Culture and Technology in the New Europe: Civic Discourse in Transformation in Post-Communist Nations*, edited by Laura Lengel, pp. 107–131. Stamford, CT: Ablex Publishing.

Iordanova, Dina. 2001. *Cinema of Flames.* London: BFI.

Iordanova, Dina. 2007. "Cashing in on Dracula: Eastern Europe's Hard Sells." *Framework* 48, no. 1 (spring): 46–63.

"Israel's Eminem Wins Fans, Angers Critics." http://www.universalmetropolis.com/magazine/articles.php?article='Israel's+Eminem'+wins+fans%2C+angers+critics.

Ito, Mizuko. 2008. "Mobilizing the Imagination in Everyday Play: The Case of Japanese Media Mixes." Forthcoming in *International Handbook of Children's*

*Media and Culture*, edited by Sonia Livingstone and Kirsten Drotner. London: Sage.

James, Beverly. 1999. "Fencing in the Past: Budapest's Statue Park Museum." *Media Culture and Society* vol. 21: 291–311.

Jameson, Fredric. 1981. *The Political Unconscious: Narrative as a Socially Symbolic Act.* Ithaca, NY: Cornell University Press.

Jameson, Fredric. 1985. "Class and Allegory in Contemporary Mass Culture: *Dog Day Afternoon* as a Political Film." *Movies and Methods*, edited by Bill Nichols, pp. 715–733. Berkeley: University of California Press.

Jameson, Fredric. 1986. "Third World Literature in the Era of Multinational Capitalism." *Social Text* 15: 65–88.

Jameson, Fredric. 1991. *Postmodernism, or, the Cultural Logic of Late Capitalism.* Durham, NC: Duke University Press.

Jameson, Fredric. 1992. *The Geopolitical Aesthetic: Cinema and Space in the World System.* Bloomington: Indiana University Press.

Jansson, André. 2002. "Spatial Phantasmagoria: The Mediatization of Tourism Experience." *European Journal of Communication* vol 17, no. 4: 429–443.

Jay, Martin. 2006. "The Ambivalent Virtues of Mendacity." In *Education and the Spirit of Time*, edited by Olli-Pekka Moisio and Juha Suoranta, pp. 91–107. Rotterdam: Sense Press.

Jeles, András. 1999. "Raszter" ("Roster"). *Filmvilág (Film World)* 42, no. 2: 8–11.

Jenkins, Henry. 2004. "The Cultural Logic of Media Convergence." *International Journal of Cultural Studies* 7 no. 1: 33–43.

Jenkins, Henry. 2006. *Fans, Bloggers and Gamers: Media Consumers in a Digital Age.* New York: New York University Press.

Johnson, Eric. 2000. "Beating to Death of Romany Mars Slovakia's Image." *United Press International*, August 25.

Johnson, Steven. 2006. *Everything Bad Is Good for You: How Today's Popular Culture Is Actually Making Us Smarter.* New York: Riverhead Trade.

Kállai, Ernö. 2000. "Cigányzenészek és külföldi lehetöségeik" ("Gysy Musicians and their Opportunities Abroad"). *Mozgó Világ ("The World in Motion")*, October. http://www.mozgovilag.hu/2000/10/okt5.htm.

Kalocsai, Csilla. 1998. "Leszbikus és meleg elméletek: identitások és identitáspolitikák" ("Lesbian and Gay Theories: Identities and Identity Politics"). *Replika* no. 33: 3. http://www.c3.hu/scripta/replika/3334/18kalo.htm.

Kant, Immanuel. 1790. *Critique of Judgement.* Oxford: Oxford University Press, 2007.

Kapitány, Gábor and Ágnes. 1995. "Changing World-Views in Hungary, 1945–1980." *Journal of Popular Culture* 29, no. 2: 33–43.

Kapur, Jyotsna. 2005. *Coining for Capital: Movies, Marketing and the Transformation of Childhood.* New Brunswick: Rutgers University Press.

Kapur, Ratna. 1999. "Cultural Politics of Fire." *Economic and Political Weekly*, May 22. http://www.cscsarchive.org.

Katrak, Ketu H. 1992. "Indian Nationalism, Gandhian 'Satyagraha,' and Representations of Female Sexuality." In *Nationalisms and Sexualities*, edited by Andrew Parker, Mary Russo, Doris Sommer, and Patricia Yaeger, pp. 395–406. New York: Routledge.

Kellner, Douglas. 2003. *Media Spectacle*. London: Routledge.

Kerényi, György. 1999. "Roma in the Hungarian Media." *Media Studies Journal* 13.3: 143.

Kinder, Marsha. 1991. *Playing with Power in Movies, Television, and Video Games: From Muppet Babies to Teenage Mutant Ninja Turtles*. Berkeley and Los Angeles: University of California Press.

Kinder, Marsha, ed. 1999. *Kids' Media Culture*. Durham: Duke University Press.

Kiossev, Aleksandar. 2000. "Megjegyzések az önkolonizáló kultúrákról," *Magyar Lettre Internationale* 37 (summer): 7–10.

Kligman, Gail, Iván Szelényi, and János Ladányi. 2002. "A Note on the Meaning of 'Underclass.'" *Roma Rights Quarterly*, no. 2: 112–114.

Knezevic, Djurdja. 2004. "Affective Nationalism." In *Transitions, Environments, Translations: Feminism in International Politics*, edited by Joan W. Scott, Cora Kaplan, and Debra Keates, pp. 65–71. London: Routledge.

Kolosi, Tamás, and Richard Rose. 1999. "Introduction: Scaling Change in Hungary." In *Hungary in Time-Space Perspective*, edited by Rudolf Andorka, Tamás Kolosi, Richard Rose, and György Vukovich, pp. 1–20. Budapest: Central European University Press.

Kovács, András Bálint. 1998. "A domináns férfi alkonya" ("The Twilight of the Dominant Male"). *Filmvilág* 41.4: 10–12.

Kovács, András Bálint. 2005. "Gábor Bódy: A Precursor of the Digital Age." In *East European Cinemas*, edited by Anikó Imre, pp. 151–164. London: Routledge.

Kremmler, Katrin. 2004. "Szervezzünk egy Leszbikus Filmnapot?" ("Shall We Organize a Lesbian Film Day?"). http://www.labrisz.hu/2/index.php?itemid =190&catid=21.

Kronja, Ivana. 2006. "The Aesthetics of Violence in Recent Serbian Cinema: Masculinity in Crisis." *Film Criticism*, spring, vol. 30, no. 3: 17–37.

Kulla, Bridget. 2002. "Why Has 'Water' Evaporated? The Controversy over Indian Filmmaker Deepa Mehta," *Off Our Backs* 32.3/4: 51–52.

Labrisz Leszbikus Egyesület. 2002. Már nem tabu. (No Longer Taboo.) Budapest: Labrisz Leszbikus Egyesület.

Lave, Jean, and Etienne Wenger. 1991. *Situated Learning: Legitimate Peripheral Participation*. Cambridge: Cambridge University Press.

Leerssen, Joep. 2006. "Nationalism and the Cultivation of Culture." *Nations and Nationalism* 12, no. 4: 559–578.

Lendvai, Erzsébet. 1998. "Animated Cartoons in Hungary." *Filmkultúra*. http://www.filmkultura.iif.hu/articles/essays/anim.textonly.ed.html.

Lengel, Laura, ed. 2000. *Culture and Technology in the New Europe. Civic Discourse in Transformation in Post-Communist Nations*. Stamford, CT: Ablex Publishing.

Lengyel, György. 1999. "The Post-Communist Economic Elite." In *A Society Transformed*, edited by Rudolf Andorka, Tamas Kolosi, Richard Rose, and Gyorgy Vukovich, pp. 85–96. Budapest, Central University Press.

Levi, Pavle. 2007. *Disintegration in Frames: Aesthetics and Ideology in the Yugoslav and Post-Yugoslav Cinema*. Stanford: Stanford University Press.

Livescu, Simona. 2003. "Play: Otherwise, A Recycled Gestalt or From Plato to Derrida: Being Differantly Playful." *CLCWeb: Comparative Literature and Culture 5*, no. 4 (December). http://clcwebjournal.lib.purdue.edu/clcweb03–4/livescu03.html.

Longinovic, Tomislav. 2005. "Playing the Western Eye: Balkan Masculinity and Post-Yugoslav War Cinema." In *East European Cinemas*, edited by Anikó Imre, pp. 35–48. London: Routledge.

Lowe, John. 1997. "Curriculum Reform in Poland: Putting New Needs into an Old System." *Educatio*, no. 4. http://www.neumann-haz.hu/tei/education/educatio/1997tel/studies/hu.prt.

Lury, Celia. 1998. *Prosthetic Culture: Photography, Memory and Identity*. London: Routledge.

Lustyik, Katalin. 2006. "Going Global? Children's Television in Transition in Central-Eastern Europe." In *European Film and Media Culture*, edited by Lennard Hojbjerg and Henrik Sondergaard. Copenhagen: Museum Tusculanum Press, University of Copenhagen.

MacCabe, Colin. 1992. "Preface" to Fredric Jameson's *The Geopolitical Aesthetic*, pp. ix–xvi. Bloomington: Indiana University Press.

Madsen, Deborah. 1996. *Allegory in America*. London: MacMillan.

Magyar, Bálint. 2004. "Elöszó" ("Foreword"). In *Médiafüzetek (Media Papers)*, edited by László Zöldi, pp. 7–8. Budapest: Enamiké.

Manovich, Lev. 1996. "On Totalitarian Interactivity. (Notes from the Enemy of the People)." http://www.manovich.net/TEXT/totalitarian.html.

Manovich, Lev. 2002. *The Language of New Media*. Cambridge, MA: The MIT Press.

Marciniak, Katarzyna. 2006. *Alienhood: Citizenship, Exile, and the Logic of Difference*. Minneapolis: University of Minnesota Press.

Marcus, George E. 2002. *The Sentimental Citizen: Emotion in Democratic Politics*. University Park: The Pennsylvania State University Press.

Marks, Laura U. 1994. "A Deleuzian Politics of Hybrid Cinema." *Screen 35*, no. 3: 244–264.

Mayne, Judith. 1990. *The Woman at the Keyhole*. Bloomington: Indiana University Press.

McChesney, Robert W. 1998, "Media Convergence and Globalisation." In *Electronic Empires: Global Media and Local Resistance*, edited by Daya Kishan Thussu, pp. 28–46. London: Arnold.

McClintock, Anne. 1995. *Imperial Leather: Race, Gender and Sexuality in the Colonial Context*. London: Routledge.

Mihancsik, Zsófia. 1999. "A láthatatlan nem: magyar nök filmen" ("The Invisible Gender: Hungarian Women in Film"). *Filmvilág* 47.7: 16–21.

Milosz, Czeslaw. 1983. *The Witness of Poetry*. Cambridge, MA: Harvard University Press.

Mitchell, W. J. T. 1994. *Picture Theory: Essays on Verbal and Visual Representation*. Chicago: University of Chicago Press.

Mitchell, W. J. T. 1998. *The Last Dinosaur Book*. Chicago: University of Chicago Press.

Mitnick, Joshua. 2003. "Israeli Hip-Hop Takes on Mideast Politics." *USA Today* (November 7). http://www.usatoday.com.

Modleski, Tania. 1991. "Femininity as Mas(s)querade." In *Feminism without Women: Culture and Criticism in a "Postfeminist" Age*, by Modleski, pp. 23–34. New York: Routledge.

Morley, David, and Kevin Robins, eds. 1995. *Spaces of Identity: Global Media, Electronic Landscapes and Cultural Boundaries*. London and New York: Routledge.

Moss, Kevin. 1995. "The Underground Closet: Political and Sexual Dissidence in East European Culture." In *Postcommunism and the Body Politic*, edited by Ellen E. Berry, pp. 229–251. New York: New York University Press.

Mul, Jos de. 2005. "The Game of Life: Narrative and Ludic Identity Formation in Computer Games." In *Handbook of Computer Game Studies*, edited by Jeffrey Goldstein and Joost Raessens, pp. 251–266. Cambridge, MA: The MIT Press.

Murasov, Jurij. (n.d.) "The Body in the Sphere of Literacy: Bakhtin, Artaud and Post-Soviet Performance Art." http://www.Artmargins.com/content/feature/murasov.html.

Naficy, Hamid. 1996. "Phobic Places and Liminal Panics: Independent Transnational Film Genre." In *Global/Local*, edited by Rob Wilson and Wimal Dissanayake, pp. 119–144. Durham: Duke University Press.

Nagy, Katalin S. 1995. "A vizualitás mint korunk gyermekbetegsége," ("Visuality: The Children's Disease of our Age"). *Írás: Tegnap és Holnap* (*Writing: Yesterday and Tomorrow*) 1, no. 4. http://www.oszk.hu/kiadvany/iras/14nk.html.

Ndalianis, Angela. 2005. *Neo-Baroque Aesthetics and Contemporary Entertainment*. Cambridge, MA: The MIT Press.

Newman, Felice. 1991. "The Passionate Landscape of Eva Szalanczky: An Introduction to *Another Love*." In *Another Love*, by Erzsébet Galgóczi; trans. Felice Newman and Ines Rieder, pp. 13–18. Pittsburgh: Cleis Press.

Nixon, Helen. 1998. "Fun and Games are Serious Business." In *Digital Diversions: Youth Culture in the Age of Multimedia*, edited by Julian Sefton-Green, pp. 21–42. London: University of London Press.

Nottingham, Michael. 2004. "Downing the Folk-Festive: Menacing Meals in the Films of Han Svankmajer." *EnterText: An Interactive Interdisciplinary E-Journal for Cultural and Historical Studies and Creative Work*, vol. 4, no. 1 (winter): 126–50.

Nowicki, Joanna. 1995. "Közép-kelet-európai sztereotípiák: vonzalom, gyanakvás és identitás" ("East-Central European Stereotypes: Attraction, Suspicion and Identity"), *Regio* 1, no. 1–2: 8–24.

Nussbaum, Martha. 1999. "The Professor of Parody." *The New Republic Online*, February 1999. http://www.tnr.com/archive/0299/022299/nussbaum 022299.html.

Nyíri, László. 1997. "A számítógép hatása az iskolára" ("The Influence of Computers on Schools"). *Educatio*, no. 4. www.neumann-haz.hu/tei/education/educatio/1997tel/studies/hu.prt.

Occhipinti, Laurie. 1996. "Two Steps Back? Anti-Feminism in Eastern Europe." *Anthropology Today* 12, no. 6: 13–18.

Olfman, Sharna. 2003a. "Introduction." In *All Work and No Play: How Educational Reforms Are Harming Our Preschoolers*, edited by Sharna Olfman, pp. 1–14. London: Praeger.

Olfman, Sharna. 2003b. "Pathogenic Trends in Early Childhood Education." In *All Work and No Play: How Educational Reforms Are Harming Our Preschoolers*, edited by Sharna Olfman, pp. 193–211. London: Praeger.

Orwell, George. 1949. *1984*. New York: Harcourt Brace Jovanovich Inc.

Panek, Sándor. 2004. "Aranybánya vagy legyőzhetetlen gépezet? A mozgóképkultúra és médiaoktatás az iskolákban" ("Gold Mine or Invincible Machinery? Motion Picture and Media Studies in the Schools"). In *Médiafüzetek (Media Papers)*, edited by László Zöldi, pp. 249–260. Budapest: Enamiké.

Panesar, Randip. 1999. "Ballyhoo in Bollywood: *Fire* Ignites Controversy in India." *Fabula* 3, no. 1: 11.

Papp, Nóra. 2005. "Ciganyirto jatek az interneten." http://www.romapage .hu/hirek/hircentrum-forummal/article/74511/1464/page/10.

Parker, Andrew, Mary Russo, Doris Sommer, and Patricia Yaeger, eds. 1992. *Nationalisms and Sexualities*. New York: Routledge.

Paul, David W., ed. 1983. *Politics, Art and Commitment in the East European Cinema*. New York: St. Martin's Press.

Paul, David W. 1989. "Hungary: The Magyar on the Bridge." In *Post New Wave Cinema in the Soviet Union and Eastern Europe*, edited by Daniel J. Goulding, pp. 172–213. Bloomington: Indiana University Press.

Paul, David W. 1994. "Szabó." In *Five Filmmakers*, edited by Daniel J. Goulding, pp. 156–208. Bloomington: Indiana University Press.

Personal Cinema Project. 2005. "The Making of Balkan Wars: The Game. A *Personal Cinema* Project." *Static*, no. 1. http://static.londonconsortium.com/issue01.

Peternák, Miklós. 1995. "A titán és a szirén" ("The Titan and the Syren"). *Filmvilág* 28, no. 10: 4.

Pethö, Ágnes. 2005. "Chaos, Intermediality, Allegory: The Cinema of Mircea Daneliuc." In *East European Cinemas*, edited by Anikó Imre, pp. 165–178. London: Routledge.

Postman, Neil. 1985. *Amusing Ourselves to Death: Public Discourse in the Age of Show Business*. New York: Viking.

"Q's Interview with Subliminal and the Shadow." 2005. *U Magazine* (April 6). http://www.tact-records.com.

Quart, Barbara. 1988. *Women Directors: The Emergence of a New Cinema*. New York: Routledge.

"Rasszista jatek az interneten," *Népszabadság Online*, February 16, 2005. http://nol.hu/cikk/352099.

Ravetto-Biagioli, Kriss. 1998. "Mytho-Poetic Cinema: Cinemas of Disappearance." *Third Text* 43: 43–57.

Ravetto-Biagioli, Kriss. 2003. "Laughing into the Abyss: Cinema and Balkanization." *Screen* 44, no. 4 (winter): 445–464.

Rich, B. Ruby. 1985. "In the Name of Feminist Film Criticism." In *Movies and Methods: An Anthology*, edited by Bill Nichols, pp. 340–356. Berkeley and Los Angeles: University of California Press.

Richardson, Michael. 2006. *Surrealism and Cinema*. Oxford: Berg.

Rogin, Michael. 1990. "'Make My Day': Spectacle as Amnesia in Imperial Politics." *Representations* 29 (winter): 99–123.

"Roma rap: avagy beindult a Fekete Vonat." 1998. *Amarodrom*. http://www.amarodrom.hu/archivum/98/vonat.html.

Russo, Mary. 1986. "Female Grotesques: Carnival and Theory." In *Feminist Studies/Critical Studes*, edited by Teresa de Lauretis. Bloomington: Indiana University Press.

Said, Edward W. 1990. "Yeats and Decolonization." In *Nationalism, Colonialism, and Literature*, by Terry Eagleton, Fredric Jameson, and Edward Said, pp. 69–98. Minneapolis: University of Minnesota Press.

Salecl, Renata. 1994. *The Spoils of Freedom: Psychoanalysis and Feminism After the Fall of Socialism*. London: Routledge.

Sándor, Beáta. 1999. "'Constantly Rewriting Herself': Lesbian Representations and Representations of Lesbians in Hungary from the 1980s to the Present." M.A. Thesis, Central European University.

Sárosi, Bálint. 1997. "Hungarian Gypsy Music: Whose Heritage?" *The Hungarian Quarterly* 38, no. 147 (autumn). http://www.net.hu/Deutsch/hungq/no147/p133.htm.

Sartre, Jean-Paul. 1969. *Being and Nothingness: An Essay on Phenomenological Ontology*, trans. Hazel E. Barnes. London: Methuen.

Schiller, Friedrich. 1954. *Letters on the Aesthetic Education of Man*, trans. Reginald Snell. New Haven: Yale University Press.

Schubert, Gusztáv. 1999a. "Fekete lyuk" ("Black Hole"). *Filmvilág* 42.1: 16–18.

Schubert, Gusztáv. 1999b. "Hült hely: Magyarország, szerelem" ("An Empty Place: Hungary, Love"). *Filmvilág* 47: 18–19.

Seiter, Ellen. 2003. "Television and the Internet." In *The Wired Homestead*, edited by Joseph Turow, pp. 93–116. Cambridge, MA: The MIT Press.

Seiter, Ellen. 2005. *The Internet Playground: Children's Access, Entertainment and Mis-Education*. New York: Peter Lang.

Sefton-Green, Julian. 1998. "Introduction: Being Young in the Digital Age." In *Digital Diversions: Youth Culture in the Age of Multimedia*, edited by Julian Sefton-Green, pp. 1–20. London: University College of London Press.

Seres, László. 2001. "Homofóbia" ("Homophobia"). *Élet és Irodalom* ("*Life and Literature*"), February. http://www.labrisz.hu/2/index.php?itemid=118& catid=21.

"SÉTA." 2004. In *Médiafüzetek* (*Media Papers*), edited by László Zöldi, pp. 218 and 248. Budapest: Enamiké.

Sherwood, Peter. 1996. "A Nation May Be Said to Live in Its Language: Some Socio-Historical Perspectives on Attitudes to Hungarian." In *The Literature of Nationalism: Essays on East European Identity*, edited by Robert B. Pynsent, pp. 27–39. Basingstoke: MacMillan.

Shohat, Ella, and Robert Stam, eds. 1994. *Unthinking Eurocentrism: Multiculturalism and the Media*. London: Routledge.

Shohat, Ella, and Robert Stam. 1996. "From the Imperial Family to the Transnational Imaginary: Media Spectatorship in the Age of Globalization." In *Global/ Local*, edited by Wimal Dissanayake and Rob Wilson, pp. 145–172. Durham: Duke University Press.

Silverman, Kaja. 1992. "White Skins, Brown Masks: The Double Mimesis, or With Lawrence of Arabia." In *Male Subjectivity at the Margins*, by Silverman, pp. 299–338. New York: Routledge.

Simms, Eva-Maria. 2003. "Play and the Transformation of Feeling: Niki's Case." In *All Work and No Play: How Educational Reforms Are Harming our Preschoolers*, edited by Sharna Olfman, pp. 177–191. London: Praeger.

Slemon, Stephen. 1987. "Monuments of Empire: Allegory/Counter-Discourse/ Post-Colonial Writing." *Kunapipi* 9, no. 3: 1–16.

Snell, Reginald. 1954. "Introduction." In Friedrich Schiller, *Letters on the Aesthetic Education of Man*, pp. 1–20. New Haven: Yale University Press.

"Sokan azt mondják egy lány ne rappeljen" ("Many People Say a Girl Should Not Rap"). 2004. *Tilos Rádió*. (February 7). http://www.ludditak.tilos.hu.

Sólyom, Attila. 2004. "Zajok szimfóniája" ("Symphony of Noises."). *Film-kultúra*. http://www.filmkultura.hu/2003/articles/films/hukkle.hu.html. Accessed on March 17.

Sparks, Colin. 2000. "Media Theory After the Fall of European Communism." In *De-Westernizing Media Studies*, edited by James Curran and Myung-Jin Park, pp. 35–49. London and New York: Routledge.

Spence, Louise, and Dennis Broe, eds. 2004. "In Focus: The New Cold War," a special section of *Cinema Journal* 43.4: 96–136.

Spivak, Gayatri Chakravorty. 1994. "Can the Subaltern Speak? *Colonial Discourse and Post-Colonial Theory: A Reader*, edited by Patrick Williams and Laura Chrisman, pp. 66–111. New York: Columbia University Press.

Spivak, Gayatri Chakravorty. 1999. "Letter to the Editor." *The New Republic*, April 19. http://foucault.info/Foucault-L/archive/msg06596.shtml.

Spyropoulos, Alexandros. 2007. "On Personal Cinema, Media and Homo Ludens." *Third Text* 21, no. 2: 171–180.

Stallabrass, Julian. 1993. "Just Gaming: Allegory and Economy in Computer Games." *New Left Review*, no. 198: 83–107.

Stam, Robert. 1989. *Subversive Pleasures: Bakhtin, Cultural Criticism and Film*. Baltimore: The Johns Hopkins University Press.

Stam, Robert, and Louise Spence. 1976. "Colonialism, Racism and Representation: An Introduction." In *Movies and Methods*, edited by Bill Nichols, pp. 632–649. Berkeley: University of California Press.

Stemmler, Susanne. 2007. " 'Sonido ciudadísmo': Black Noise Andalusian Style in Contemporary Spain." In *Sonic Interventions*, edited by Joy Smith, Sylvia Mieszkowski, and Marijke de Valck, pp. 241–264. Amsterdam: Rodopi.

Strinati, Dominic. 1995. *An Introduction to Theories of Popular Culture*. London: Routledge.

Strukov, Vlad. 2005. "The Performativity of Fear." *Static*, no. 1. http://static .londonconsortium.com/issue01.

Suleiman, Susan Rubin. 1997. "The Politics of Postmodernism After the Wall (Or, What Do We Do When the 'Ethnic Cleansing' Starts?)." In *International Postmodernism: Theory and Practice* edited by Hans Bertens and Douwe Fokkema, pp. 50–64. John Benjamins: Philadelphia.

Sümegi, Noémi. 2005. "Romakép-zavar" ('Troubled Roma Images'). *Heti Válasz*, June 23. http://www.romapage.hu/hirek/hircentrum-forummal/article/ 75165/165.

"SuperStar (Czech Idol) Is Romany Vlastimil Horvath." 2005. *Ceska Tisková Kancelár*. June 14.

Sutton-Smith, Brian. 1997. *The Ambiguity of Play*. Cambridge, MA: Harvard University Press.

Syed, Javid. 2002. "Queering India." *Trikone Magazine* 13, no. 3: 1–18.

Szilágyi, Ákos. 1982. "Kettös szorítottság kínjában. Beszélgetés Makk Károllyal" ("In the Agony of a Double Bind: A Conversation with Károly Makk"). *Filmvilág* 22, no. 5: 11–14.

Taussig, Michael. 1993. *Mimesis and Alterity: A Particular History of the Senses.* London: Routledge.

"Tiltakozás a TV2 *Bazi nagy roma lagzi* címü müsora miatt." 2003. *RomaPage.* http://www/romapage.hu/hirek/index.php?kozep=rsk777.htm.

Todorova, Maria. 1997. *Imagining the Balkans.* Oxford: Oxford University Press.

Töttössy, Beatrice. 1994. "Hungarian Postmodernity and Postcoloniality: The Epistemology of a Literature." *Canadian Review of Comparative Literature/ Revue Canadienne de Littérature Comparée* 22.3–4: 881–91.

Tully, James. 1999. "The Agonic Freedom of Citizens." *Economy and Society* 28, no. 2 (May): 161–182.

Ugresic, Dubravka. 1996. "The Confiscation of Memory," trans. Celia Hawkesworth. *New Left Review* 218: 26–39.

Vajda, Miklós. 1988. "Introduction." In *Eternal Moment*, by Sándor Weöres, pp. 13–19. London: Anvil Press.

Vasecka, Michal. 2001. "Roma." *Eurozine.* http://www.eurozine.com/article/2001 –03–12–vasecka-en.html.

Verstraete, Ginette. 2003. "Heading for Europe: Tourism and the Global Itinerary of an Idea." In *Mobilizing Place, Placing Mobility*, edited by Ginette Verstraete and Tim Cresswell, pp. 33–52. Amsterdam: Rodopi.

Watson, Peggy. 1993. "The Rise of Masculinism in Eastern Europe." *New Left Review* I/198 (March–April): 71–82.

Waugh, Thomas. 2001. "Queer Bollywood, or 'I'm the Player, You're the Naïve One?': Patterns of Sexual Subversion in Recent Indian Popular Cinema." In *Keyframes*, edited by Amy Villajero and Matthew Tinkcom, pp. 280–290. London and New York: Routledge.

Wells, Paul. 2002. "Animated Anxiety: Jan Svankmajer, Surrealism and the 'agit-scare.'" In *Kinoeye*, vol. 2, no. 16 (October 21). www.kinoeye.org/02/16/wells16 .php.

Williams, Bruce. 2002. "A Mirror of Desire: Looking Lesbian in María Luisa Bemberg's *I, the Worst of All.*" *Quarterly Review of Film and Video* 19: 133–143.

Willis, Susan. 1999. "Imagining Dinosaurs." In *Girls, Boys, Books, Toys: Gender in Children's Literature and Culture*, edited by Beverly Lyon Clark and Margaret R. Higonnet, pp. 183–195. Baltimore: The Johns Hopkins University Press.

Wilson, Frank R. 2003. "Handmade Minds in the Digital Age." In *All Work and No Play: How Educational Reforms Are Harming Our Preschoolers*, edited by Sharna Olfman, pp. 111–122. London: Praeger.

Wilson, William Julius. 1980. *The Declining Significance of Race: Blacks and Changing American Institutions*. Chicago: University of Chicago Press.

Wittgeinstein, Ludwig. 1974. *On Certainty*, trans. Denis Paul and G. E. M. Anscombe. Oxford: Blackwell.

Young, Neil. (n.d.) "Hukkle." http://www.jigsawlounge.co.uk/film/hukkle.html.

Yuval-Davis, Nira. 1998. "Gender and Nation." In *Space, Gender, Knowledge: Feminist Readings*, edited by Linda McDowell and Joanne P. Sharp, pp. 404–408. Hodder Arnold.

Žižek, Slavoj. 1994. *The Metastases of Enjoyment: Six Essays on Woman and Causality*. London: Verso.

Žižek, Slavoj. 1998. "A Leftist Plea for 'Eurocentrism.'" *Critical Inquiry* 24.4: 988–1009.

Zöldi, László. 2003. "A médiaoktatás ellentmondásai" ("The Contradictions of Media Education"). In *Médiafüzetek* (*Media Papers*), edited by László Zöldi, pp. 11–18. Budapest: Enamiké.

Zoonen, Liesbet van. 2004. "Imagining the Fan Democracy." *European Journal of Communication* 19, no. 1: 39–52.

Zsugán, István. 1982. "Riport a cannes-i filmfesztiválról" ("Report from the Cannes Film Festival"). *Filmvilág* 25, no. 7: 15–19.

Zsugán, István. 1985. "Egy azonosságzavar története" ("The Story of an Identity Confusion"). *Filmvilág* 27.2: 12–17.

# Index